The Greatest Baseball Debates
of Two Centuries

Brushbacks and Knockdowns

Allen Barra

Thomas Dunne Books   St. Martin's Press   🙝   New York

THOMAS DUNNE BOOKS.
An imprint of St. Martin's Press.

www.stmartins.com

ISBN 0-312-32247-X
EAN 978-0312-32247-2

First Edition: May 2004

10 9 8 7 6 5 4 3 2 1

To my aunt, Louise Palma,
who never learned much about baseball
but taught me the fun of a good argument

Contents

Introduction   xi

1. Sultan of Swat vs. Splendid Splinter; or If Ted Is the   1
   Greatest Hitter, Why Is Babe the Greatest Player?

2. The Greatest Team Sports Player of the Twentieth   29
   Century; or Half This Chapter Is 90 Percent Mental

3. Robin Roberts (and Eddie Mathews and   57
   Ernie Banks and Whitey Ford) and the All-Star
   Team of the 1950s; or Me Versus 200 Writers

4. Two Guys From Chicago; or Why Ron Santo   101
   and Minnie Minoso Are the Two Best Players
   Not in the Hall of Fame

5. Competitive Balance 2; or Wrath of the Con   111

Contents

6. Where Have All the All-Stars Gone? 139

7. Don't Blame the Yankees; or Yankees Town, 205
Red Sox Press

8. The Strange Case of Barry Bonds 259

Introduction

Someone once said that the only sequels better than the originals are *Huckleberry Finn* and *The Godfather Part II*. (I might add *The Road Warrior* to that list.) These works have at least one thing in common—namely, that they broadened and expanded the themes of the originals. *Brushbacks and Knockdowns* follows proudly in their tradition.

With the suggestions and encouragement of my editor at Thomas Dunne Books, Pete Wolverton, in this book I've attempted to get deeper into some issues than I was able to do in the short-chapter format of *Clearing the Bases*, and in the process examine some topics—competitive balance, revenue sharing, steroids—that I had room to mention only in passing in the previous book.

My thanks to several editors who worked on the stories from which the chapters in this book originated and whose own rigorous debating skills honed my own: Scott Veale and Michael

Introduction

Anderson of *The New York Times;* Eric Gibson, Barbara Phillips, Stuart Ferguson, Erin Friar, and Dick Tofel of *The Wall Street Journal;* Gary Kamiya and King Kaufman of Salon.com; Ward Harkavy of *The Village Voice;* Bryan Curtis of Slate.com; Nathan Ward of *Library Journal;* Richard Snow of *American Heritage;* Bob Carlton of *The Birmingham News;* Scott Eyman of *The West Palm Beach Post;* Steve Wasserman of *The Los Angeles Times;* Ed Gray of *The Arkansas Democrat-Gazette;* Fritz Lanham of *The Houston Chronicle;* Cheryl Chapman of *The Dallas Morning News;* Will Carroll of *Baseball Prospectus;* Richard Aregood of *The Newark Star-Ledger;* Gene Seymour of *New York Newsday* (whose son, Chafin, has taught us both something about a good argument); Andrew Zimbalist, with whom I'll never argue baseball economics again; Anna Campbell, who doesn't argue much but who always asks the right questions; my cousins Rick Schofield and Joe Anello, who have refined argument to an art form; and Art Bourgeau, who asks the best rhetorical questions of any debater I've ever known.

Thanks to Roger Kahn for arguing me out of some bad positions; Jesus Diaz of *The Village Voice* for arguing me into some good ones; Rob Neyer of ESPN.com for suggesting some new ones; and Margaret Whitton for suggesting a chapter called "Don't Blame the Yankees."

Also, thanks to: Bob Costas for always playing devil's advocate; Marvin Miller for always returning the call; George Will for his kind comments, though we'll never agree on Mantle and Mays; Jay Mandel, my agent at William Morris, who would make a great editor if he ever gets tired of agenting; Ray Robinson for always taking time to offer historical perspective; Doug Pappas, editor of the SABR newsletter, who returned every call; Mike Leary of *The Baltimore Sun* and formerly of *The Philadelphia Inquirer,* who first suggested that I do *Clearing the Bases;*

Bert Sugar for being a kvetch supreme; Kevin Baker for editing, so to speak, several of these chapters over the phone; Bill James for continuing to be Bill James; Charles Pierce for being the best sportswriter in America; Joe Rinaldi of St. Martin's for being the best publicist I've ever worked with; Coach T. J. Troup, who knows almost as much about baseball as he does about football; and both the late George Plimpton and the late Leonard Koppett for their kindness and encouragement over the years. Though I never met him, I'd like to thank Branch Rickey, whose *Baseball in America*, written nearly forty years ago, touched on so many of the issues discussed in this book.

Finally, thanks to Beverly Barton and Mary Grace McCord, who taught me about courage, and to G. K. Chesterton for getting my head back together every night.

1

Sultan of Swat vs. Splendid Splinter
or
If Ted Is the Greatest Hitter,
Why Is Babe the Greatest Player?

Who is the greatest baseball player who ever lived?

Now—who is the greatest *hitter* who ever lived?

The answer to the first question, of course, is Babe Ruth. Every baseball fan knows that, right? The answer to the second is Ted Williams. Every baseball fan knows that too, right?

I'm not saying that those are necessarily the answers I would give or you would give—though I'll lay it out right now that I do regard Ted Williams as the greatest hitter who ever lived, and though I may argue for someone else as a greater player, I'm not going to argue terribly hard *against* Ruth—but they are certainly the answers that you'd *expect* most baseball fans to give, perhaps fewer now than, say, sixty or fifty or even ten years ago, but almost certainly still the answers that most baseball fans would endorse.

A quick survey of my family, friends, and colleagues on these questions merely confirms what I already believed: At

least 60 percent of all people who call themselves baseball fans
would call Babe Ruth the greatest player who ever lived and Ted
Williams the greatest hitter. Moreover, nearly everyone that I
asked *believed both propositions to be true,* that Ruth was the
greatest player and Ted Williams the greatest hitter.

Have you ever thought about those two questions at the
same time? Did it ever occur to you that there might be something of a contradiction in accepting both statements as true?
It didn't occur to me until I began mulling over the question
of whether or not Barry Bonds over the last three seasons has
been the greatest hitter *and* the greatest player in baseball
history.

For the time being, I want to leave Barry Bonds out of this.
(More on Bonds later in this book.) I suppose I could just as easily rephrase the questions to "Who was the greatest player of the
last century?" and "Who was the greatest hitter of the twentieth
century?" But I'm not going to. The notion of Ruth as the greatest player in baseball history and Williams the greatest hitter has
been received wisdom in baseball for so long that I think we can
dispense with any qualifications and simply deal with them as
we have grown to accept them.

So, I guess you figured by now that what I'm wondering is:
If we all pretty much agree that Babe Ruth was the greatest
player, how can we all think Ted Williams was the greatest *hitter*? Or, stated a different way, why don't we think Babe Ruth
was a greater hitter than Ted Williams? Or yet another: If Ted
Williams was a better hitter than Ruth, why don't we regard him
as the greater player?

Let's define our terms at the outset. If we mean "greater" in
the sense of importance, as being of greater mythical stature,
there is no argument that Ruth wins hand down over Williams
or anyone else who ever played the game. No Japanese soldier

ever led a banzai charge at an American machine gun yelling, "Die, Red Sox, to hell with Ted Williams!" I'm sure that is what some people mean when they say that Babe Ruth was the greatest player in baseball history, but I'm equally sure that many also mean it in the sense of *better,* as in most valuable, as in would help you win the most ball games. This is the sense in which I mean "greater," and the sense I intend to discuss it here.

Let's start by asking why Ted Williams is regarded as a better hitter than Babe Ruth. Note that it's never said this way—you almost never hear anyone say "Ted Williams was a better hitter than Babe Ruth," they just say that "Ted Williams was the greatest hitter who ever lived." But if we're saying that Ted Williams is the greatest hitter who ever lived, we are saying that he's a better hitter than Babe Ruth, aren't we? I don't know what else greater or better hitter could mean. Darn it—now we have to stop again and define what we mean by the *best* or *better* hitter. Do we mean it in the sense of more consistent, as in "more consistent; makes contact more often" and maybe "reaches base more often"?

If that's what we mean, then Williams gets a slight edge in career statistics, having posted a .344 lifetime batting average in 2,292 major league games to the Babe's .342 in 2,503 games and a .482 on-base average to Ruth's .474. Ruth struck out 1,330 times in 8,399 at-bats, or once every 6.3 at-bats, while Williams struck out just 709 times in 7.706 at-bats, or once every 10.9 times at bat.

This doesn't necessarily make Williams a better hitter than Ruth from the standpoint of consistency or ability to reach base—we all know there are other factors to be taken into consideration, such as park effects and conditions in the times they played—but it does mean that if you accept consistency, making contact, and ability to reach base as the primary attributes of a great hitter, then someone taking Ruth's part in the debate would have to present some evidence that undermines Williams's evident superiority.

On the other hand, if we mean best hitter in the sense of best power hitter, the basic stats favor Ruth, though not by so great a margin as some might assume. Ruth, as we all know, hit 714 home runs, one for every 11.8 times at bat. Williams hit 521 home runs, or one for every 14.8 at-bats. Ruth's career slugging average was .690, Williams's was .634.

So, then, Ruth was, on basic stats, more superior to Williams as a power hitter than Williams was superior to Ruth in reaching base. The handiest and most reliable statistic for combining the two basic yardsticks of baseball hitting is SLOB, which is Slugging Average times On-Base Average. Most baseball analysts like to add them into a stat they refer to as either OBA or OBP, depending upon whether you prefer the term "average" or "percentage." My old economics professor at the University of Alabama in Birmingham, George Ignatin, insisted, after much research and experimentation on our part, that multiplying the two provided a result that correlated better with team scoring than adding.

Around the same time—the early '70s—that George and I were hashing out SLOB, Dick Cramer, a Philadelphia-area research scientist, came up with the same formula and called it Batter's Run Average. I never figured out who came up with it first, but it really doesn't matter. The formula for both SLOB and BRA is:

> **(Hits + Walks + Hit By Pitch)** divided by
> **(At-bats + Walks + Hit By Pitch)** multiplied by
> **(Total Bases divided by At-Bats)**

George likes the term "multiplistic." That's his explanation for the effect that multiplying the two stats produces and why it gives a slightly better picture of their run-producing potential than adding the two stats.

To connect SLOB to our discussion, let's take Babe Ruth's best mark. In 1920, he posted an on-base average of .532 and a slugging average of .847 for a fabulous SLOB of .4506, or, if you move the decimal two spaces to the left, 45.06, which means that in 1921 Babe Ruth "produced" or "created" 45 runs for every 100 at-bats. For his career, Ruth had a SLOB of .3271 or produced 32.7 runs per 100 at-bats.

Needless to say, Babe ranks first on the all time lists. Williams is second, with 30.60. That's pretty close. By the way, Williams's seasonal high in SLOB was 1941, the year he hit .406, posting an on-base average of .551 and a slugging average of .735 for a SLOB of 40.50.

We probably shouldn't go any farther without taking a look at their career stats as listed in baseball's official encyclopedia, *Total Baseball*.

	G	AB	HR	R	RBI	BA	OBA	SA
Ruth	2,503	8,399	714	2,161	2,201	.342	.474	.690
Williams	2,292	7,706	521	1,798	1,839	.344	.482	.634

Ruth, it may be argued, lost a couple of prime years in his hitting stats to his pitching talent, which we'll discuss in more detail later. From his rookie season in 1914, when he pitched in four games, through 1919, when he pitched in 17 games, Babe totaled 158 games, 144 of them starts. It's difficult to say how many home runs he lost because of his pitching. From 1914 through 1918 he did manage to hit 21 home runs, and in 1919, as he was phasing out the pitching part of his career (from 1920 to the end of his career he would pitch in just five more games, four of them starts), he hit 29 home runs. From 1914 through 1918, Ruth batted 678 times, so in that period he averaged a home run once every 32.3 times at bat.

I haven't seen any comparative studies of what other leading hitters averaged during the same period, and I'm not going to slow things down here any more than I have to by doing one now. Suffice it to say that while it could be argued that Ruth would have hit home runs at a more frequent rate had he been a starting outfielder instead of a pinch hitter and spot outfielder (and, in 1918, he played 59 games in the outfield), it isn't likely he would have hit home runs at a *much* greater rate than he had in the previous couple of seasons. Conditions just weren't right then for Babe Ruth to be Babe Ruth.

Why? Because the Ruthian revolution hadn't happened yet. Ruth is often mistakenly credited with single-handedly taking baseball from the dead ball to the lively ball era. In point of fact, baseball was heading toward the lively ball era—and would have gotten there eventually—with or without Ruth. In 1917, the American League hit just .248 with 133 home runs; the league's earned run average was 2.67. In 1918, the year Ruth won his first home run title with 11, things began to perk up: The league hit .254, and though, for some mysterious reason, there were only 96 home runs, the league ERA rose to 2.78.

In 1919, when Ruth astonished the baseball world by hitting 29 home runs, the overall league batting average had shot up 15 points to .269 and the league's ERA to an eye-opening 2.23 with an overall 240 home runs—in other words, not counting Ruth, the American League had more than twice as many home runs in 1919 as it had in 1918.

By 1920 the bats were booming. The American League hit .284, the league ERA had swelled to 3.79, and, led by Ruth's gargantuan total of 54 home runs, the league as a whole hit 369 home runs. *That's 314 without Ruth, up from 211 without Ruth the previous year.* Clearly, Babe Ruth was influencing the way a lot of hitters were hitting, but just as clearly Babe was the beneficiary of a trend created by numerous factors, from the outlawing of the spit ball to—as I believe Bill James was the first to point out—a greater supply of fresh, clean, lively baseballs, at least after 1920 when Ray Chapman was hit in the head and killed by a baseball that was so dirty it was hard to see.

The point is that after 1917 *everyone* was hitting baseballs more often. In the National League, batting averages went from .250 in 1917 to .255 in 1918 to .258 in 1919, and then, in 1920, to .270. NL hitters had 139 home runs in 1918; in 1919 the figure rose to 207, and in 1920 to 261. You would really have to stretch things to say that Babe Ruth alone was responsible for all this power hitting. After all, in an age when there was no TV, how many NL hitters even *saw* Babe Ruth?

Perhaps one of the primary reasons why Ruth's hits tended to go further than everyone else's was suggested by Branch Rickey in *The American Diamond:*

Babe Ruth not only changed modern baseball with his home run hitting but he influenced bat design. Ruth, Cobb, Sissler, and Speaker all used bats forty ounces or more in weight, but Ruth's home run records began a trend to lighter bats. Other players wishing to emulate his swing and not having his girth or power decided they could duplicate his swing with lighter bats. Rogers Hornsby initiated modern bat styling and effected the transition from the old large-handled bats, with small barrels and the weight more evenly distributed, to the first modern bat. Hornsby's bat had a comparatively large barrel tapering gracefully to a small handle. When Babe Ruth took this shape and added his weight out at the head end of the bat and accentuated the gradually tapering handle, it added considerable whip when swung. Today the whip effect is more prominent than it ever was, because the handles are thinner than ever. Roger Maris's bat has a narrower handle than a Little Leaguer's.

So does Barry Bonds's bat, a matter we'll get to in a later chapter. So did Ted Williams's bat. Williams was one of the first passionate advocates of whip-handled bats.

But I digress. What I want to do is indicate what Ruth's numbers might have looked like had he come up to the big leagues as an outfielder rather than as a pitcher. Let's assume for fun that instead of batting 678 times from 1914 through 1918 and hitting just 21 homers, Ruth had batted 1,950 times—that's just under 400 at-bats per season—and, at the same ratio of 1 home run for every 32.1 times . . . Well, no, that's not fair. If Babe had been starting in the outfield every day he *would* have hit home runs at a greater rate. Not nearly so well as he did from 1919 on, because nobody could hit the ball that far that consistently in the dead ball era; but Babe, had he played regularly at that time, would almost certainly have had better hitting ratios than he had while switching every couple of days from the pitcher's mound to the outfield.

Let's take the average of one home run for every 32.1 times at bat from 1914 through 1918, and the average of one home run for every 11.1 at-bats from 1919 through the end of his career, and just split the difference—let's say that if Ruth had come up as an outfielder, from 1914 through 1918 he would have averaged a home run every 21.6 times at bat for 1,950 at-bats. That would give him 90 home runs for those five years instead of 21, and it's probably safe to say, about 250 RBIs over that same period rather than the 116 he did have, with roughly the same increase in runs scored. I think it's also safe to say that playing regularly at that time would have cost him 3 or 4 points off his career batting average because of how much tougher it was for everyone to hit back then.

So, if Ruth had come up as an outfielder in 1914, it's a good bet his basic career stats would probably look something like this:

	BA	HR	R	RBI
Ruth (Actual)	.342	714	2,174	2,213
Ruth (Projected)	.338	783	2,324	2,347

If Babe Ruth had come up in 1914 as an outfielder, dead ball and all, he would almost certainly still be the major league career leader in home runs, RBIs, and runs scored. If you wanted to argue that he'd have wound up with over 800 home runs, I'd probably concede it. The guy was pretty good.

So was Ted Williams. The Splinter came up as a cocky twenty-year-old outfielder in 1939. How cocky? A Red Sox veteran told him, "Just wait till you see (Jimmie) Foxx hit." "Wait," Williams shot back, "till *Foxx* sees *me* hit."

Foxx was probably one of the four best hitters—along with Ruth, Lou Gehrig, and Rogers Hornsby—of the 1920s and '30s, and in fact would finish his career with 15 more home runs than Williams. It is not recorded what Foxx thought when he saw Williams hit, but he certainly ought to have been impressed. In his first season Williams hit .327 with 31 home runs and a league-leading 145 RBIs. After that he got better.

For his next seven seasons, 1940–42 and 1946–49, Williams established a record of hitting dominance that rivals or surpasses any seven-season stretch in baseball history except Ruth's in the 1920s. From '40 to '42 and from '46 to '49, Williams led the American League in doubles twice, home runs four times, total bases five times, runs scored six times, runs batted in three times, batting average four times, on-base average seven times, and slugging six times.

For six consecutive seasons, from '41 to '42 and from '46 to '49, Williams made a clean sweep of the two most important basic hitting statistics in baseball, on-base average and slugging average, leading the league in both categories each year. Eight times in his career, including 1951 and 1957, Williams led the American League in both categories. Only Ruth has topped this, leading the league in both categories nine times.

With Ted Williams, though, there are mitigating circumstances. As every baseball fan knows, Ted Williams lost almost all of five seasons to military service. As not every baseball fan knows, Williams was frequently injured; in only one of his seasons did he play in all of the Red Sox games, and only four times in his career did he play as many as 150. Injuries cost him at least 60 games in 1950 and more than 80 from '54 and '55.

We can't do anything about the injuries, but we can at least give him a little credit for what he might have done had it not been for the two military stints. Did I say a "little" credit? Heck, giving Ted Williams his just historical due is one of the things this book is about. Of all the "What ifs" in baseball history, there may be none quite so intriguing as "What if Ted Williams hadn't spent five seasons in the military?"

In 1941, the young Ted Williams, who turned twenty-three as the season wound down, had one of the most fabulous seasons of any hitter ever to play the game. As just about anyone reading this book knows, he became the last player to hit over .400, and he led the league in most home runs hit in one's home park as well as most home runs hit on the road, runs scored, walks, batting, on-base average, and slugging. The next season, his last before the end of the war, his batting average dipped 50 points—for some reason, probably more night games, batting statistics in the American League dipped sharply from 1941 to '42 with batting averages going from .266 to .257 and slugging averages dropping from .389 to .357. But he still led the league at .356. He also led the league in home runs again, most home runs both at home and on the road, total bases, runs scored, runs batted in, walks, on-base, and slugging average.

That's what Ted Williams did in his twenty-third and twenty-fourth years. Then he went off to war. Yes, I know, there are far larger concerns in times of war than what one's batting average might have been. But this isn't a book about war, it's a book about baseball, so permit me to indulge in my fantasies—*our* fantasies, I presume, or you would not have read this far.

So here we have Ted Williams for 1941 and 1942, age twenty-three and twenty-four, averaging, for the two seasons, 36.5 home runs, 138 runs scored, 128.5 RBIs, batting average of .380. Is it fair to say that he would have averaged those same numbers for the next three seasons if he hadn't been serving his country? Is it fair to assume that? Are you kidding? He would have *averaged* those numbers? Ted Williams would have been at his *absolute physical peak* at age twenty-five, twenty-six, and twenty-seven. Not only is it fair to say he probably would have *surpassed* those numbers, it's reasonable to speculate that he would have obliterated them.

When he came out of the service in 1946, after three years of baseball inactivity, he hit 38 home runs and led the league in total bases, runs scored, walks, on-base average, and slugging average, while hitting .342. The next year, he led the league in hitting with .343 as well as pacing the league in home runs, total bases, runs scored, runs batted in, walks, slugging, and on-base average.

I don't know what is more unbelievable: what Ted Williams accomplished in his two seasons before he went into the service or what he accomplished in the two seasons after he came home, with three years of rust to shake off. You can't argue that he was "better" after he came out. He was *fantastic* when he came out. I didn't even get to his 1949 season, when he hit a career-high 43 home runs (leading the league both at home and on the road) and established career highs in total bases, runs scored, runs batted in, and walks. But he wasn't quite the hitter he had been for the two seasons before he went into the Navy Air Corps.

If we want to get an idea of what Ted Williams's career stats might be like had it not been for World War II, suppose we take his two seasons before service and his first season after and average them out. In 1941, '42, and '46 Ted Williams played in 443 games, batted 1,492 times, got 547 hits, hit 111 home runs, and drove in 380 runs. That averages out to .367, 36 home runs and 127 RBIs per season.

Look what this does to Williams's career numbers:

	G	AB	HR	RBI	BA
Actual (nineteen seasons)	2,292	7,706	521	1,839	.344
Projected (including '41, '42, and '46)	2,735	9,198	632	2,219	.348

By the way, you may have noticed that just averaging out Williams's projected RBI total puts him 6 RBIs ahead of what Babe Ruth's actual numbers are.

Of course, Williams didn't just miss time during World War II, he missed a bunch of time in the Korean War when he served in the Marine air wing. Williams left baseball for the Korean War April 30, 1952, and returned on August 6, 1953. In those two seasons, he played in a total of just 43 games, hitting 14 home runs, driving in 37 runs, and hitting, for those two years .406. (Yup! the same average he had for the 1941 season!) Tempting as it is, we just can't assume that he would have continued to average a home run every three games and hit .400 at ages thirty-four and thirty-five.

Let's instead give him credit for what he did, and try to give him reasonable credit for what he might have averaged for the remainder of those two seasons had he continued to play major league ball. In 1951, Williams played in 148 games, hit 30 home runs in 531 at-bats, drove in 126 runs, and hit .318, his second-lowest batting average (after 1950, when he hit .317) until 1959, his next-to-last season, when he hit just .254. In 1954, after his Korean stint, he played in just 117 games, with 386 at-bats, hit 29 home runs, with 89 RBIs, and batted .345.

Leaving off the fractions, that averages out to about 132 games per season, 29 home runs, 107 RBIs, and a .329 batting average. But we already have Williams's stats for 43 games in '52 and '53, so let's subtract 43 games from the 264 games we're projecting he might have had during '51 and '52, which leaves 222 games. What we're saying is that for those missed 222 games, based on what he did the year before and the year after, Williams can be fairly given credit for a home run every 15.5 at-bats, an additional 59 *home runs for the two seasons.*

Likewise for RBIs: Williams played 43 games in '52 and '53. Giving him credit for an additional 222 games and an additional 816 at-bats, he would reasonably have driven in an additional 191 RBIs.

All right then, if we give Babe Ruth five years as a hitter that he "lost" as a pitcher and restore for Ted Williams the better parts of five seasons that he lost in World War II and the Korean War, there's a very good chance that the career at-bats, homers, and RBIs of the two men would look like this:

	AB	HR	RBI	BA
Babe Ruth Projected Career	10,349	783	2,347	.338
Ted Williams Projected Career	10,014	691	2,410	.346

Ted Williams is catching up to Babe Ruth. Has he surpassed him?

Williams's career on-base average was 8 points higher than Ruth's, .482 to .474. Williams's career batting average was 2 points higher than Ruth's, .344 to .342, and he walked a fraction more often, .881 walks per game to Ruth's .824. In our new projected numbers, Williams out-hits Ruth by 8 points, and the gap between them in walks would have grown still larger, which means that if we give Ruth back the five seasons that he lost to the pitching mound and give Ted Williams back the five seasons he lost in wartime, more than likely Williams's career on-base average would have been not 8 points higher than Ruth's but as much as *15 or 16 points* higher. That is one hell of a lot of points for anyone's career on-base average to be higher than Babe Ruth's.

What about slugging? For their careers, Ruth outslugged Williams by 56 points, .690 to .634. But in our projected scenario Williams would have picked up a few points and Babe would have lost a few. About 5 points both ways seems reasonable, which means that the projected Babe might have outslugged the projected Ted by, oh, let's say 46 points.

So, if we do a projected SLOB of the two, we come up with these numbers: 32.20 for Ruth and 31.06 for Williams. Or, rounded off another way, it means a batting order of "Projected Babes" would have totaled about 32 runs per 100 at-bats, and a lineup of "Projected Teds" about 31 runs per 100 at-bats. Whew!

These, of course, are merely best estimates. We can't know exactly what they would have done had they both had those precious five seasons restored. But I think it's safe to draw two conclusions: One, that Ted Williams comes a lot closer to being Babe Ruth's equal than it might seem from just looking at the raw numbers of their actual careers; and, two, that even allowing for those restored seasons, we still don't have any objective evidence that Ted Williams was, as most baseball fans seem to believe, a better hitter than Babe Ruth.

Are there perhaps some other perspectives from which to compare the two greatest hitters in baseball history? Most baseball analysts agree that what a hitter does on the road—in all the other ballparks he plays in—is a better reflection of his ability than his home stats, as his home park may unfairly inflate or deflate his numbers.

Here are the career road stats for Babe and Ted:

ROAD STATS, CAREER

	AB	H	BB	2B	3B	HR	BA	OBA	SA
Ruth	4,366	1,475	1019	269	66	367	.338	.463	.682
Williams	3,819	1,251	987	206	36	273	.328	.466	.615

Remember, this gives Ruth an advantage of 547 at-bats. Giving Williams the same number of at-bats as Ruth and using Williams's percentages for 3,819 at-bats, the career road stats would be very close to this:

	AB	H	BB	2B	3B	HR	BA	OBA	SA
Ruth	4,366	1,475	1,019	269	66	367	.338	.463	.682
Williams	4,366	1,430	1,128	236	41	312	.328	.466	.615

Let's stop a moment to reflect. Do you think on the whole the numbers a hitter compiles on the road are a better reflection of his ability than those he compiles in his home park? *I* do.

If that's true, then it looks as if Babe has now pulled substantially ahead of Ted in the unofficial race for Greatest Hitter of All Time, because it must be said that Williams's statistics got a solid boost from Fenway Park. The House That Ruth Built was indeed built *for* Ruth, but he hit home runs only marginally better there than he did at other American League ballparks of his era. From his first game at Yankee Stadium in 1923 to his last in 1934, Babe hit 259 home runs at home and 252 in the rest of the AL parks. That's not really an advantage at all, as you'd expect any player to perform a little better in his home park. For his career overall, Ruth actually hit more home runs on the road—367 to 347.

However, taking into account everything else, it can't be denied that Ruth's numbers at home are better than on the road. His career batting average was 9 points better than his road average (.347 to .338), his home slugging average was .698 to a road .682, and his home on-base average was .480, to a road .463. Multiplying his slugging times on-base averages to get a SLOB, we find that Ruth has 33.50 for his career at home to 31.58 on the road. That's not a huge difference, but it does indicate that Ruth produced about 2 runs more per 100 at-bats—1.92 to be exact—at home than on the road.

For Ted Williams, the difference was more substantial. Oddly enough, Williams hit fewer home runs at Fenway Park—248 to 273—than he did in all the rest of the AL ballparks. But in every other category he was significantly better at Fenway than on the road. Williams hit .361 at Fenway and .328 on the road; he had 319 doubles at home to 208 when out of town. I don't know what would account for this enormous difference— Williams hit 53 percent more doubles at home than on the road—and that gap constitutes most of the difference between his effectiveness at home and on the road. (I would love to see an ambitious researcher for the Society for American Baseball Research devote some time to this puzzle.)

In any event, Williams's home slugging percentage was .652 to .615 on the road, and his home on-base average was a breathtaking .495, which is 29 points higher than his road OBA (which was plenty good enough). This means that Ted's career SLOB at Fenway was 32.27 to 28.66 everywhere else, for a difference of 3.61 more runs per 100 at-bats.

So, even if we do Williams the favor of granting him, for the sake of argument, the same number of road at-bats as Ruth, thus increasing his hit, walk, double, triple, and home run totals, it doesn't change his *percentages.* Outside their respective home parks, Ruth outhit Williams by 10 points, had an on-base average just 3 points lower than Williams, and outslugged him by an impressive 67 points.

I still can't find, try as I might, any statistical evidence that Ted Williams was a better hitter than Babe Ruth.

Let's try another perspective. How do they compare at *peak* value? And how do we define "peak"? Are twelve seasons a fair sampling? Let's look at how they compare in their twelve best seasons, as ranked by *Total Baseball.* And since we've already established road stats as a more accurate barometer than total stats, let's stick with them.

BABE RUTH

Year	G	AB	H	BB	2B	3B	HR	BA	OBA	SA
1919	67	232	74	49	15	6	20	.319	.438	.694
1920	76	254	91	87	15	3	25	.358	.522	.736
1921	74	285	101	65	20	9	27	.354	.474	.772
1923	76	276	104	78	19	6	22	.377	.514	.728
1924	75	269	101	76	21	3	22	.375	.513	.721
1926	77	254	96	70	17	3	24	.378	.512	.752
1927	78	287	98	76	19	4	32	.341	.479	.770
1928	77	276	87	76	21	4	25	.315	.463	.692
1929	75	281	100	36	19	3	25	.356	.429	.712
1930	73	274	95	71	15	4	23	.347	.481	.682
1931	70	267	103	65	20	3	22	.386	.506	.730
1932	61	218	78	59	7	3	22	.358	.495	.720
Totals	*879*	*3,173*	*1,128*	*808*	*208*	*48*	*289*	*.356*	*.486*	*.725*

Ruth's SLOB for his 12 best seasons is 35.24, while Williams's is 30.61. This means, on paper at least, a difference of about 4.63 runs per 100 at-bats. This, I think, pretty much finishes the objective part of the argument in favor of Ruth. There are a couple of minor factors I could toss into the argument, such as Ruth's road statistics being swelled a bit by his getting to play 10 or so games a year in Fenway Park, which was a hitter's paradise, whereas Williams would play about the same number per season in Yankee Stadium, which was just about neutral.

Also, as we saw, Williams lost three prime years, perhaps *the* three years of his physical prime, to World War II. As we've seen, if we give him credit for those three seasons based on what he did before and after he got out of the military, his

TED WILLIAMS

Year	G	AB	H	BB	2B	3B	HR	BA	OBA	SA
1939	74	288	90	55	22	6	17	.313	.423	.608
1940	68	264	92	49	15	9	14	.348	.450	.633
1941	68	213	81	65	12	1	18	.380	.525	.699
1942	75	261	93	81	13	2	20	.356	.509	.651
1946	74	248	78	83	16	4	20	.315	.486	.653
1947	75	251	89	78	16	3	16	.355	.508	.633
1948	71	270	100	60	21	2	16	.370	.485	.641
1949	78	294	99	71	12	2	20	.337	.466	.595
1954	59	200	64	64	11	1	13	.320	.485	.580
1956	64	195	64	43	9	0	14	.328	.450	.590
1957	69	214	80	67	9	1	26	.374	.523	.790
1958	63	204	67	41	9	0	16	.328	.441	.608
Totals	*838*	*2,902*	*997*	*757*	*165*	*31*	*210*	*.344*	*.479*	*.639*

overall stats, particularly his "quality" stats—meaning his batting average, on-base average, and slugging average—would look a little better. (Giving him credit for time lost in Korea would increase his totals but wouldn't really affect his quality stats.) But giving Ted all the breaks isn't going to close that gap with Ruth of 4.61 per 100 at-bats. If we split the difference—and that seems generous—Babe is still up about 2.3 runs per 100 at-bats.

What about the argument, then, that Babe Ruth was a greater *player* than Ted Williams? Of course, that's not the way people say it—they just say that Babe Ruth is the greatest player of all time, or something like that. But if Ruth was the greatest player of all time, then he was greater than Williams, and if many of the people aren't saying that they think Ruth was a better *hitter* than Williams but simply that he was a greater *player*, they must be referring to Ruth's contributions outside of the batter's box.

As we all know, Babe Ruth was a great pitcher before he was a great hitter. How good was he? Well, in *Total Baseball*'s rankings, he is listed for the 1916 season—in which he went 23-12 and led the league with an ERA of 1.75 and in shutouts with 9—as the most valuable player in the game. Not the most valuable *pitcher*, the most valuable *player*.

The year after that he won 24 games, led the league with 35 complete games, and posted an ERA of 2.01. (*Total Baseball* ranks him as the third best pitcher in the league in 1917 and the fifth most valuable player.) His career won-lost percentage was .671, just a few points behind that of Lefty Grove, who most analysts regard as one of the four or five best pitchers in baseball history. Not that Ruth would have finished his career with a won-lost percentage as high as .671, but it's still pretty impressive.

The problem here is that we can't consider Ruth's value as a pitcher and an outfielder *at the same time.* We have to consider him first as a pitcher, then as an outfielder and great slugger, and the fact is that great as he was on the mound, he was even greater as a regular player.

But try as I might, I can't see what the argument is for Babe Ruth's value as a regular player outside of his hitting. Ruth has a lingering reputation as an all-around player that I simply cannot understand. For his career he is known to have stolen 123 bases and to have been thrown out 117 times for a terrible success rate of only 51 percent—and that includes the 1918 and '19 seasons, when he is known to have stolen 13 bases but for which no "caught stealing" information has been located. If you eliminate those two seasons and just take into account the seasons for which we have both stolen and caught info, the success rate is 110 stolen to 117 caught for a miserable 48.5 percent. On the bases, Ruth contributed no runs; he *cost* his team runs, a bunch of them.

For Ted Williams, the percentage looks slightly better. In eighteen seasons he stole 24 bases and was thrown out 17 times for 59 percent. Clearly, Williams was no base-stealer, but I don't see how anyone can say that Babe Ruth was, either. Branch Rickey, probably the most astute judge of talent in baseball history, praised Ruth as a man who could "steal a base," but unlike nearly every other observation Rickey made, I can't find any validity in this particular statement.

It's true that in Ruth's time the rewards for stealing were higher because the primitive gloves of the era often allowed throws to bounce into the outfield where the runner could take an extra base. Even allowing for that, though, I fail to see how anyone could make a case for Babe Ruth's value as a base-stealer. My guess is that the only real difference between Ruth and Williams as base-stealers is the eras they played: In Ruth's time, nearly everyone was expected to try to steal, and when Williams played, bigger, slower sluggers were simply not expected to. If I try to assign some value to Williams and Ruth as base-stealers, Williams is going to come out ahead, not necessarily because he was a better base runner than Ruth, but simply because in the time in which he played it was understood that it was simply better *not* to have him steal.

The fairest thing I can think of in regards to Ruth's and

Williams's base running abilities is to simply remove them from the debate and call the whole thing a wash.

What about their respective abilities as fielders? Once again, Ruth has a reputation as an outfielder that is baffling from a twenty-first-century perspective. ("Ruth was a good fielder," said Branch Rickey.) For his career, Ruth's range factor was 2.16 chances in the outfield per 9 defensive innings, which was .21 below the league average. His fielding average of .968 seems low by modern standards, but fielding percentages were lower in his time; Ruth was actually 2 points above the league fielding average for his position.

Some say Ruth was a better outfielder when he was younger, lighter, and faster; but from his last two years with the Red Sox through his first nine years with the Yankees—the ninth being 1928 when he played in all his team's games for the only time in his career (he would never again play in more than 144)—*he was below the league average in chances per game in 8 of 11 seasons.* How much ground could he have been covering if nearly every other player at his position was getting to more balls?

What about that great throwing arm? Well, Babe was in double figures in assists eleven times in his career, which seems pretty good, but he never led the league in assists.

Williams had a reputation as a mediocre fielder, though in fact his fielding statistics in left field are pretty much the same as Ruth's in right field. His career fielding average was .974, 3 points below the league average for his position, and his range factor was 2.05 chances per nine innings, significantly lower than the league average of 2.41.

Both those numbers are deceiving. First, Williams made 19 of his career 113 errors in his rookie season, after which he was much more consistent. Second, his career range factor is greatly affected by his last eight seasons, when he was slowed by age, constant injury, and rust from inactivity. After 1953, he never averaged over 2 chances per nine innings; before that, he was over 2 chances a game every season.

There's a third reason why Williams's fielding numbers might make him seem worse than he was: Fenway Park. Because of the high, monstrous green wall in a short left, left fielders at Fenway Park simply get fewer chances per game. For what it's worth, Carl Yastrzemski, who was considered much faster and a much better outfielder than Ted Williams, averaged 2.09 chances a game in his career to Williams's 2.05.

Williams didn't have a particularly strong throwing arm. He did record double figures in assists 7 times, all in his first ten seasons, probably more of a tribute to his learning how to play bounces off the wall than to his arm, and in 1951 he led the league in double plays with 6, which is something Ruth never did.

Several observers of Williams's defensive play thought he was much better than he was given credit for; in my father's tattered copy of *Baseball Stars of 1950*, Ed Rummill wrote that through constant practice and study of the treacherous caroms produced by the Green Monster, Williams "made himself a fine defensive outfielder." Dominic DiMaggio, Williams's teammate in center field for several seasons and one of the great outfielders of his time, always insisted that Williams was better than his reputation.

We're left, then, with two outfielders, neither of whom was outstanding—one was probably overrated, Ruth, and one seems to have been a bit underrated, Williams. Who was more the more valuable defensive player? We could call in more observers here, but then that would take us deeper into the realm of the subjective. On the basis of the evidence there doesn't seem to have been enough of a difference between Ruth and Williams in the field on which to base a decisive judgment. My guess is that if Ruth and Williams were graded by some cosmic yardstick that could accurately evaluate their value, they'd both get a C or C+.

That's it. I can't see any objective evidence that Ted Williams was a greater hitter than Babe Ruth, although most baseball fans seem to think he was. Nor can I see any evidence that Babe Ruth was a greater player than Williams, except for a little more value at-bat, though most fans seem to think so.

And after all this, you probably still think Ted Williams was the greatest hitter that ever lived. And you know what? So do I.

One thing I haven't considered is how each man's batting numbers looked in relation to their league's. I don't want to spend much time on this because I don't think it's all that important. To begin with, there's no way that Ruth doesn't win that comparison. Let's look at the differences between Ruth and Williams and their leagues in what the *STATS, Inc. All-Time Major League Handbook* says were their best seasons.

In what are arguably his three best seasons, Babe Ruth outhit the league, on average, by just over 96 points. His on-base average was just over 182 points higher than the league's, and he outslugged them on average by—keep your socks up—almost 425 points.

In what are probably Ted Williams's three best seasons, on average he outhit his league by 78 points, his on-base average

1920	BA	OBA	SA
Ruth	.376	.532	.847
AL	.284	.343	.387
Diff.	+.092	+.189	+.460

1921	BA	OBA	SA
Ruth	.378	.512	.846
AL	.292	.352	.408
Diff.	+.086	+.160	+.438

1923	BA	OBA	SA
Ruth	.393	.545	.764
AL	.282	.346	.388
Diff.	+.111	+.199	.376

1941	BA	OBA	SA
Williams	.406	.553	.735
AL	.266	.339	.389
Diff.	.140	.214	.346

1946	BA	OBA	SA
Williams	.342	.497	.667
AL	.256	.326	.364
Diff.	.086	.171	.303

1949	BA	OBA	SA
Williams	.343	.490	.650
AL	.263	.351	.379
Diff.	.080	.139	.271

was 174 points higher, and he outslugged the league by 307 points.

There's just no way that Ted Williams or anyone else is going to be able to compete with Ruth in an against-the-league comparison. And with good reason. When Ruth led the AL with 54 home runs in 1920, the number two man was the St. Louis Browns' George Sissler with 19. When he led the league with 59 home runs in 1921, the number two man was the Browns' Ken Williams, who had 24. In 1923, when Ruth led the league with 41 home runs, Ken Williams was again second with 29.

In 1941, when Ted Williams led the league with 37 home runs, the Yankees' Charlie Keller was second with 33, the Yankees' Tommy Heinrich was third with 31, and the Yankees' Joe DiMaggio was fourth with 30 . . . Well, you get the picture.

By the time Williams was at his peak, the game had changed radically. There were more good power hitters and no single hitter was dominating.

We all know this, and yet we never remember it when talking about Babe Ruth—except when we think about Ted Williams. You seldom hear anyone say, "Gosh, imagine what Mickey Mantle or Willie Mays or Hank Aaron or Alex Rodriguez or Barry Bonds would have done if they had been playing back in the 1920s!" Okay, you *do* hear some people ask questions like that, but you seldom hear them try to offer a logical answer. Myself, I still hear baseball fans who say things like "Alex Rodriguez would have hit .400 with 60 home runs in 1927." The same people *also* say that Babe Ruth was the greatest player who ever lived.

Clearly the conditions Ruth played under were more favorable to compiling great batting statistics than those at any other time in baseball history—with the possible exception of whatever factors have contributed to the conditions of Barry Bonds's last three seasons (a subject we'll get to later). Clearly, when fans insist that Ted Williams was the greatest hitter ever, what they're saying is, "If Ted Williams had played at the same time as Babe Ruth, or if Babe Ruth had played at the same time as Ted Williams, Williams would have the better numbers and be recognized as the greater hitter."

I can't say for certain that that's true, but if it is, then Ted Williams deserves to be recognized as the greatest—i.e., the most valuable—player in baseball history.

Do I think Ted Williams was the greatest hitter who ever lived? Yes, I do. Do I think he was the greatest player who ever lived? No, I don't. Why? I don't know.

Perhaps I just can't reconcile calling a player the greatest ever who didn't excel in any other area of the game besides hitting, no matter how important hitting is. Perhaps, like most baseball fans, I've been saying, "Babe Ruth was the greatest player and Ted Williams the greater hitter" over and over in my mind for so long that I've simply learned to live with the contradiction. To paraphrase Walt Whitman, do I contradict myself? Very well, then, I contradict myself.

2

The Greatest Team Sports Player of the Twentieth Century

or

Half This Chapter Is 90 Percent Mental

In 1999, anticipating all the end-of-the-millennium nonsense, *ESPN Magazine* invited me to participate in a special issue that would address two questions: One, who was the most dominant athlete of the twentieth century? And two, who was the greatest team sports player of the century? Regarding the first question, I chose Muhammad Ali—why not? After much discussion, all the writers involved agreed to drop the second.

It wasn't a good idea, and the reasons why should have been obvious from the start, beginning with the point that if you didn't choose a boxer or golfer or tennis player or perhaps a bicycle racer—in other words, if you chose a team sports player—there is no real reason why the same athlete couldn't top both lists, and then what was the point in having two polls? Why couldn't the most dominant team athlete also be the greatest team sports player?

Still, the distinction has continued to intrigue me over the years. Is it possible to isolate the qualities that make a great "team player," and how might they differ from a great team athlete who is simply "dominant"? Does an athlete's being dominant add or subtract to his credentials as a "team player"? And, in what is probably the toughest question of all to answer once you get into serious analysis, how does one compare the qualities of players in different sports?

The answer to the last question, of course, is that you can't, not in any meaningful way. But we argue these kind of things because they're fun, right? Not a day goes by when someone on a subway or bus or standing at the water cooler doesn't argue with someone else the relative greatness of Babe Ruth and Michael Jordan or Joe Montana versus Wayne Gretzky. Why can't you attempt to apply logic to the question and *still* have fun with it? Of course, given the vagueness of the definitions we are using, I suppose only a fool would attempt a long analysis of the team sports question, so, well, here I go.

First off, when I began to discuss the topic of greatest team sports player with my colleagues I discovered a built-in prejudice against both baseball and football players. (Some of them championed the choice of a hockey player. While I enjoy hockey, I don't know enough about it to argue for or against a hockey player, so I'm leaving hockey out of the debate.) Simplified, the argument for not choosing a baseball player as the greatest team-sports athlete is that one baseball player doesn't have enough impact on his team—not the way a basketball player, who is one of only five in the lineup, impacts a game.

That may be true, stated a certain way: Even Babe Ruth was just one of nine men in a batting order. But I don't see any reason why that should disqualify a baseball player from being included in the debate simply because the nature of the game makes him less of a factor in the outcome. It's true that you can use a basketball player (or, for that matter, a running back in football) as often as you want while Babe Ruth only gets up to bat four or five times a game, but so what? A baseball team doesn't need to win eighty percent of its games to be dominant the way a basketball or football team does. Usually sixty percent will do, and a baseball player's value should be measured by how much he contributes to that sixty percent.

The argument against choosing a football player for greatest team sports player had to do with the fact that the impact of quarterbacks and runners is so much greater than that of the other positions—how do you compare the value of a quarterback to that of a right guard? But, again, that's the nature of the game. If we can't find a way to measure the impact of an offensive guard or inside linebacker, then we'll stick to passers and runners.

Who are the major candidates in each of the three major sports, and what criteria should we go by in choosing them?

To me, it is obvious that a great team sports player must first be, by any definition and whatever else he might be, a great player on his own merits. I don't just mean a good player who is endowed by his fans with loads of immeasurable "intangibles." Give me an undeniably great player, one who objectively and verifiably can be proven to be great, and I'll be happy to sort though the evidence and see if I can find some intangibles. I'm not saying intangibles don't exist or don't count. I think when we call someone a "team player" we are implying that his skills or qualities go some way towards making his teammates better and that he makes them better *as a team,* in ways that can't just be measured by statistics.

But when I'm choosing the *greatest* team sports player, I want to make my choice from among the ranks of players who are regarded as great *before* the question of intangibles comes into play. If I have to, I'll toss in intangibles as a tiebreaker.

The place to start looking for the greatest winners in team sports is on championship teams, so if we started with basketball, for instance, while I might conclude that Wilt Chamberlain is the "greatest" or most "dominant" basketball player of all time—and I probably would, if you pressed me—I wouldn't pick him in this debate because he won "only" two championships.

Or more to the point, I wouldn't pick him over his great rival, Bill Russell, who won 11 championships in thirteen seasons, even though Chamberlain's personal statistics are far more impressive than Russell's. In fact, Russell's all-around ability, his intelligence, his play-making skills, and his defensive genius, not all of which can be measured by statistics such as blocked shots and steals, make him an ideal choice. The eleven championship rings don't make a bad argument, either.

The only problem with choosing Bill Russell as our greatest team basketball player is that it seems to punish some players with comparable team skills simply for being better players. Obviously, we are talking about Michael Jordan. Jordan clearly had many of the same "team" skills on offense and defense as Russell, and just as clearly he was a better—well, let's say more dominant—player. If he didn't pass off the ball more often than he did, or at least as often as Russell, it's because he was the greatest shooter of his time. Why penalize him for not giving the ball more often to players who would have scored fewer points?

There are other points to consider. Jordan, for instance, earned six championship rings in fifteen seasons, five fewer rings than Russell, but given the greater number of playoff series Jordan's teams had to play through to win their championships, is six rings in fifteen seasons really a less impressive figure? I would go with Michael Jordan over Bill Russell as the greatest team player in basketball history. But I'm not going to argue too loudly if you choose Russell.

How do you frame the argument in football? First off, I'm not comfortable arguing about players from before my time, players who I not only never saw but to whom I can't apply any yardsticks. Unfortunately, this rules out what is probably the golden age of football *as a game,* by which I mean the era when players had to play on both sides of the ball. In other words, a time when they had to be *football players,* football players who had to block and tackle, and not just quarterbacks or free safeties or tight ends or nickel backs who exercised a single skill.

You know what I mean. Have you noticed that nowadays when people argue about football players they never say "Who's the best player in the game?" the way they do with baseball or basketball players? Instead, they ask "Who's the best passer?" or "Who's the best one-on-one cover man?" That's what football has evolved into in the last five decades of the twentieth century, and though I don't like it, that's the way I have to deal with it. The modern game is a game of specialists, and it's dominated by quarterbacks and running backs.

Of the two positions, I think quarterback is by far more important, which is to say that modern football is dominated by passing, not running. Some people don't see eye to eye with me on this, but I think that most fans and observers of the game would agree with me that the quarterback has less to do with individual achievement and more to do with team skills and qualities than the running back. Certainly a quarterback has more to do with making his teammates' skills better than a running back, if only because no receiver can look good with a bad passer. And if intangibles in the form of nerve and improvisational skill and inspirational value are key factors in the winning of football games, then a quarterback is the man most likely to possess them.

Who, then, are our top "team" quarterbacks? Dan Marino is often credited with being the game's greatest passer, but he never won a Super Bowl ring. Do you really feel confident with him going for you in the championship game? I don't, or at least not as much as some other quarterbacks I can name.

Many consider John Elway to be the best athlete among quarterbacks of his time, and many would choose him as the best ever at the position. He certainly led some of the game's most legendary fourth-quarter comebacks, but he also suffered some truly humiliating title game defeats. Do we simply give him credit for the games he won and write off the ones he lost to his team's poor play? Elway did finally win two championships in the final years of his career, but not until he played for a coach who transformed him into a *team* quarterback who didn't try to do it all himself. If John Elway had been able to start his pro career with a coach like Bill Walsh, there might not be a debate as to who was the best quarterback ever.

Joe Montana *did* get to start his career with Bill Walsh, and if he wasn't the most talented quarterback ever to play, I'm still okay with his selection as the best ever. He won four Super Bowls with the '49ers and even made winners out of the Kansas City Chiefs late in his career.

Many rank Johnny Unitas with or ahead of Montana. Unitas defined the position of quarterback in the modern game—unless you want to credit that to Otto Graham, who preceded Unitas but played a game that few of us would recognize as modern pro football—but I have a little trouble picking Unitas over Montana.

Though Unitas is now recalled as a great "big game" quarterback, he won his reputation largely on the basis of the famous sudden-death win over the Giants in 1958, which is generally regarded as the start of the modern NFL. The next year he beat the Giants again, but those were the only two championships Unitas ever won. In the 1960s he was dominated by Bart Starr and the Green Bay Packers, who repeatedly beat Unitas and the Colts in key games as well as winning key games against teams who the Colts lost to.

In fact, Starr played for the championship of the NFL six times in eight years and lost only once—to the Philadelphia Eagles in 1960, on their home field, by a field goal. Football writers who came of age with Unitas often wrote off Starr's performance by saying that the Packers were simply a dominant team under Vince Lombardi and *should* have won, but in retrospect there wasn't that much difference between the Colts and the Packers in the '60s except in big games—and except when they played each other. I just don't see how Bart Starr's amazing record from 1960 through 1967 can be written off to Lombardi or Packer "dominance." In most seasons and in most of their key games, the reason the Packers won was because Bart Starr was better than the guy taking the snaps on the other team.

My picks for Greatest Team Sport Athletes of the last century are Bill Russell and Michael Jordan in basketball and Joe Montana and Bart Starr in football. I'll give Jordan the edge over Russell because he was a greater player and, from what I have been able to determine, possessed of at least comparable team skills. I'm going to give Starr the edge over Montana because he played in and won more championships, the ultimate yardstick of leadership, but also because in the game he played quarterbacks had to call most of their own plays—and the quality of intelligence cannot be underestimated in team sports.

Who do you like in baseball? Well, Babe Ruth is always a safe choice, and a darn good one. Still, as a Yankee, Ruth won "just" four World Series, and his skills were more geared to individual achievement than making his teammates better. In a sport where so many championships were won by the Yankees, it's hard to find a non-Yankee who really qualifies.

Most modern fans would pick Willie Mays as the best all-around player in the second half of the twentieth century, if not of all time. In addition, everyone who played with him is pretty much in agreement that Willie was "a great clubhouse guy." But Mays's Giants won just 3 pennants and only one World Series. (Willie also made a solid contribution to the Giants' 1971 play-off team and was at least on the roster for the Mets' 1973 National League pennant.)

Still, there are many great players who are bigger winners than Mays, and most of them are Yankees. For instance, Mickey Mantle, who was a huge presence on seven championship teams. Mantle's individual skills were fabulous, and he had "team" skills as well, such as the ability to bunt from either side of the plate, to begin a big inning by drawing a walk, and steal a base in a tight situation. Why so many people speak of Michael Jordan as the most "dominant" modern team sports player and never think of Mickey Mantle is beyond me. Don't Mantle's *seven* World Series rings count for something?

By "modern," of course, most people mean the second half of the twentieth century, but if you consider the first half, Joe DiMaggio makes a handsome choice. His Yankees won nine championships in Joe's thirteen seasons, a pretty good argument for DiMaggio's candidacy right there. DiMaggio was one of the greatest all-around players the game ever saw. He was regarded by friends and rivals as a great clutch performer, and whatever the mysterious quality is that inspires a team, DiMaggio had in abundance. Even the books that treat DiMaggio in a negative light, such as Richard Ben Cramer's *Joe DiMaggio—The Hero's Life,* quote teammates who spoke of DiMaggio with reverence.

"When Dago was in the lineup," one said, "we always thought we were going to win." And they did.

There was another Yankee who, like DiMaggio, had nine World Series rings and who, like Mantle, won three Most Valuable Player awards. He also played on three other pennant-winning teams.

Actually, Yogi Berra played for sixteen pennant-winning teams and ten World Series winners, but Yogi isn't a greedy man, and if he knew I was writing this chapter he would probably suggest that I confine my argument to seasons where he played in over 100 games. There were certainly enough of those to deal with.

I've established that a player must have great credentials at three levels to be considered for my team sports player of the century title. Yogi has the greatest record as a winner of any player mentioned in this debate. Not even Bill Russell had his team play in the postseason fourteen times—so that takes care of the first. The second can be dealt with just as quickly: Was Yogi undeniably a great player? *Of course.* At the toughest position to find a good player at in baseball—and maybe in all three major sports—Yogi Berra was, arguably, the greatest player in his position in his game's history.

The catcher Yogi was most often compared to in his playing days, of course, was his crosstown rival, Roy Campanella. Campy didn't get to start in the big leagues till 1948, when he played about half a season. In 1948 he was already twenty-seven. If Campanella had been able to join the Dodgers in '46, he almost certainly would be included in this comparison. (The record, as I mention in the chapter on the All-Star Team of the 1950s, indicates that at his peak Campy could certainly be regarded as Yogi's or anyone else's equal or near equal). As it stands, only four catchers had ten or more truly outstanding seasons and deserve to vie for the title of best-of-century.

Mickey Cochrane and Bill Dickey compete with each other for the title of best catcher in the first half of the century, and in the second half, virtually all experts who don't go with Berra choose Johnny Bench. Berra and Bench are easier to compare to each other than either is to Dickey or Cochrane, who, in comparison, played in a radically different game.

Berra and Bench actually square off quite nicely. Here's their career numbers at the plate (and my thanks to both men for having the decency to play almost the same number of games during their careers).

	G	AB	HR	RBI	R	BB	SO	GDP	BA	OBA	SA
Berra	2,120	7,555	358	1,430	1,174	704	414	146	.285	.348	.482
Beach	2,158	7,658	389	1,376	1,091	891	1,278	201	.267	.342	.476

SO = Strikeouts
GDP = Grounded Into Double Play

By the way, both men played other positions: Yogi put in 260 games as an outfielder, while Bench played 111 in the outfield, 195 at third, and another 145 at first. I saw no reason not to include all their batting numbers here. We're talking about team sports players, and the ability to switch positions should help, not hurt, a player's standing as a team player.

If you asked most baseball fans and writers today who the greatest catcher in baseball history was, they would probably answer Johnny Bench, with Yogi Berra a close second. Bench may well have been the greatest, and there is a lot more to the argument than these plain figures. But anyone making a case for Bench would have to argue past these figures first.

Yogi played in 38 fewer games and hit 31 fewer home runs than Bench, but he also drove in 54 more runs and scored 83 more. Bench walked 187 more times, which is significant, and Berra struck out 864 fewer times, which may or may not be significant. It certainly *sounds* better to say someone struck out 864 fewer times, but what that means in terms of actual runs is difficult to say. Since major leaguers in the second half of the last century caught about 97 percent of the balls hit to them, it might mean that the extra balls put in play by Berra produced maybe 25 errors more than Bench's batted balls. Would that add up to perhaps one additional run per season for Berra's teams? Maybe, maybe not.

In any event, look at the categories Yogi leads Bench in: batting average, by 18 points; on-base average by six; and slugging average, also by six. Figured by SLOB, or slugging average times on base average, Yogi produced 16.7 runs per 100 at bats to Bench's 16.3. Not much of a gap there, and it certainly fits into the category of possible margin for error. But until a system is discovered that ranks Bench slightly ahead of Berra instead of slightly behind him, why would we automatically rank Johnny Bench ahead of a man who played for ten World Series winners?

What about their relative worth as defensive catchers? Fielding statistics, of course, are never as definite as batting stats, and it is easier to make sense of Berra's and Bench's batting numbers than their fielding numbers. This is particularly true as regards stolen bases, since runners simply didn't attempt many steals in the '50s and went wild at the time Bench was catching in the late '60s and early '70s. We do have their reputations among their contemporaries to go by, though, and by consensus they were both considered among the top few defensive catchers in their times.

For what it's worth, the defensive numbers seem to me to be all on Yogi's side. (The numbers in parentheses indicate how many times they led the league.)

	G	PO	AST	DP	FA	LFA
Berra	1,697	8,738 (8)	798 (5)	175 (6)	.989 (2)	.987
Bench	1,742	9,249 (2)	850 (1)	127 (1)	.990 (1)	.987

Okay, so fielding numbers are vague; they don't offer a clear picture of which man was a better defensive catcher, though one thing is clear: Berra led his league in these fielding categories more often than Bench. So perhaps you want to throw the fielding stats out the window. Fine; but what, then, are you going to base your argument for Bench's superiority on? I'm not saying that there is a statistical basis for saying Yogi was better, either at bat or in the field. I'm saying I can't see the basis for coming down on either side.

I *can* see a clear difference between either Berra and Bench and either Bill Dickey or Mickey Cochrane. Hitting stats such as batting average and home runs and the conditions that create them change radically from one era to another, so it makes no sense to argue that Mickey Cochrane was a better hitter than Berra because his lifetime batting average of .320 was 35 points higher than Berra's, or to claim that Bench was a more productive hitter than Dickey solely on the basis of his having hit 187 more home runs.

One good way of measuring a hitter's effectiveness, though, is to look at how he ranked among his peers. For instance, *Total Baseball* ranks the top five hitters in every year since 1871 in runs, hits, doubles, triples, home runs, total bases, runs batted in, runs produced (runs plus RBIs), bases on balls, batting average, on-base average, slugging percentage, and their own complex evaluation system, Total Player Rating (TPR). Catchers aren't expected to lead their leagues in key hitting categories; the defensive job is just too demanding on legs and backs. But Berra and Bench show up an amazing number of times in the top five spots, not just for catchers, but for anybody. Let's do a year-by-year search, starting with Yogi:

1949—fifth in slugging percentage
1950—fifth in runs, fourth in hits, third in total bases, third in RBIs, second in runs scored, **second in TPR**
1951—fourth in total bases, **fifth in TPR**
1952—fourth in runs, third in HRs, fifth in RBIs, **fourth in TPR**
1953—fourth in HRs, fifth in total bases, fifth in RBIs, third in slugging, **third in TPR**
1954—fourth in total bases, second in RBIs, third in runs produced, fifth in batting average, fifth in slugging, **fifth in TPR**
1955—third in RBIs
1956—third in HRs, third in RBIs, fourth in runs produced, fifth in slugging average, **third in TPR**

Those are Yogi's seven best seasons, and I think that, relative to his era, it's the most impressive batting display ever put on by a catcher. Johnny Bench's is almost as impressive:

1970—first in HRs, second in total bases, first in RBIs, second in runs produced, **second in TPR**
1972—third in total bases, first in RBIs, fifth in runs produced, third in walks, third in slugging, **third in TPR**

1973—fourth in RBIs

1974—third in runs, third in doubles, second in HRs, fourth in total bases, first in RBIs, first in runs produced, fourth in slugging

1975—fourth in doubles, fourth in homers, second in RBIs, fifth in runs produced, fourth in slugging, *third in TPR*

1977—fifth in slugging

Bench's prime years, like Berra's, span eight seasons. It's easy to see why many people regard Bench as the greater catcher, or at least the greater hitter. At his best, Bench was better than Yogi, finishing relatively higher than Berra in the power categories—HRs, RBIs, and slugging average—in several seasons. But note Yogi's consistency. He shows up in something in every year for eight straight seasons, while in '71 and '76 Bench fails to place anywhere in the top five in anything.

Whether you agree with me or not, you must concede that, as hitters, both Berra and Bench leave Cochrane and Dickey in the dust.

Cochrane had a pretty good run from 1930 to 1935. In 1930, he was fifth in batting and fifth in TPR; in '31 he was fourth in batting and fifth in TPR; in 1932 he was fifth in walks, fifth in on-base average, and fourth in TPR; in 1933 he was second in walks, first in on-base average, fourth in slugging and fifth in TPR. In 1934 he was fourth in on-base average, and in 1935 he was fifth in on-base average.

Dickey's best seasons were from 1936 to 1939, when he finished, respectively, fifth, fourth, fifth, and fifth in TPR. But the only hitting categories he ever placed in were batting average (third) and slugging average (fifth) in 1936 and RBIs (fourth) in 1937.

I think it's safe to say that in their own time Yogi Berra and Johnny Bench were better hitters than Mickey Cochrane and Bill Dickey were in theirs. I think it's also safe to say that Berra and Bench were the two most valuable catchers of the century. Their hitting and fielding numbers are too close to declare either one a clear winner, so let's call the statistical comparison a draw and move on to the question of "team skills."

Now we move into the realm of what is generally referred to as "intangibles." I usually hate debates involving intangibles, not because I don't believe that intangible qualities don't exist in some form, but because they are so difficult to identify. But whatever you believe intangibles are, and however you want to measure them, you have to agree that if anyone had them, Yogi did.

Let's start with the idea of "clutch" performance. I am skeptical about "clutch" performance because I don't know how to measure it, and I've never seen a calculation for it that I thought was reliable. Yet I can't discount the evidence that some players raise the level of their game in big games. Year after year, Bill Russell performed above the level of his own high standards to hold the game's greatest player, Wilt Chamberlain, to a standoff in postseason play. In five NFL championship games Bart Starr outperformed his own quality numbers in championship games against tougher opposition than he faced during the regular season and outperformed more celebrated quarterbacks on the other teams. Can we simply disregard this evidence and call what happened season after season a fluke, or do we conclude that these men raised the level of their play in the biggest games?

In Yogi's case, we have the World Series to consider. As Branch Rickey pointed out, Yogi played the equivalent of nearly half a season just in the World Series. In 75 games he set the

World Series record for most hits, 71, and batted .274 with 12 home runs, 10 doubles, 32 walks, 39 RBIs, and 41 runs. His slugging average was .452, 30 points off his career mark, and his .354 on-base average was 6 points better than his career stat.

How good was Yogi in postseason play? Well, every baseball fans knows that Reggie Jackson is "Mr. October"—that's the way he signs his baseballs. Yet, the postseason records of Yogi and Reggie are quite comparable. Jackson played in seventeen postseason series, five of them World Series, a total of 77 games, two more than Yogi, and 281 at bats, 22 more than Berra. His postseason batting average is .278, just 4 points higher than Yogi, and his on-base average of .354 is the same. Jackson has a significant edge in slugging average, .527 to .452, but a big chunk of the edge in Jackson's postseason statistics is due not only to one series, the 1977 World Series against the Dodgers, but a single game in that series—in which Reggie hit 3 home runs. He batted .450 with 5 home runs and 8 runs batted in for the '77 Series. Without that single game, Jackson's career postseason slugging average drops below .490.

Yogi wasn't a better postseason hitter than Reggie Jackson, but there wasn't that much difference between them, and on defense Reggie didn't catch any perfect games.

Then there is the quality of leadership. When Joe DiMaggio began with the Yankees, Lou Gehrig and Bill Dickey shared the burden of team leadership. It wasn't till he returned from World War II that DiMaggio had to become the heart and soul of the Yankees by himself, a responsibility he handled splendidly. By 1948 DiMaggio's burden was lightened by the maturation of Berra, who started assuming the everyday catching duties. In 1949 injuries held DiMaggio to just 76 games (though he batted .346). Yogi caught 116 games, drove in 91 runs, and began to be looked on by the rest of the team as the on-field leader.

DiMaggio made something of a comeback in 1951, playing 139 games, batting .301, driving in 122 runs, and leading the AL in slugging at .585. However, the Yankees' best player in '51 was Berra, who caught 148 games, hit .322, and drove in 124 runs. By 1951 DiMaggio had badly faded, hitting just .263 with 12 home runs and 71 RBIs. Mantle, a rookie that year, had almost identical numbers to DiMaggio, batting .267 with 13 home runs and 65 RBIs. It was Berra who carried the team, catching 141 games, batting .294, hitting 27 home runs, and winning the MVP award.

From '52 through '55 Mantle and Berra were neck-and-neck for the title of most valuable Yankee, with Yogi winning back-to-back MVP awards in '54 and '55. In '56, Mantle pulled ahead and stayed there for the rest of the decade, though Yogi was second in the '56 MVP voting.

One could go back through those MVP years and raise arguments about whether Berra or Mantle should have won them in a couple of those seasons, but that would be irrelevant to this discussion. The point is that Berra's support in the voting is a strong indication of how he was regarded in those years by the writers and players—who, after all, influenced the writers—when it came to what is heaped together under the heading of "intangibles." One of those intangible qualities, perhaps the most important a catcher can possess, is the ability to handle a pitching staff. Everyone agrees that this is an almost impossible quality to give an exact measurement to, and everyone agrees that great pitchers make it easier for a catcher to look great.

How many truly great pitchers did Yogi Berra work with? I think Whitey Ford qualifies as great from just about any perspective, but what other Yankee pitchers could justifiably be called great, from the late '40s when Berra assumed the regular catching duties till the end of the next decade?

Allie Reynolds, as I remark in another chapter, certainly came close. But despite some flashes of greatness with the Indians, and despite working with an outstanding defensive catcher, Jim Hegan, Reynolds didn't become a consistently effective pitcher till he came to the Yankees. In addition to better fielding and coaching, one of the likely reasons Reynolds brought his game together was his ability to work well with Berra, who caught 51 games in '47, 71 in '48, and 109 in '49. There is no clear evidence that Yogi made a star out of Reynolds or Eddie Lopat or Vic Raschi or Tommy Byrne, the Yankees' four starting aces of the post-WWII period, or any of the Yankees' other pitchers, but look at how they all improved as Berra eased into the Yankees' first-string catcher position:

Year	Reynolds		Lopat		Raschi		Byrne		Berra
	Team	W-L	Team	W-L	Team	W-L	Team	W-L	GmsCaught
'46	Cle	11-15	CWS	13-13	NYY	2-0	NYY	0-1	6
'47	NYY	19-8	CWS	16-13	NYY	7-2	NYY	0-0	51
'48	NYY	16-7	NYY	17-11	NYY	19-8	NYY	8-5	71
'49	NYY	17-6	NYY	15-10	NYY	21-10	NYY	15-7	109
'50	NYY	16-12	NYY	18-8	NYY	21-8	NYY	15-9	148
'51	NYY	17-8	NYY	21-9	NYY	21-10	2Tms*	6-11	141

*NYY, StL-A

This isn't scientific, but when you see the records of these four good-to-very-good-but-not-great pitchers alongside Yogi's increasing total of games caught, it's hard to escape the conclusion that they matured together. Tommy Byrne's case stands out even more than the others. In '51 the Yankees traded Byrne to the Browns after arm trouble limited him to just nine ineffective appearances and a 2-1 record. He was just 4-10 for the rest of the season with St. Louis. In '53 he bounced from the White Sox to the Senators, going 2-5 with an ERA of 6.16. At the tail end of '54, the Yankees reacquired him and he went 3-2 with an ERA of 2.70 for 5 starts. In '55 he had his best season, starting 22 games, going 16-5, with an ERA of 3.15.

Yes, he had some arm trouble, and with the Yankees he was with a much better team. But a huge portion of that better team, both at bat and behind the plate, was Yogi Berra. Byrne had some effectiveness in both '56 and '57 with the Yankees, mostly as a relief pitcher, but when you add it all up, Tommy Byrne not only pitched ineffectively when he was outside New York, he had all of his best seasons when Yogi Berra was his catcher.

And so did most of the Yankees' other pitchers in the '50s. From 1954 to 1959, the last season Berra served as the Yankees' workhorse catcher before giving way to Elston Howard, the Yankees won four more pennants and two more World Series, and in one of the two years they didn't win the pennant, 1954, they won 103 games. Their pitching staffs in those seasons consisted of Whitey Ford, a couple of aging veterans, and a long list of career mediocrities who had a couple of good seasons with the Yankees and then faded into obscurity. Even Yankee fans can't remember most of their names. Season by season, the most important ones were:

1954

The staff included Ed Lopat and Allie Reynolds, hanging on in '54 (Reynolds's last season, Lopat's next to last), Johnny Sain (playing out a productive three-year stretch with the Yanks; the next season, after a few appearances, he would be dealt to Kansas City), Bob Grim, Tom Morgan, Harry Byrd, and Jim McDonald. Let's look carefully at the last four:

- Grim was 20-6 for the Yankees in his rookie season of '54; for the next three seasons he was plagued by arm trouble but was effective when he could pitch, winning 25 games, losing 14, and by 1957 making the transition into a reliever (he led the AL in saves with 19 that year). For the rest of his career, for four other teams, he was a combined 16-20.
- Tom Morgan was a combination starter-reliever for the Yankees from 1950 to 1956, when he was dealt to— you guessed it—Kansas City. For his five seasons in New York, he was 38-22, with his best season coming in 1954 when he started 17 games and went 11-5. He lasted in the big leagues for six more seasons, winning 29 and losing 25.
- Harry Byrd was with the Yankees just one season, winning 9 and losing 7 in 21 starts and posting the best ERA of his career, 2.99. For the rest of his six seasons in the bigs he was 37-47 with an ERA of over 4 runs per game.
- Jim McDonald was with the Yankees for three of his nine major league seasons, '52–'54, when, as a reliever and spot starter, he was a combined 16-12 with an ERA under 4 runs for all three seasons. For the rest of his career he was 8-15, and his overall ERA was 4.27.

There you go. Four more guys who, for whatever reasons, pitched very well when Yogi Berra was behind the plate and very lousy when anyone else caught them. Let's move on to '55.

1955

The Yankees rebounded from their second-place finish in '54 to beat out the Indians by three games for the American League pennant. After Whitey Ford (18-7) the staff was paced by—

- "Bullet Bob" Turley, who had compiled a three-year record of 16 wins and 22 losses with the Cardinals and Orioles, but was to go 76-44 from 1955 to 1960 with the Yankees before arm trouble reduced him to spot starting and middle innings relief. In 1945, with the Orioles, he was 14-15 with an ERA of 3.46; in this first year with the Yankees and Yogi he was 17-13 with an ERA of 3.06.
- Don Larsen, whose perfect game in the 1956 World Series is always regarded as a colossal fluke, which, of course, it was. But for four seasons, from 1955 through 1958, Larsen was a pretty good pitcher for the Yankees, both as a starter and a reliever, after enduring two horrible seasons with the St. Louis Browns and then with their incarnation in Baltimore, where he won 10 games and lost 33 with an ERA of over 4.20. In 1955, Larsen started 13 games for the Yankees, went 9-2, and saved two others, posting an ERA of 3.06. Overall, in his four good seasons in New York, Larsen went 39-17 and his ERA never exceeded 3.74. In '59, he dipped to 6-7, and the next year the Yankees dealt him to—need you ask?—Kansas City, where he was 1-10 with an ERA of 5.38.
- Johnny Kucks was a rookie in '55 and started in 13 games, relieved in 16, and had an 8-7 record and a respectable 3.41 ERA. Nineteen fifty-six was his best

year, when Yogi and the Yankees coaxed an 18-9 record out of him. Overall, in four seasons and a part of a fifth with the Yankees, he was 42-35 with 6 saves. In 1959 the Yankees traded him to—have I already mentioned this?—Kansas City, where, for the next two years, he was 12-21 with an ERA of over 4 runs per game.

- Jim Konstanty—yes, the Jim Konstanty who won the MVP award for the Phillies in 1950. After going 16-7 for the Phils at the beginning of the decade, Konstanty was 23-24 over the next three seasons with an overall ERA in that span of over 4 runs per game. In '54, when he was 37, the Phillies traded him to the Yankees, where he made nine relief appearances, saving 2, and recorded an ERA of 0.98. In '55 he was again sensational for the Yankees, winning 7 and losing 2 in 45 relief appearances. He saved 11 games and posted the best seasonal ERA of his career, 2.32. The next season the Yankees dealt him to the Cardinals (the Athletics' phone must have been busy), where he closed out his career.

1956

This time the Yankees not only won the pennant but the World Series as well. Ford, of course, was the ace that year at 19-6. The staff was fleshed out by Kucks (18-9), Larsen (11-5), Turley (8-4), Byrne (7-3), Grim (6-1), and the new addition of Tom Sturdivant (16-8).

Sturdivant pitched in 33 games as a rookie with the Yanks in '55 with an excellent ERA of 3.16. The next season he started 17 games and relieved in 15, winning 16 and saving 5 with an ERA of 3.30. In '57 he had his best year, pitching exclusively as a starter, leading the AL in won-lost percentage (16-6, or .727), with his career best ERA, 2.54. That was about it for Tom. After a disappointing '58 season, 3-6, and a slow start in '59, the Yankees dumped him on—am I starting to sound like a broken record here?—Kansas City, where he went 2-6. He pitched indifferently for 6 seasons after leaving the Yanks, never approaching the 32-14 record he had in '56–'57.

1957

The Yankees won the pennant, but lost the World Series to the Braves. The most significant addition to the staff was Bobby Shantz, who had won the MVP award in 1952 for the lowly Philadelphia A's when he went 24-7, but then had spent the next four seasons struggling with arm trouble and had a won-lost record of 13-26. The Yankees squeezed four more good seasons out of him—two ('57–'58) as a spot starter and reliever and two ('59–'60) almost exclusively as a reliever. In '57 he was brilliant, starting 21 games, going 11-5, saving 5, and leading the league with a 2.45 ERA. Over the next three seasons he was 19-13 with 14 saves, recording ERAs of 3.36, 2.38, and 2.79. In '61 the Yankees traded him to Pittsburgh, and he spent his last four seasons bouncing around the National League. Shantz is an exception to most of the Yankees' pitching trades of the '50s and early '60s. He had been a great starter, at least for one season in Philadelphia, and after he left New York he was actually a useful reliever right up until the end. Still, it was with the Yankees that he turned things around.

1958

The Yanks again won it all. The pitching staff was paced by "Bullet Bob" Turley (21-7), who had his best season and walked off with the Cy Young award. Whitey Ford, at 14-7, was the *only other pitcher to win more than 9 games.* Perhaps more than any other of the Yankees' pennant-winning seasons with Berra as the regular catcher, the Yankees staff was an incredible pastiche of one-shot wonders and also-rans. Let's go down the list:

- Duke Maas. Duke had a record of 19-32 with the Tigers and Athletics before the Yankees acquired him early in the '58 season. He promptly went 7-3 for them with an ERA of 3.82. Maas wasn't much of a pitcher, but he lasted with the Yanks for two more full seasons and part of a third before retiring in early 1961. From '59–'60, incredibly, he managed to win 19 and lose only 9.
- Ryne Duran. Duran, of course is one of the great weird stories of the '50s and '60s. A terrifying fastball pitcher, he suffered from bad eyesight. In a brief (one game) appearance with the Orioles in '54 and 42 innings with—is there an echo in here?—Kansas City in '57, Duran had an ERA of 5.3 runs per 9 innings. In 1958, after coming to New York, he did an immediate about-face with a 6-4 won-lost record, a league-leading 20 saves, and a spectacular 2.20 ERA. In '59, despite a 3-5 won-lost record, he was even more effective, with an ERA of 1.88. After a bad spring and slow start in 1961 the Yankees let him go to the expansion Angels, where he went on to lose 12 of 18 games and collect only 2 saves, with a horrendous ERA

of 5.18. He hung around for four more seasons, having some success in '63 with the Phillies (6-2, ERA 3.30), but he won only one more major league game after that.

- Art Ditmar. Ditmar was one of the most amazing Yankee success stories of the 1950s. From '54 through '56 he struggled with the (natch!) Athletics—winning 25, losing 38, and watching his career ERA climb precariously toward 5 runs per 9 innings. In 1957 he came to the Bronx, went 8-3 with 6 saves, and saw his ERA drop to 2.35. In '58, the Yankees' last championship season under Casey Stengel, he was a useful pitcher, going 9-8 in 13 starts and saving 4 games with an acceptable 3.42 ERA. From '59 through the first month of '61, Ditmar was 30-21 before leaving New York for—stop me if you've heard this one—Kansas City—where over the next 2 seasons he was 0-7 with an ERA of nearly 6 runs per game.

Have I left anyone out? Oh, yeah, I almost forgot. There was Zach Monroe. I don't know anything about Zach except that his first season in baseball was 1958, that he started 6 games for the Yankees and went 4-2 with a very good ERA of 3.26. The following season he pitched in 3 innings and was out of baseball forever. (The upside is that he never got traded to Kansas City).

There are, of course, all kinds of reasons why all these pitchers had their best years with the Yankees: better hitting (though that doesn't explain the improved ERAs), better fielding, better coaching, and Casey Stengel's shrewd application of their mostly modest talents. But there is one connection common to all of them that is more direct: Yogi Berra. Yogi worked with just one undeniably great pitcher in his career, Whitey Ford, and in

1951 and '52 when Ford was in the service Yogi was at his peak, winning the MVP award in '51.

Throughout the late '40s and most of the '50s the Yankees had the best pitching in baseball, even though they seldom had the best pitchers. In most years the Yankees' staffs consisted of one- or two-year wonders, faded veterans who discovered a little gas left in their tanks, and also-rans who had a good season or two squeezed out of them and then moved on to obscurity. All of them, no matter what their talent or background or fate, shared two things: World Series money and a catcher. Not Mickey Cochrane nor Bill Dickey nor Johnny Bench ever displayed anything like Yogi's talent for handling a pitching staff. They might have, if they had been faced with the same circumstances and the same talent to work with. But they didn't have the chance; Yogi did, and he won—seasonal games, pennants, World Series rings—more than any other catcher. In fact, more than any other baseball player of the century.

If Yogi Berra's record as handler of Yankee pitching staffs isn't a clear indication of an extraordinary talent for leadership, then we may as well dispense with the word altogether.

A few years ago at an Old-Timers game at Yankee Stadium I asked Whitey Ford how he came to be called "The Chairman Of the Board." "Everyone," he told me, "regarded me as a cocky kid when I came up, and that's the way they continued to see me throughout my career. I acted that way 'cause I figured it gave me an edge. I didn't throw as fast as some guys and I didn't have as big a curve as some, but I acted as if I was confident, and that's the way people regarded me, especially the hitters, the ones I really wanted to impress. Well, I wasn't confident, not really. It was Yogi who was confident, and Yogi that made me feel that way. With anyone else as my catcher, I wouldn't have been the same pitcher."

In the 11 years that Yogi Berra was the New York Yankees' regular catcher, the team won nine pennants, seven World Series, and had one second-place finish in 1954, winning 103 of 154 games. Overall, Yogi made contributions to three other pennant winners and one World Series winner by playing a capable left field (how many catchers can you think of who began and ended their careers in left field?), pinch-hitting, and backing up the regular catchers.

Yogi Berra was, arguably, the greatest ever at baseball's toughest position, the position that wears out players faster than any other. He was a great clutch performer, however you want to define the word. He was so well regarded by teammates, foes, fans, and writers that he was voted onto *fifteen* All-Star teams. His leadership skills are evidenced by the records of nearly every pitcher he ever worked with. He was one of the great winners, maybe the greatest, in American sports history.

The question of who was the greatest "team" player in baseball during the last century can't be debated the way you would debate a question like "Who's the greatest player ever?" or "Who's the greatest pitcher?" By nature, the question demands too subjective an interpretation. But interpret "team player" and "team skills" however you like, and then apply your standards to Yogi Berra. I think he meets more of the criteria than any player the game ever produced.

For my money, Yogi Berra was the most valuable team player in any sport in the twentieth century.

3

Robin Roberts (and Eddie Mathews and Ernie Banks and Whitey Ford) and the All-Star Team of the 1950s or Me Versus 200 Writers

Route 18, which runs by Old Bridge, New Jersey, is a quaint two-lane road connecting Menlo Park (that's Thomas Edison's Menlo Park) to Route 9, immortalized by Bruce Springsteen in "Born To Run": *Sprung from cages out on Highway 9.*

If you should ever drive down it—and I'm not really suggesting that you go there for that purpose, as there isn't much to see except scrub and pine trees that immediately identify the area as the outgrowth of Appalachia it was known as before housing developments were built for Manhattan commuters— you'll see a charming little ballpark that proclaims itself "Home of The Old Bridge Little League." On the walls you'll notice some stenciled portraits of baseball greats such as Babe Ruth, Lou Gehrig, Joe DiMaggio—this was and largely still is Yankee country—as well as Honus Wagner and Ty Cobb. As I write this sentence, they have been on that wall for 41 years. I'm the one who put them there.

Well, not by myself, and not all of them. Sometime back, I don't know when (my family moved away in 1965), someone painted pictures of then-current stars, the oldest of whom was Willie Mays and the youngest Rod Carew, so the new ones were probably added in the late '60s or early '70s. But the original portraits were done by the director of the Old Bridge Little League, whose name I have long forgotten, and they were copied from a book I loaned him, one of my all-time favorite baseball books, *Big-Time Baseball*.

Big-Time Baseball was an eight-by-eleven-inch softcover book printed for several years—I don't know for how many, but I have the '59, '60, '61, and '62 editions—by the Hart Publishing Company in New York, and edited for years by a veteran sportswriter for the Associated Press named Ben Olan. The last edition I saw (which I bought at a card and memorabilia show in Houston, Texas) doesn't mention Olan's name but says "compiled by Michael H. Hart," presumably of the Hart Publishing Company, though exactly what it was he compiled is unclear, since 90 percent of the book is the same text as the previous editions.

I hear people talking all the time about ways to get younger kids interested in baseball. Personally, I think it's a fruitless task. Kids today seem completely absorbed in skateboarding and video games, and are not much involved with team sports at all, except for soccer, which all the kids of my acquaintance would stop playing if their mothers stopped forcing them to, and lacrosse, which they lose interest in before their senior year in high school. But if it was possible to interest kids in baseball again, it would almost surely have to start by getting them to *read* about baseball. That was the genius of *Big-Time Baseball* and books like it, which opened up the game for me and many of my friends when we were at an impressionable age.

My first edition was the 1960 volume, which my mom got for me while we were on vacation in Atlantic City. I was scarcely old enough to read it, but, like the Superman and Batman comics of my youth, they *compelled* me to read. There were chapters headed "The Hall of Records" (with items such as "Alexander pitched 16 shutouts in one season"), "The Hall of Blunders" ("Mike Grady made four errors on one batted ball"), and "Big Moments of the Big Time" (where I first learned that Carl Hubbell struck out Babe Ruth, Lou Gehrig, Jimmie Foxx, Al Simmons, and Joe Cronin in a row in the 1934 All-Star Game). There was a chapter, the first such I had ever seen, on statistics, which listed all the batting champions, all the 200-game winners, and every Hall of Famer from 1901 to 1959.

There was also a great chapter on baseball's zanies, where I learned all the apocryphal stories about Babe Herman, Dizzy Dean, and Lefty Gomez, with full-page pictures of "Today's Stars," including a posed shot of Dick Stewart smiling as he gloved a ground ball. ("Must have been one of the few he caught all season," my father quipped.) Then there was the All-Star Team of All Time, picked by a committee of "164 top-flight sportswriters of the country's leading newspapers as well as 76 nationally-known public figures." (I'd love to know who the public figures were. The introductory text implies that there was some connection with Cooperstown, but nothing is specified.)

Whoever selected the All-Star Team of All Time, there weren't many surprises. In fact, any reasonably knowledgeable fan, if asked to guess who such a committee might pick on an all-time team in 1959, could probably have guessed all nine players. The pitcher was Walter Johnson, the catcher Bill Dickey, Lou Gehrig was at first, Rogers Hornsby at second, Honus Wagner at short, Pie Traynor at third, Babe Ruth in right, Ty Cobb in center, and Joe DiMaggio in left. Today, many historians might favor Mickey Cochrane over Dickey and maybe Jimmy Collins over Pie Traynor at third; the only eye-opener was that Cobb made center field over DiMaggio, a selection I found inexplicable even then. The accompanying portrait sketches by an artist named Sydney Weiss were the ones that wound up on the wall at the Old Bridge Little League field entrance. It never occurred to me until I wrote this sentence that we of the Old Bridge Little League might have owed Mr. Weiss's estate some royalties.

That chapter in *Big-Time Baseball* was my introduction to the immortals, but another chapter, "The All-Star Team of the Decade," was my introduction to arguing about baseball. Not right away, because I wasn't old enough to have heard of, let alone to have seen the players who were chosen, but I memorized their names, and within a few years I was smarting off to my friends and saying things like "Do you know who was the best third baseman of the nineteen fifties?" And when they didn't get it—and they never did—when I told them and they expressed disbelief, I shot back, "Well, that's not what 'some two hundred sportswriters and editors of the country's leading newspapers' thought."

Forty years later, it's hard for me to recall the impact this poll had on me. The introductory text (presumably written by Olan) explains that "Ballots were submitted from the four corners of the U.S.A. A total of one hundred and thirty-seven cities are represented—ranging from Aberdeen, South Dakota, to Youngstown, Ohio. Sports scribes from forty-one states and the District of Columbia pondered a select list of stars before rendering their verdict. The results of the vote add up to an honor roll of the best in baseball in recent years—the All-Star Team of the Past Decade."

In later years I would get to meet some of the men who voted in the poll, and I never failed to tell them how much it meant to me in my youth: the *Atlanta Journal's* Furman Bischer, the *Birmingham News's* Zipp Newman, the *Columbus (Ohio) Dispatch's* Paul Hornung (who always enjoyed fans confusing him with the Notre Dame and Green Bay Packers football star), the *Los Angeles Times's* Paul Zimmerman (who later became the famous football writer for *Sports Illustrated*), the *Newark Evening News's* Hy Goldberg (whom I met when I won a prize for delivering the most copies of his paper), the *St. Louis Post-Dispatch's* Bob Broeg (who was probably the worst reactionary of any sportswriter in my generation) and at least a score of others.

Without an exception, they all remembered the All-Star Team of the Past Decade, and without exception, I found out to my surprise, they all said that if they had to do it over, they would have made some different choices.

I never did figure out how "164 top-flight sportswriters" and "76 nationally-known public figures" added up to the advertised 200, but here, selected by some 200 sportswriters and editors of the country's leading newspapers, are the first, second, and third all-star teams of the 1950s:

THE *BIG-TIME BASEBALL* ALL-STAR TEAM OF THE 1950s

	First Team	Second Team	Third Team
First Base	Gil Hodges	Mickey Vernon	Ted Kluszewski
Second Base	Nellie Fox	Red Schoendienst	Jackie Robinson
Shortstop	Phil Rizzuto	Pee Wee Reese	Ernie Banks
Third Base	George Kell	Ed Mathews	Al Rosen

Brushbacks and Knockdowns

(continued)

	First Team	Second Team	Third Team
Outfield	Ted Williams	Mickey Mantle	Al Kaline
	Stan Musial	Hank Aaron	Jackie Jensen
	Willie Mays	Duke Snider	Richie Ashburn
Catcher	Yogi Berra	Roy Campanella	Del Crandall
Left-Handed Pitcher	Warren Spahn	Whitey Ford	Billy Pierce
Right-Handed Pitcher	Allie Reynolds	Robin Roberts	Early Wynn
Relief Pitcher	Elroy Face	Jim Konstanty	Hoyt Wilhelm
Pinch Hitter	Johnny Mize	Enos Slaughter	Dusty Rhodes
Manager	Casey Stengel	Al Lopez	Leo Durocher

Big-Time Baseball was my introduction to baseball analysis, and for years, right on into college, I regarded both of its all-star team polls, both the All-Star Team of All Time and The All-Star Team of the Past Decade, as sacred. I simply accepted as an act of faith the idea that smart baseball men who were close to the players in time, who had actually seen them play, would know exactly how to evaluate and rate them. It never occurred to me that they might be too close to the subject to see the big picture.

One day, putting books and things from my room in my parents' house in storage, I came across my old copies of *Big-Time Baseball* and flipped open to the All-Star Team of the Past Decade. For the first time, I realized that *I* could have picked a better all-star team than the 200 leading sportswriters and editors did. It took me twenty-two years to get around to it, but here's my All-Star Team of the 1950s, matched against the country's top 200 sportswriters.

First Base

"Gil Hodges," the text says, "was an out-and-out runaway for first base, scoring 523 points, more than 200 better than his closest competitor, Mickey Vernon, who had 291. Ted Kluszewski took third place with 213."

I don't know that anyone has ever asked the question before, and if not, this is as good a place as any: Why weren't there any truly great first basemen in the 1950s? I mean, there were certainly some very good first basemen, and there's certainly nothing disgraceful about the selection of Gil Hodges as the best in the decade, but where were the George Sislers, Bill Terrys, Lou Gehrigs, Jimmie Foxxes, and Hank Greenbergs of earlier times and the Willie McCoveys, Harmon Killebrews, Orlando Cepedas, Eddie Murrays, Keith Hernandezes, Mark McGwires, Jeff Bagwells, Rafael Palmeiros, and Fred McGriffs of later decades?

Since about 1915 or so, in the era of slower-moving baseballs and inferior gloves, first base has generally been considered the least-demanding defensive position, which means that most first basemen are free to concentrate on their hitting. Yet, the 1950s, which were generally a time of de-emphasized base running and power hitting, produced not one truly great power hitter.

Gil Hodges was a very good player, perhaps one of the 25 or 30 best first basemen of all time, but not a great player and, thus, in my estimation—and, apparently, in that of most Hall of Fame voters—not a genuine Hall of Famer. I wouldn't go to the barricades to keep Hodges out, and I see no rule that would not permit voters to simply vote him in on the basis of his having been a good player *and* an excellent manager, having guided the '69 Miracle Mets to baseball immortality. But it is as a player that we are concerned with here, and Hodges, for all his skill and admirable personal qualities, was simply not a great player.

Was he the best first baseman of the 1950s? Probably. The voters chose him over Mickey Vernon, a now-forgotten player who had some outstanding seasons (and some inexplicably poor ones) with the Washington Senators between 1939 and 1955, taking time out for World War II. (He finished up as a semiregular with Boston, Cleveland, Milwaukee, and Pittsburgh from 1957 to 1960.) Vernon was a good, solid player who won batting titles in 1946 (.353) and 1953 (.337); he led the league in doubles three times, fielding percentage four times, and was in double figures in stolen bases five times, unusual for anyone in that era and highly unusual for a first baseman.

The problem is that those highlights make Vernon's career sound better than it was: For 20 years in the big leagues, he hit just .286 and his power was not outstanding, just 172 home runs, including only one season with 20 or more, though he probably would have fared much better had he not played his home games in D.C.'s cavernous Griffith Stadium. On the whole, I'd have to rate him pretty close to Hodges, but Gil has to get something for all those pennants he helped the Dodgers win.

I suppose the argument could go either way: What if Vernon had played on the Dodgers and Hodges had played for the lowly Senators? But Hodges *did* play on the Dodgers and they *did* win a lot of pennants, and I don't see any sound reason why he should be docked for that fact.

For my first baseman of the '50s, I'm going to pick the writers' *third* pick, Ted Kluszewski, not because I think he was better than Hodges, but because I bragged that I could pick a better all-star team than the writers, and Kluszewski is about the best pick I can make at first base. For peak value, which includes the 1950 season (when he hit 25 home runs, drove in 111 runs, and batted .307) and 1953 through 1956 (when he made four consecutive all-star teams, sharing the roster in the first three with Hodges and in which he averaged 42 home runs, 116 RBIs, and a .315 batting average), "Big Klu" was at least Hodges's equal.

Although he was not known as an outstanding first baseman, for a big guy (he was listed at 6'4", but people who remember him from the period say that the weight of 225 currently listed by *Total Baseball* is a little low) he was at least technically sound. He led the National League's first basemen in fielding percentage for five consecutive seasons, from '52 to '55.

Why did Ted Kluszewski not achieve true greatness? Most accounts of the period cite chronic back trouble. He was an incredibly strong man with huge biceps. My father used to tell me that he read in the papers where Klu had to slit the red sleeves on his Cincinnati uniform to fit his arms through, and from the pictures I've seen, that was probably true. Like many players who are fixed on bodybuilding, he seemed to be on the brittle side and missed numerous games due to injury. I can't compensate him for what he might have done, but I can't see why, for at least five seasons, he couldn't be considered as good as Hodges, if not a little better.

Still, for long-term service, advantage to the 200 Writers, by a little.

Second Base

"There was an extremely tight tussle for honors at second," reads *Big-Time Baseball*. "Nellie Fox finally squeaked through to victory over Red Schoendienst by the hairline margin of 3 points, 351 to 348. A respectable third was Jackie Robinson, his supporters giving him 317."

The voters certainly got the margin between Jacob Nelson ("Nellie") Fox and Albert ("Red") Schoendienst right; in terms of career value, they were almost exactly the same player, and if Red hadn't contracted tuberculosis in 1958 at age thirty-five, he would probably have nosed Fox out. (He missed almost the entire 1959 season fighting off the disease, after which he had three productive seasons with the St. Louis Cardinals as a reserve player.)

Let's look at their career statistics:

	G	H	HR	R	RBI	BA	OBA	SA	DP	Range	FA
Nellie '47–'65	2,367	2,663	35	1,279	790	.288	.348	.363	1,619	5.57	.984
Red '45–'63	2,216	2,449	84	1,223	773	.289	.337	.387	1,368	5.62	.983

Fox played a handful of games at first and third base, while Schoendienst played 39 at third, 49 at shortstop, and 123 in the outfield. All fielding statistics in the above comparison are from their games at second base, where Fox put in 2,295 while Schoendienst played 1,834. Schoendienst actually averaged slightly more double plays per game at second base, .75 to Fox's .71. (Forgive me for just listing him under just "Red," but it's easier than spelling out Schoendienst every time.)

Fox got to more balls per nine defensive innings than the average second baseman in the American League, 5.57 to 5.42, and was 7 points above the AL in fielding average, .984 to .977. Red was almost identical, getting to 5.62 balls per game to the NL average for second basemen of 5.51, and his career fielding average of .983 was 8 points above the NL average of .975.

I believe, with Branch Rickey, that "nothing can be done with fielding statistics." There are so many factors to consider—the type of pitching staffs on their teams and the regularity with which they produced ground balls, the fielding range of the shortstops and first basemen they played alongside, etc. But I can't imagine that when two guys playing at the same time for so long are this close that any detailed study is going to reveal much of a difference in their performance. I'd have to say that from the available evidence that Red and Nellie were just about in a dead heat in the field.

At bat? Well, you can see how close the numbers are. If you figure it by SLOB—slugging average times on-base average—Schoendienst has a slight edge, 13.04 to Fox's 12.62, or roughly speaking, about 0.4 more of a run per 100 at-bats for Red. Both were considered to be smart base runners but bad base stealers: Nellie stole just 76 bases in 156 attempts for a dismal 49 percent success rate while Red was a little better, 89 out of 116 for a success rate of 55 percent. I don't really see the point of trying to figure who contributed more runs with their base stealing. Nellie grounded into 175 double plays in 2,367 games. Red grounded into 5 more double plays in 151 fewer games, so, slight edge for Nellie.

All in all, the numbers are so close that I don't know how anyone could make a clear choice of Fox as the better second baseman. Yet Nellie, who won a razor-sharp decision over Red in The All-Star Team of the 1950s poll, is far better remembered today. Why is that?

I can think of only one good reason: Nellie finished the decade stronger than Red. Red got his first World Series ring in 1946 with the Cardinals, batting .281 and leading the National League second basemen in fielding percentage at .984. He made a substantial contribution to the Braves' world championship drive in 1957, playing in 93 games and hitting .310 for them. (Overall, he batted .309 for the season and led the league with 200 hits, the only time he topped the NL in that category.) He made a solid if unspectacular contribution to the Braves' 1958 pennant drive, hitting .262 in 106 games and leading the league's second-sackers in fielding at .987. But the TB was starting to get to him then, and he would only play five games into 1959 and would never again play more than ninety-eight in a season. Red never won an MVP award, and neither of the world championship teams he played on quite captured the public imagination like the 1959 Chicago White Sox.

The White Sox capped the decade by winning the American League pennant, and Nellie Fox, considered by many to be the spark plug of that team, won the American League MVP award. The Sox were known collectively as the "Hitless Wonders" and "The Go-Go Sox" because they hit a league-low 97 home runs and stole a league-high 113 bases, led by Luis Aparacio's 56. That historical perception of the '59 Sox is a bit off, because Comiskey Park was one of the worst hitters' parks in baseball. Nonetheless, writers who followed the White Sox all season long perceived Nellie Fox to be the primary factor in the pennant win, and from all accounts I've read, the players thought so too. As Kevin Costner's Crash Davis says in *Bull Durham,* "The reason a team *thinks* it's winning *is* the reason it's winning."

Was Nellie Fox better or more valuable than Red Schoendienst? Nellie was a hard-nosed, aggressive ballplayer, popular with both the fans and press. His image is immortalized in the Hartland statue, originally issued in 1960, which shows him making the pivot to first on a double play, a huge lump in his cheek from the chaw of tobacco. The tobacco would eventually kill him; he died of cancer in 1975 at the age of forty-eight. I sent a copy of the reissued Hartland to my friend, the novelist Barry Gifford, who is best known for the novel *Wild At Heart,* but who first came to my attention as the author of the lovely cult book about Wrigley Field, *The Neighborhood of Baseball.* The book is primarily about the Cubs, but Fox was Barry's favorite player as a boy. "Every time I look at that statue and see that bulge in Nellie's cheek," he once told me, "my heart hurts." It now sits on the desk in his work studio in Oakland, California.

I would never imply that Nellie Fox didn't deserve all the affection he holds in the memories of fans and writers who saw him play. It's just that I can't see any clear reason why he would rank higher on any career evaluation than Red Schoendienst. If I chose Red as my second baseman for the '50s, I'd have to give myself a tie with the 200 Writers.

But I'm not going to choose Red Schoendienst as my second baseman of the '50s. I'm going to choose the man they put on the Third Team, Jackie Robinson.

I'm going to give the 200 best baseball writers of the '50s a break here. I'm going to assume that they all knew that Jackie Robinson was a far better ballplayer than either Nellie Fox or Red Schoendienst. The only conceivable reason I can see why he wasn't at the top of their list is because he only played for three full seasons at the position (1950, '51, and '52) and then just 36 games at second base over his last four seasons.

If that's the way the writers wanted to vote, so be it. However, Robinson made third place on their list, which means he was eligible, and if he's eligible, then I'm grabbin' him for my team.

In the three seasons Robinson spent at second base in the 1950s, he exhibited something that neither Nellie nor Red did in their entire careers: real, unequivocal greatness. In those three seasons, he batted, respectively, .328, .338, and .308. In 1952 he led the league in on-base percentage at .440. He averaged 17 home runs, 81 runs batted in, and 103 runs scored for three seasons. He averaged 20 stolen bases per year, a very high total in that non-running era. These are offensive numbers that neither Red nor Nellie ever came close to. Nor, for those three seasons, does he give away anything to either Nellie or Red in the field. In '50, '51, and '52 Robinson led the National League in double plays; in '50 and '51 he led the league in fielding percentage; and in 1950 he led the league in putouts, assists, and range factor as well.

It's plain silly to argue otherwise: If Jackie Robinson is eligible for this poll, then you take him.

At second base, big advantage to me.

Shortstop

This is where I start to clean up. The 200 Writers chose Phil Rizzuto for the first team and Pee Wee Reese for the second. I don't get it.

I'm not going to revive the old "Should Phil Rizzuto Be In The Hall of Fame?" argument. Since the Hall of Fame voters (or at least the Veterans Committee) wanted him in so badly, it's fine with me. Without trying too hard, I can find some other players in the Hall who are less worthy. But Phil Rizzuto was *not* a better shortstop or more valuable player than Pee Wee Reese, particularly not in the 1950s.

In 1950 Rizzuto had a sensational season, batting .324, scoring 125 runs, and somehow managing, from his leadoff spot, to drive in 66. He even hit 7 home runs. He was awarded the Most Valuable Player Award, and as far as I can see, deservedly so. But those numbers were hugely uncharacteristic of Rizzuto's career. Phil hit .307 as a rookie in 1941 at age twenty-four and .284 the following season, and it's very likely that he left some or all of his best seasons in the service from 1943 through 1945. I'll give him all the credit he deserves for that.

Outside 1941 and 1950, though, Rizzuto never hit over .300, and in only one other season, 1948, did he hit as many as 6 home runs. His batting averages for '51 through '54, the last in which he would play more than 81 games, were .274, .254, .271, and .195. He hit exactly 2 home runs in each of those four seasons. If you put a gun to my head I wouldn't understand why Jackie Robinson, who had three sensational seasons in his position in the '50s, finished third in this poll, while Phil Rizzuto, who has just one sensational season in the decade at his position, finished first.

Pee Wee Reese, on the other hand, played seven full seasons at shortstop in the '50s (and an eighth and final season, in which he played 103 games, if you want to count that, though nearly three-fourths of those were at third base). He wasn't a sensational hitter in the '50s, but he was better than Rizzuto, hitting, respectively, .260, .286, .272, .271, .309, .282, and .257. For those seven seasons he averaged 11.5 home runs per season, a couple of which I'm sure could be accounted for by the friendly confines of his home park, Ebbets Field. Still, Pee Wee outslugged the Scooter every season except 1950.

One thing about those 200 Writers: When they blew a call, they blew it big. In point of objective fact, neither Phil Rizzuto nor Pee Wee Reese was anywhere near the most valuable shortstop of the 1950s. The best by a wide margin was their third pick, Ernie Banks.

This is so obvious that I don't really need to cite any exotic statistics to back it up. Ernie Banks played every game at shortstop for six seasons in the 1950s. From 1954 through 1959 he hit with spectacular power, averaging 37 home runs per season. And that average is watered down by the total of just 19 he hit in his rookie year of '54.

It has been pointed out that Ernie's batting stats got a substantial boost from the games he played in his home park, Wrigley Field. That's true, but on the road from '54 through '59 he hit 94 home runs, which projects over six full seasons to 188 homers. Thirty-one home runs per season is the kind of power that Rizzuto and Reese wouldn't have approached if you took all of their home runs and lumped them *together.*

Banks's fielding statistics at shortstop are pretty decent. He had exactly the same range factor of 5 chances per game as the rest of the league's shortstops over his career, which is a tad better than Pee Wee managed (5.03 to the NL's 5.11) and not quite as good as Rizzuto (5.21 to the AL's 5.09), though it's very likely that part of Banks's range factor can be attributed to the lousy Chicago pitching that allowed so many balls to be hit. Still, Ernie was sure-handed: He led the league's shortstops in fielding average three times, and for his career was 7 points (.969 to .962) better than average.

I'm not going to try to tell you that Ernie Banks was a better fielding shortstop than either Phil or Pee Wee, but when considering overall value, the point is irrelevant. There is simply nothing that Phil and Pee Wee could have done in the field that could have made up the difference between those two and Ernie Banks at the plate.

Advantage to me—big, big time.

Third Base

This was by far the strangest pick made by the 200 Writers, even stranger than their second base and shortstop selections. Over the years I have had fun asking several of my friends and colleagues "Can you guess who the 200 leading sportswriters of the 1950s picked at third base?" Not only have none of them ever guessed the answer, scarcely any of them ever heard of the winner when I gave them the answer.

I don't mean to be dismissive of George Kell. Actually, I don't really know enough about him to be dismissive. The record book says that he was a pretty good ballplayer, hitting .306 for his career and even leading the American League in batting at .343 in 1949, the first time any third baseman had ever won a batting crown. He led the league in hits and doubles in both 1950 and '51 while playing for the Tigers, for whom he had most of his best seasons.

Kell didn't have much power. He hit more than 10 home runs only once (hitting 12 when he was with the Red Sox in 1953, with 9 of them hit in Fenway Park). Kell hit over .300 five times in the '50s, including .340 in 1950, the year after he won the batting title. He seems to have been a very good third baseman, averaging exactly as many chances per game (3.21) as the rest of the league's sackers during his career, but finishing a whopping 15 points higher in fielding average (.969 to .954). Apparently he couldn't run a lick, stealing just 51 of 87 bases in 87 tries for his 15 years in the bigs. Given the sparseness of talent at that position in the first half of the twentieth century, I'd guess that overall he was probably one of the ten or fifteen best third basemen the game had seen up to that time and one of the top 25 or 30 of all time.

I haven't a clue as to why George Kell was the first choice at third base in the All-Star Team of the 1950s while Al Rosen was chosen number three.

For five seasons, from 1950 through 1954, Al Rosen touched greatness. As much as "Pistol Pete" Reiser, Herb Score, or Don Mattingly, he merits consideration for what he might have done if not for injuries. (In Rosen's case, the injury was to his back, which made his last two seasons, '55 and '56, a torture and which forced him into an early retirement at age thirty-two.) Before that, he was probably headed for recognition as the best player in the American League up to that time at third base, with the possible exception of Home Run Baker, who was a heck of a player in his own time (1908–1922), though not always recognized as such. Rosen *might* have been the best third baseman in either league up to that time.

From '50 through '54 he averaged 31 home runs and 114 runs batted in per season, hitting over .300 three times. In 1953, he had one of the greatest seasons of any third baseman ever, hitting 43 home runs, scoring 115 runs, driving in 145, and leading the league in both on-base and slugging average. George Kell never had a season like that. Mike Schmidt and George Brett had a couple of seasons like that, but not many.

Still, I'm not going to choose Al Rosen as my third baseman of the '50s. Instead I'm going with the 200 Writers' number two guy, Eddie Mathews. (In *Big-Time Baseball* he is identified in several places as "Ed," just as his friend and teammate Hank Aaron is always identifed in the '50s as "Henry." Don't ask me why.)

Al Rosen was the best American League third baseman of the '50s, but the best in the game during the decade, and one of the four or five best players at that position in the game's history, was Eddie Mathews. He was one of the three best ever, not far behind Mike Schmidt and George Brett.

From 1952 to the end of the decade, Eddie Mathews was one of the best power hitters in the game, hitting over 40 home runs four times and leading the league in both 1953 and 1959. He hit for a respectable average (over .300 in both 1953 and 1959) and was a whiz at drawing walks, 80 or more for six straight years from '53 through the end of the decade, leading the league with 109 in 1955.

Though he didn't have great running speed, he helped his team enormously by *not* hitting into double plays. From his rookie season of 1952 to the end of the decade, he grounded into an average of just 6.75 double plays per season. Let's put that into perspective: In Hank Aaron's first eight seasons, 1954–61, he grounded into an average of *16.4 double plays per season.*

Mathews was a capable if unspectacular third baseman, averaging exactly the same number of chances per game, 3.02, as did the rest of the league's third sackers over the same stretch. His career fielding average was 6 points higher than the league average for the same position (.956 to .950). George Kell seems to have been a little better in the field, but there is no conceivable way he could have done anything with a glove to close the gap between himself and Eddie Mathews as hitters.

The Kell selection is so puzzling to me that I'm going to refer to the only evidence I have as to why it was made. The text on his page in *Big-Time Baseball* reads "The soft-spoken, affable country boy from Swiftan, Arkansas, was called *the Quarterback at the Plate* [Ital. theirs]. He was a guy who used his bean. He could bunt and he could drag a bunt; he could hit behind the runner, and he could poke one to right field; he could hit straightaway and he could raise a high, long drive. He was a crackerjack fielder, a keen batter, and an ideal team player. In short, he was a baseball man's dream of what a third-sacker should be."

Okay, I'm willing to concede that George Kell was a fine third baseman and one of those rare players whose value cannot be measured by statistics alone. I'd love to have a player like him on my team. But George Kell, no matter what his contributions on and off the field, was *not* a more valuable player than Al Rosen at his best, and he wasn't anywhere near as valuable as Eddie Mathews at almost any time during his career.

The selection of Kell as the third baseman of the '50s (and the selection of Fox at second and Rizzuto at short) indicates a mindset that was prevalent then and that lingers even now, more than four decades later. Namely, that a third baseman (or shortstop or second baseman) wasn't expected to be much of a hitter, but just a good glove man who could make contact and execute the occasional hit-and-run play. *George Kell was a '50s baseball man's dream of what a third- sacker should be.*

Kell was a good hitter, one of the better hitters to play third base in either league up to that point in the game's history. But somehow, so the mindset went from 1900 through the '50s, if you were a really *great* hitter, as Ernie Banks and Eddie Mathews were, you weren't really an *authentic* shortstop or third baseman, even if you played the position well. I think that that mindset was probably responsible for keeping scores of good hitters from playing those positions until the 1970s.

At third base, advantage me again, by a wide margin.

Outfield

First off, I want to say that the spelling of Mickey Mantle's first name as Mickie on The All-Star Team of the 1950s is not a mistake, or at least not mine. That's the way it's spelled in *Big-Time Baseball*. In the interest of historical accuracy, I thought I'd reproduce it for you here. Even as a kid I couldn't help but wonder if that misspelling indicated just a tad of disrespect for Mantle, just a small failure to grasp his true greatness.

Well, we'll get to that in a minute. Meanwhile, how should we compare outfields? The 200 Writers never specified which outfielders would play which positions, but I think it's pretty obvious from looking at the first and second team that Willie Mays and either Mickie—sorry, I mean Mickey—Mantle or Duke Snider would play the position for the second team. Snider was a superb center fielder, probably a shade better than Mantle, at least taken on the evidence of their entire careers, though in the early and midfifties Mantle's speed probably gave him the edge.

In the 1950s, before accumulated injuries slowed him down,

Mantle was a streak in the outfield, often said to have been the fastest player in the game at the time. Since it's my team, I'm going to take Mantle and put him in center field. Logically then, the comparison of my team with that of the 200 Writers begins with a comparison of Mickey and Willie.

I hope at least some of you were drawn to this book because you enjoyed *Clearing the Bases*—currently available in trade paperback from St. Martin's, by the way, in case you missed it. (Most major bookstores should have it, and if they don't, Amazon.com or any other Internet book service can rustle you up a copy in no time.) In *Clearing the Bases*, I devoted a long chapter to a comparison of Mantle and Mays, my two favorite ballplayers and heroes of my boyhood. Let me refer briefly to that now.

I concluded, emphatically, that at their respective peaks, Mantle was the superior ballplayer, and that all other things being equal, a batting order and an outfield of Mantles would defeat a batting order and an outfield of Mayses if all other things were equal. I left it to the reader to decide whether he would define peak as five, ten, or twelve best seasons. I'm not denying that Mays was more valuable on the strength of his long career; the point of the essay was to determine who was the best at their relative peaks.

I admit, no matter how you figure it, it's close. But it's not quite as close if you go by just the '50s. First of all, Mantle was an established star (though not yet a superstar) in '52 and '53, when he hit, respectively, .311 with 23 home runs and then .295 with 21 home runs. In the spacious Yankee Stadium outfield, he was terrific, posting a 2.60 and then 2.78 range factor against the league's average of 2.40 and 2.43 for those two seasons. He struck out a lot—he led the league with 111 in '52—but he made contributions in other ways, such as *not* grounding into double plays, just 7 for those two seasons.

Is it fair to compare them in terms of decade-long value when Mays, after his 1951 rookie season, lost almost all of two years to the Army and didn't play his first full season until 1954? I don't know, but there's no reason not to compare the two of them on the basis of what they did from '54 through '59.

It's close in '54: Mays, out of the army, took off like a rocket and led the National League in batting at .345 (his only career batting title) and slugging average at .667, as well as triples with 13. He had 41 home runs, 110 runs batted in, and in the outfield led the National League with 9 double plays. His range was sensational—he averaged 3.10 catches per game in center field to the league's average of 2.36. This was probably one of Willie's two best seasons, along with '55, but nonetheless it's very, very close.

On the surface Mantle's season doesn't seem nearly as impressive—27 home runs and 102 RBIs to go with a .300 batting average. However, there are mitigating factors. For instance, Mantle grounded into just 3 double plays to Mays's 12, led the league with 129 runs scored, and walked 102 times to Mays's 66. I'm going to give Mays the edge in '54, but only by what amounts to a handful of runs.

In '55, Mays's season again looks much better than Mantle's and sensational from any perspective. He led the league with 51 home runs, drove in 127 runs, batted .317, led the league in triples with 13 and total bases with 382, and even stole 24 bases in 28 attempts. Mantle was pretty good, too. He led the American League in home runs with 37, drove in 99 runs, and hit .306. He led the league with 11 triples and 113 walks and stole 8 of 9 bases.

Mays led the NL in slugging average with .659, while Mantle led the AL at .611; but Mantle also led the AL in on-base average with a healthy .431, fully 31 points higher than Mays.

Once again, Mantle made minor contributions that went largely unnoticed by the baseball press. For instance, grounding into a ridiculously low 4 double plays (Mays in comparison had 12). It's pretty close in '55, so I'm not going to call it.

But the next three seasons are all Mantle's. The years 1956 and '57 add up to one of the great two-year runs the game has ever seen, with Mickey reaching heights. Mays had the weakest season of his prime years in '56, hitting just .296 and driving in just 84 runs (though he did steal a career high 40 bases, an impressive total for that period). It doesn't matter, though, what kind of season Mays had that year, because at his peak Willie never had a season like Mantle did in 1956. Babe Ruth and Ted Williams and Ty Cobb and Honus Wagner, at their absolute best, scarcely had seasons like Mickey Mantle in 1956.

Mick led the AL in home runs, RBIs, batting, runs scored, total bases, and slugging, the last number a breathtaking .705. The *STATS, Inc. All-Time Major League Handbook* credits him with 174 "runs created" that year, exactly as many as Ted Williams in 1948, his highest total. Mays's highest runs created total was 146 in '55.

Baseball analysts love to argue over which was Mantle's better season, '56 or '57. In 1957 American League pitchers simply would not pitch to Mickey in any situation where they absolutely did not have to, walking him 146 times, 34 more than the previous season. As a result, his home run total dropped to 34, which numerous sportswriters found disappointing after predicting that he'd make a run at Ruth's record of 60 home runs in '57. He upped his average by 12 points to a career high .365, led the AL in runs scored for the second straight season and the third time in the decade, stole 16 bases in 19 tries, and grounded into the ridiculously low total of just 3 double plays.

Was Mick better in '56 or '57? *STATS, Inc.* credits him with

174 runs created in '56, 155 in '57. *Total Baseball*'s complex ranking system prefers '57. Ranked by SLOB, slugging average times on-base, they are close, 32.9 runs per 100 at bats in '56 to 34.2 the following year. Which Mickey do you think was best? Like Satch said, you pays your money and takes your choice.

Willie Mays, by the way, was a superb ballplayer in 1957, hitting .333 with 35 home runs, a league-leading 38 stolen bases, and a league-leading slugging average of .626. But Mantle out-slugged him by nine points, and his on-base average was a whopping 104 points better, .515 to .411.

Those two seasons, along with Mantle's performance in 1961 and '62 (though we aren't using them in this comparison), really ought to settle the issue of whether Mantle was better than Mays at their respective peaks. As for the remaining two years of the '50s, it's a toss. In 1958 Mantle led the AL in homers, total bases, runs (for the third year in a row and the third time in four seasons), walks, stole 18 bases in 21 attempts, and hit .304. Willie was terrific, too, hitting a career high .347, with 29 home runs and NL leading totals in stolen bases and runs scored. I'm not enough of an expert to tell who was better that season, and I don't really see enough of a possible difference to pursue the question further. I'll call 1958 a draw.

In 1959 Mays was very good, hitting .313, 34 homers, and 104 RBIs, with 27 stolen bases (leading the NL for a fourth straight year). Mantle had what was probably the worst season of his prime years, battling injuries and hitting just .285 with 31 home runs (though managing to steal 21 bases in 24 attempts). Yet, looked at from some perspectives their performance wasn't that far apart: Mantle had a slugging average of .514 and an on-base average of .390, for a SLOB of 20.0, while Mays had a slugging average of .555 and an on-base average of .381, for a SLOB of 21.1. It seems hard to believe that a player with a .285 average and 31 home runs could contribute just one fewer run per 100 at bats than a player with a .313 average and 34 home runs, but the evidence indicates that objectively there wasn't that much difference in 1959 between Mantle and Mays.

For the decade of the '50s, then, I might be generous and call the six seasons between 1954 and 1959 a split; I might be more generous and give Mays a slight edge for their rookie seasons of 1951 (in which Mays batted .274 with 21 home runs in 121 games and Mantle hit .267 with 13 home runs in just 96 games). But do I discount Mantle's two fine seasons in 1952 and '53 altogether? Even if I do, I'm left with the fact that at their respective bests, Mantle was better, and by a wide margin.

Sorry, 200 Writers of my youth, but Mickey Mantle was the greatest ballplayer of the 1950s, better than Willie Mays, though not by a lot, and worthy, no matter how you look at it, of being on that All-Star Team of the 1950s.

I've spent a lot of time on Mantle vs. Mays because, quite honestly, I think it is the only outfield spot where the 200 Writers have a chance to win. I can almost hear some of you guffaw; do I really think Duke Snider and Hank Aaron, great as they were, were better than Ted Williams and Stan Musial? No, not really. But after acknowledging that all comparisons of ballplayers are in some sense flawed by our lack of complete knowledge—Do we really know who was the best clutch hitter? Can we really evaluate and compare the performances of two players on radically different teams in different types of ballparks?—we are left with the fact that, what the heck, silly as this exercise may be, we have still agreed to undertake it, and if we are going to derive any benefit from it we must follow the rules of the game as they are set before us. It may be unfair to compare Williams and Musial with Snider and Aaron solely on the basis of their 1950s performances, but I didn't start this, and in any event the point is to see how well I can spot the best players in the time frame I have been given.

And by those standards, my team—and my outfield—kicks butt on the one chosen by the 200 Writers. Duke Snider may not have been a superstar for the ages like Williams, but from 1950 through 1959 he was one heck of a player, leading hitters in both leagues in both home runs (326) and RBIs (1,031). Ted Williams had the highest batting average for the decade, .336, but I really don't know how you can make a case that he was more valuable over the ten-year period than any one of the other five outfielders in this comparison.

Williams, it must be mentioned, got shafted in the draft and lost most of '52 and '53 to the Korean War, for which we must cut him some slack. And he did win two batting titles, in 1957 and '58. His 1957 hitting performance, of course, was amazing; at age thirty-nine he hit .388, outhitting the American League by 133 points. But in the '50s Williams played in as many as 136 games only once, in 1956. In only one season, 1951, did he drive in as many as 100 runs. He was still a terrific hitter almost all through the decade, posting just one bad season, 1959, when he hit .254 (though he would rebound to hit .316 with 29 home runs in his next and final season). However, increasingly as the decade went on, he was capable of making almost no contribution to his team outside of the batter's box— and as an all-around player Williams wasn't exactly Mays or even Mantle in his youth.

As age and injury took their toll Ted Williams became something of a liability in the field and on the bases (one can easily imagine him switching to DH in his last few years, if he had played in the modern game).

In contrast, Duke Snider was one of the game's most complete performers during the '50s, a terrific power hitter, a fine center fielder, and a capable base runner. Five times in the decade he hit 40 or more home runs, and six times he drove in more than 100 runs. Six times he hit over .300, going as high as .341 in 1954. I'm not going to make an elaborate argument to prove Snider was Williams's near equal on an all-time list, but if you had to choose one of them to play on your team from 1950 through '59, who would you pick? If you didn't pick Snider, you're nuts; you're doing what the 200 Writers did in 1959, refusing to look at the cold facts and going by Williams's reputation from 1939 through 1949.

All right, then, I say I'm two up on the 200 Writers in the outfield at two spots. Plus, I've got *two* center fielders to their one. So, am I going to go on the offensive for Hank Aaron over Stan Musial? No. I'm going to just declare it a draw and move on. Stan was a great player for every year of the decade except 1959, when like Williams, age and injury combined to inflict his worst season on him (.255, though he would hit .275, .288, and, finally, .330 in his last season, all with fair power). He led the league in batting four times in the '50s, in runs four times, and RBIs once. He was a good if not great outfielder, but if you choose him on your all-fifties team it's for his bat, since only five times in the decade did he play in as many as 100 games in the outfield.

Hank Aaron played only six seasons in the '50s, the first one good and the rest truly great. He led the NL in hits twice, batting twice, home runs once, RBIs once, runs once, and total bases three times. In short, he was Hank Aaron, a little younger and a little faster than the one who was to surge towards Babe Ruth's career home run record in the '60s and '70s. From '54 through '59 he was a better outfielder and base runner than Musial. Unless you simply want to award the position to Musial because Aaron didn't begin playing until '54, you'll have to concede that Aaron is at least Musial's match for the '50s.

For the sake of argument, I'll give the 200 Writers a slight edge in this one, at this position, though if you want to switch them and compare Snider to Musial—edge to Musial for the decade, though not by a wide margin—I'm still going to take Hank Aaron in the '50s over Ted Williams in the '50s. So, no matter how you look at it—well, at least, no matter how *I* look at it—I win in two of the three outfield spots.

Those are the matchups for the basic eight positions. What's the tally so far? I'll concede the 200 Writers a slight edge at catcher—more on that in a moment. I'll also concede them first base, and, grudgingly, one of the outfield spots. I'm giving myself a slight edge at one outfield spot (Mantle vs. Mays) and a slightly bigger edge at one of the others (Snider vs. Williams), and I'm claiming *big fat margins of victory for myself* at second, third, and short.

Catcher

Yogi Berra beat out Roy Campanella for the first spot in the poll, 506 points to 412. Now, I'm not going to argue against Yogi Berra for any reason. I already discussed my almost-neighbor (he lives in Montclair, New Jersey, a couple of miles from my home in South Orange) in the previous chapter. Suffice it to say that I have no quarrel with anyone who wants to pick Yogi over Johnny Bench or Mickey Cochrane or Roy Campanella or anyone else as the best all-around catcher of all time.

But really, how much of a difference was there between Yogi and Campy at their best? Both men broke into the Bigs in 1948—Yogi at age twenty-three, Campy at twenty-seven. (He certainly would have made it a couple years earlier if not for segregation.) In 1957, his last season, Campanella was thirty-six, already old for a catcher, so it's fair to say that his career statistics probably don't reflect his real ability.

Still, let's take him and Yogi from 1950 through 1957:

	Games	AB	HR	RBIs	Walks	BA
Yogi	1,143	4,309	215	838	453	.290
Campy	1,002	3,490	211	729	430	.276

Yogi gets a slight edge in everything, largely because being a bit younger, he was able to catch more games in the '50s. Note, though, that Yogi had to appear in 141 more games in order to get just 23 more walks and bat 819 more times just to hit 4 more home runs. Yogi was more durable; Campy was a better power hitter.

They were both pretty good catchers. Campy led the National League in putouts six times in his ten seasons. Yogi led eight times in roughly twelve full seasons of catching. Berra led the American League in assists three times, while Campy led the NL once. Campanella led the NL in double plays twice, Yogi six times. Campanella led his league's catchers in fielding average twice; Yogi led his league's catchers once.

Both men were winners with several pennants on their list of credentials. Both were team leaders and reputed to be great clutch performers. Both were regarded as excellent handlers of pitchers.

I'm going to give Yogi the edge here, but by the slimmest of margins. Advantage, 200 Writers, by a little.

Relief Pitchers

I won't take issue with the selection of Casey Stengel as the all-50s manager, a subject for another essay at another time, and

I really don't care that much about pinch hitters, but I want to say a word about the selection of Elroy Face as the decade's best relief pitcher with Jim Konstanty as the number two selection and Hoyt Wilhelm limping in at number three.

First, the case of Konstanty. Konstanty was essentially a one-year wonder, one of the most celebrated in baseball history. He was arguably the most valuable player on the Philadelphia Phillies' 1950 pennant-winning "Whiz Kids." It's odd, in retrospect, that he should be one of the best-remembered players on a team of kids, considering that he was thirty-three in 1950. His 16-7 won-lost record and 22 saves earned him the NL's Most Valuable Player award and went a long way towards convincing big league managers and pitching coaches that a genuine relief specialist might be something more than simply an ex-starter who blew his arm out.

Due to a combination of age, arm trouble, and bad luck, Konstanty never came close to duplicating his 1950 season—in fact, he would win more than 7 games in only one subsequent season, 1953, when he went 14-10 with the Phillies as a combination starter-reliever. In a different era, one that recognized the value of great relievers, Jim Konstanty might have been a great pitcher, but as the record stands, he had only one great season and thus has no business finishing second in the 200 writers' poll.

I'm not going to call Elroy Face a one-year wonder, but if not for his 1959 season when, through a combination of skill (he was one of the pioneers of the fork ball, which evolved into what we now call the split-fingered fast ball), luck, and a different system for recording wins than now exists, he put together a truly amazing 18-1 record for the Pittsburgh Pirates. He was very good in other seasons, particularly 1962, when he led the league with 28 saves and posted a 1.88 ERA. But what he did in the '60s isn't relevant to this discussion.

In 1958, the year before his amazing run, he was very good, going 5-2 with an ERA of 2.89 and leading the league with 20 saves. From 1953 through '57, though, he was unremarkable, losing 7 more games than he won and collecting just 21 saves over four seasons. Not once in that four-year span was his ERA under 3 runs per 9 innings.

Hoyt Wilhelm, like Elroy Face, was the popularizer of an odd pitch—in Hoyt's case the knuckleball. He was not a great reliever for all of the '50s, but he had four seasons from 1952 through 1959 where he posted an ERA of under 2.50, making 432 relief appearances in addition to 32 starts (the latter in '58 and '59, when he was used as a starter and reliever). His won-lost record from '52 through '57, when he was used exclusively in relief, was 62-50 and he saved 58 games. I suppose it's close to a tossup, but I just don't see how you can say that in the 1950s Elroy Face was a more valuable relief pitcher than Hoyt Wilhelm.

In fact, I'm stumped as to why the writers picked Wilhelm third. Whatever you make of his record, he was certainly good for a longer period than Konstanty. The only thing I can imagine is that Wilhelm got caught between two extraordinary seasons at each end of the decade—the first one being Konstanty's 16-win MVP season in 1950, which opened people's eyes to the potentials of relief pitching, and Face's equally remarkable 18-win season in 1959, which established a reliever's value beyond question. There is perhaps one more point to be made: namely, a perception that Wilhelm's real career as a reliever didn't start until the 1960s. (He surely would have been selected as the best relief pitcher on an all-star team of that decade.)

But by any statistical method I can find, Wilhelm had more value as a reliever in the 1950s than either Elroy Face or Jim Konstanty.

Advantage: me, by a slim margin.

Left-Handed Pitchers

Warren Spahn, of course. The 200 Writers win this one. I'd have to be a contrarian even beyond my reputation to argue with the selection of a man who won 363 games in twenty-one years, 20 or more in thirteen seasons, and was probably one of the five or six or seven greatest starting pitchers in baseball history. In eight of ten seasons in the '50s, Spahn won 20 or more games. He led the NL in victories five times in the decade (and four consecutive times from 1958 to 1961). He led his league in strikeouts from '50 to '53, in complete games four times, and ERA twice. If he was available for my All-Star Team of the 1950s, I'd take him.

But you're not going to tell me that I'm not getting an excellent consolation prize in Whitey Ford. A peculiarity of Ford's career is that he was a stronger pitcher in the early '60s than what were considered his prime years when he made his major league debut in 1950 at age twenty-two. In '61 and '63 he led the league in both games started and innings pitched and recorded his only 20-win seasons, going 25-4 in '61 and 24-7 in '63. From '61 through '64 he was close to invincible, recording 83 wins against a mere 25 losses for a dizzying .769 won-lost percentage.

That was in the first four years of the '60s, but in the '50s he was pretty good, too. Despite having his career interrupted for two crucial years during the Korean War, Ford, in 1950 and then from 1953–59, was 121-50 for a .708 won-lost percentage. Though he led the league in ERA twice, '56 and '58, and in wins (81) in '55, Ford never had a 20-win season in the '50s.

Why? Largely because of the way Casey Stengel used him. We know how good Warren Spahn was, but we'll never know how good Whitey Ford was because precise statistics hadn't yet been developed to measure his kind of value. Stengel seldom used a set rotation and quite often saved Ford to face the

Yankees' strongest foes, sometimes on just two days' rest (if he had only gone, say, six or seven innings in the previous start). Stengel would even pull Ford after five or so innings if he thought he might need him in relief in an upcoming game. Not until Ralph Houk replaced Casey as the Yankees' manager after the 1960 season did the baseball world find out that, yes, Whitey Ford was capable of winning 20 games in a season, and in fact was capable of winning 25. Not only that, but Stengel frequently used him in relief, 37 times during the decade. (*STATS, Inc.* credits him with 7 saves).

Possibly because he was handsome and blonde, and a pugnacious, unapologetic New Yorker, and a true-blue Yankee, Ford stirred some resentment in fans of other teams in the '50s and '60s. Somehow, the idea developed that Ford wasn't "tough," that he seldom was able to finish his own starts.

Stengel himself was responsible for some of this attitude. In a 1960 copy of *Baseball Digest* I found in my father's library, Casey sounds almost apologetic for Ford: "Complete games don't mean as much as they used to. I mean, look how many games Whitey Ford won for me, and he didn't finish many of them." (Casey may have had it in for Whitey. Ford was extremely bitter about not being allowed to start the first game of the 1960 World Series against the Pirates, in which he pitched two shutouts. Consequently, he wasn't available to start the seventh and final game, which the Pirates won on Bill Mazeroski's home run.)

Well, Casey, if you're reading this—wherever you are—let me suggest that Ford might have finished a few more games for you had he not been finishing games for your other pitchers. Let me also suggest that the notion that Ford wasn't a good finisher doesn't have much basis in fact. When he was allowed to, Ford was very good at finishing his own starts; in both 1955 and '56 he completed 18 games, leading the league in '55. He wasn't quite in Spahn's class as a finisher, but he wasn't given the opportunity to be.

Anyway, you can't simply write off Ford's sensational won-lost percentages by saying he pitched for the Yankees. Lots of other good pitchers started games for the Yankees in the 1950s, and none of them are in the Hall of Fame.

I'm not going to argue against the choice of Warren Spahn as the '50s' best left-hander, but I also can't find anything negative to say about the starting pitcher with the best won-lost percentage of the twentieth century. Someday, perhaps, someone will go through Ford's career under Casey Stengel game by game, looking at who he beat, and then we'll have a better idea how good he really was.

Even with the information we have, though, Ford's greatness is obvious. He was 9-1 in his rookie season in 1950 and 18-6 in '53, his first year out of the service. Is it reasonable to assume that had he pitched in '51 and '52 he would have been, say, just 15-7 each season? In that case, he would have wound up with at least 266 victories in his career. My guess is that if he had pitched his whole career under someone like Ralph Houk, he would have been a consistent twenty-game winner and would have finished with over 300 victories. I think he was one of the twenty to twenty-five best starting pitchers of the twentieth century.

Advantage to 200 Writers by a slim margin.

Right-Handed Pitcher

This is where I nail it down, where I tip the scales so strongly in my favor that even if you disagree with me on one of the other selections, I still win big.

Let me start by conceding that Allie Reynolds was one of

the most amazing pitchers of the forties or fifties, in some ways *the* most amazing. Perhaps more than any other pitcher of his time—maybe even more so than Whitey Ford—plain statistics can't reveal Allie Reynolds's true value.

To begin with, the "Big Chief" (Reynolds was part Cherokee Indian from Oklahoma) didn't begin to mature as a pitcher until he was thirty years old and the Yankees acquired him from—really, you can look this up—the Cleveland Indians. At that point he had won just 51 of 98 career decisions. Even that's not quite as good as it looks, as he had spent all the war years pitching to many batters who couldn't have earned roster spots had there not been a war. (Allie was exempt from service because of a knee injury suffered when he was a track star in college.) He'd had only one truly good season, 1945, when he won 18 and lost 12, despite leading the league with 130 walks.

Reynolds didn't actually pitch poorly up to that time, his highest ERA being 3.88 in 1946, his last year with Cleveland. But he seemed to be pitching without purpose. Immediately after coming to New York Reynolds turned things around. In '48 and '49 he was a combined 33-13 as a starter and picked up 4 saves in the bullpen. From '50 through '54 he won 79 games and lost 39, leading the AL with a terrific 2.06 ERA in 1952 as well as in strikeouts with 160 and shutouts with 6. In those five seasons, he also collected 35 saves, which gives you an idea of how Stengel was using him.

He had a reputation as one of the best big game pitchers of his time, and his Bob Gibson-like World Series record—7-2 with a 2.79 ERA and two shutouts—backs this up. And that doesn't count 3½ perfect innings in game four of the '49 Series, in which he earned a save. In game six of the '52 Series, he earned a save, and in game seven the next day, he started, got the win, and saved the Series for the Yanks.

According to Casey Stengel, Reynolds was the best pitcher "at starting and relieving I've ever managed. In fact, I'd go further and tell you he's the best at the two things that I've ever seen." As with so many Stengel quotes, it's difficult to decipher that one. I can't believe Casey was actually saying Reynolds was the best starting pitcher he'd ever seen, but he may well have been the best reliever. Reynolds would later claim that Casey wanted to make a reliever out of him, but couldn't replace him in the Yankees' rotation.

Reynolds's last season was 1954, when at age thirty-nine he won 13 of 17 decisions and saved 4 games in relief. The Yankees actually offered him a cut in salary—*thanks, Allie, for all those great World Series performances, but what did you do last year when we finished second?*—and he found he could make more money as head baseball coach at Oklahoma State.

For all his ability and versatility, though, Reynolds got the nod from the 200 Writers for two main reasons that don't necessarily make him the best right-hander of the '50s. The first, of course, was his pitching in the World Series. The second was the two no-hitters he threw in the 1951 season. It can be said with reasonable certainty that he was the best pitcher on a team that won five consecutive world championships, and if nothing else, that would be a strong argument for his greatness.

Reynolds won 182 games in his career, losing 107 for an excellent .630 won-lost percentage. It would have been interesting to see what would have happened had he been paid a decent wage and stuck around for a couple more years as a reliever. He might have cracked 200 victories and made the Hall of Fame, but without free agency, Reynolds had no choice but to accept the Yankees' pay cut or find another job. The man could have used Marvin Miller to head the players' union about two decades earlier.

So could Robin Roberts, the man who eventually went out and got Marvin Miller. If he had just thought to do that ten years earlier, Roberts might have staked a claim for himself as the greatest starting pitcher since World War II. As it was, he came close. I'd certainly place him in the top ten since World War II, and maybe even one of the top seven or eight in that span. Ah, but what might have been!

Was Robin Roberts the unluckiest great pitcher in baseball history? Of course he was; he pitched the prime of his life away, from age twenty-two to thirty-five, for the Philadelphia Phillies. At least Walter Johnson got to pitch in *two* World Series.

How good was Robin Roberts? In his eight best seasons as a starter, from 1950 through '56 and then again in '58, he was over 100 percentage points per season better than his team. Here's the breakdown:

Year	W-L	Pct.	Phillies Pct.	Diff.
1950	20-11	.645	.591	.054
1951	21-16	.583	.474	.109
1952	28-7	.800	.565	.235
1953	23-16	.590	.539	.051
1954	23-15	.605	.487	.118
1955	23-14	.622	.500	.122
1956	19-18	.514	.461	.053
1958	17-14	.548	.448	.100

I searched around for someone to compare him to, but no one else quite works. Walter Johnson, in what might be considered his eight best seasons (1911 through 1913, 1915 through

1916, 1918, and 1924 through 1925) was 145.8 points better than the Senators, but the game that Roberts pitched in was probably more balanced and competitive than Johnson's.

In any event, won-lost percentage against one's team is a tricky stat; the better a pitcher's staffmates are, the less of a chance he has of finishing high above his team in relative won-lost percentage. A testament to Whitey Ford's greatness is that he was a member of what was almost always an excellent staff, and yet, from his first year out of the service in 1953 till the end of the decade, he was still .76 percentage points higher than the Yankees, a team that won five pennants in those seven seasons.

But when his staffmates and the rest of his teammates are awful, a pitcher would seem to have a zero chance. Who can measure the physical and psychological stress of pitching year after year for a team that cannot score runs or make fundamental plays? How much does it take out of a pitcher to know that he must finish nearly every game he starts to have even a decent chance to win? How does a pitcher motivate himself year after year when it is evident that the team's management has no intention of improving the team, but is simply content to put him out there game after game and pocket the extra cash he earns them when he pitches? There aren't any statistics available that can tell us that.

How bad were the Phillies in the 1950s? Got a minute?

- In 1951 the Whiz Kids faded into Phizz Kids, finishing fifth, 8 games under .500. They were fifth in the NL in runs scored, and, thanks largely to Roberts's league-leading 315 innings pitched and 3.03 ERA, fifth in the league in team ERA.
- In '52, the Phils rebounded to finish a respectable 20 games over .500—87-67—though they finished just

fourth, 9½ games behind the Dodgers. In reality, the Phillies were a .500 team with an incredible starting pitcher who had one of the handful of great seasons posted by a starter in the last century. Roberts was 28-7 for a team that was otherwise 59-60.

How unlucky was Robin Roberts? Let's stop for a moment and reflect on a now-forgotten little historical oddity. In 1952, Philadelphia's other team, the Athletics, were three years away from moving to Kansas City. There were no Cy Young awards then, but writers had fewer qualms then than now about giving the Most Valuable Player award to a pitcher. In 1952, they gave it to the A's Bobby Shantz, who had a great season. Let's compare Shantz's season to Roberts's.

	W-L	ERA	G	CG	IP	H	SO	BB
Shantz	24-7	2.48	33	27	279.2	230	152	63
Roberts	28-7	2.59	37	30	330.0	292	148	45

Now let's look at them relative to their leagues:

	ERA	LERA	Diff	Pct	TeamPct	Diff
Shantz	2.48	3.67	1.19	.774	.513	.261
Roberts	2.59	3.73	1.14	.800	.565	.235

How do you call a contest this close? Roberts gave up about half a hit more per game than Shantz, but his walks-to-innings-pitched ratio was better. Their ERAs in relation to their leagues are almost identical, with Shantz winning by a hair, but then Roberts pitched in 4 more games, completed 3 more, and went nearly 51 more innings. He did, after all, win 4 more games than

Shantz, though Shantz's won-lost percentage in relation to his team's is slightly better.

Who gets the Cy Young? Myself, I'd chose Roberts, but I might be a little prejudiced here. But they didn't have Cy Young awards back then. They only had MVP awards, and considering that Roberts's team was within striking distance of the pennant for much of the season, I'd say that if you were going to give it to one of the two, it'd have to be Robin Roberts, whose wins, after all, meant something.

That's not even my point, though. Shantz was a solid major league pitcher who lasted 18 years and won 119 games, hanging on the last few seasons to pitch in relief. Aside from his '51 season, when he won 18 games, he never before or after won as many as 12 games in a major league season.

Robin Roberts comes along and wins 28 games for a team that was otherwise .500, and who pops in out of nowhere to win the MVP award he should have gotten, but a guy playing in the *same city* having the *only* great season of his career?

And you know what? Roberts may not have been any better in '52 than he was in '53, when he outpitched his previous performance in innings (a staggering 346.2 to 330 in '52) and posted a considerably more impressive ERA in relation to the league (his 2.75 that season was 1.54 lower than the National League's ERA, which ballooned to 4.29.)

Nineteen fifty-three is pretty much covered above, but it should be noted that primarily because of Roberts, who completed 33 games, the Phillies led the NL in that category with 76. The Braves with Warren Spahn, who was second in the league with 24, were the only other team in the league to have more than 51.

Don't you wonder why a team that finished 22 games behind the league leader would need their ace to complete 33 games?

Couldn't they bring up a couple of rookies from Reading to spot the guy a little rest?

- In '54 Roberts led the league in victories (23), starts, complete games, innings pitched, and strikeouts for a team that finished four games under .500 and finished seventh out of eight teams in runs scored.
- In his last great season, 1955, he *again* led the league in wins with 23 and *again* led the league in starts, complete games, and innings pitched for a team that was otherwise 54-63.

It has been suggested that in the era of free agency teams sign pitchers for three- and four-year contracts and then tend to overwork them because they want to get their money's worth. Who knows whether the guy will still be with you when the contract is up and why do you care how many games he pitches for someone else? But what was the Phillies' excuse for working Robin Roberts so miserably hard? From 1950 through 1955 Roberts pitched *over 300 innings every season,* leading the league from '51 through '55.

Warren Spahn, one of the most durable pitchers the game has ever seen, led the NL just four times in innings pitched over a twenty-three-year span, surpassing 300 just twice. You might have thought that the 1956 season, in which Roberts's record dipped to 19-18 (for a team that was otherwise 52-65), might have been a word to the wise. But who's ever used the word "wise" in connection with the Phillies' management? In '56 a struggling Roberts, only thirty years old, was still allowed to go 297 innings and complete 22 games.

Roberts's glory years were over. In '57 he led the league in losses with 22, but was still allowed to pitch 249 innings. He rebounded slightly the next year at 17-14, his ERA dropping back down to 3.24 from 4.07 the previous year. However, pitching 269 innings was far too heavy a workload.

He struggled through the rest of the decade trying to win the way he had always won, with a belt-high fastball that had lost considerable heat from the long strain. In 1962, having learned a couple of new pitches, he began a productive three seasons with the Baltimore Orioles, winning 37 and losing 29. He retired in '66 after pitching for both Houston and Chicago. One of his last actions was to help seek out Marvin Miller, a retired chief economist from the Steelworkers' Union, to head the Players Association. Within ten years, Miller had achieved free agency for the players. Imagine if Roberts had had a chance to play for a better team fifteen or even ten years earlier.

To me, the real question is not so much how many games would Robin Roberts have won had he pitched for the New York Yankees instead of the Phillies. The question is how many more productive seasons, and thus how many more games, would he have won had he not been forced to pitch so many innings before the age of thirty. His career record was 286-245 for a won-lost percentage of .539. In a fairer world these figures would be more like 330-201 for a winning percentage of .621. *At least.*

Robin Roberts was probably the best pitcher in his league and maybe all of professional baseball for six seasons, from 1950 through 1955. About how many pitchers can you say that they were the best in the game for six straight years? With all due respect to Allie Reynolds, Robin Roberts was far and away the best right-handed pitcher in the National League in the 1950s, *and with all due respect to Warren Spahn, he was the best pitcher, right or left, in the league from 1950 through 1955.*

Advantage me, by a solid margin.

Here, then, are the All-Star Teams of the 1950s, the first chosen by the 200 best baseball writers and editors in the country and the second by me. You decide which team is better—just keep in mind that we're talking about how good these players were on the basis of their performances from 1950 through 1959.

(And out of courtesy to both the writers and Mickey Mantle, this time I'm spelling his first name correctly.)

	200 Writers	Barra
First Base	Gil Hodges	Ted Kluszewski
Second Base	Nellie Fox	Jackie Robinson
Shortstop	Phil Rizzuto	Ernie Banks
Third Base	George Kell	Eddie Mathews
Outfield	Ted Williams	Duke Snider
	Stan Musial	Hank Aaron
	Willie Mays	Mickey Mantle
Catcher	Yogi Berra	Roy Campanella
Left-Handed Pitcher	Warren Spahn	Whitey Ford
Right-Handed Pitcher	Allie Reynolds	Robin Roberts
Relief Pitcher	Elroy Face	Hoyt Wilhelm

I think that if you could take all of the above players and average out their '50s performance and then flesh out the rest of the rosters with clones, my team would finish five or six games ahead of their team at the end of a season.

Does that make me smarter than the 200 writers and editors whose opinions I worshipped as a boy? No, not by a long shot. There's two things I learned from this exercise. One is to be at least a bit skeptical about consensus opinions, even those expressed by experts. All experts are subject to the prejudices and prevailing notions of their time and often have just as much of a problem as the rest of us putting their areas of expertise into perspective.

The second thing I learned is that just because you have the shoulders of others to climb on when viewing the past doesn't mean that you're smarter than they are. I wouldn't have started along the lines of thinking I use when analyzing ballplayers today if not for the men whose opinions I pondered over when I was a kid. And lest I get too arrogant about this, I'm going to keep reminding myself that there will be some young smart-asses out there who may be pointing out what I overlooked in my analysis a few decades down the pike.

Anyway, to Ben Olan, the editor of *Big-Time Baseball,* whoever he was and wherever he is, my sincerest thanks for introducing me to the game of baseball. This chapter has been a blast, and believe me, after nearly forty years, it's a relief to get all this off my chest.

4

Two Guys From Chicago
or
Why Ron Santo and Minnie Minoso Are the Two Best Players Not in the Hall of Fame

In 1993 and '94 I wrote a series of articles for various papers, including the *Village Voice* and the *Philadelphia Inquirer*, advocating Richie Ashburn for the Hall of Fame. In all of them I used some variation of the phrase, "Richie Ashburn is the best player *not* in the Hall of Fame."

After Ashburn was finally elected in 1995, I got a letter from a baseball fan in Birmingham, Alabama, named Lamar Smith, who asked me, "Okay, *now* who's the best player not in the Hall of Fame?"

That's a good question, and although I wrote several columns for the *Wall Street Journal* on the subject of the Hall of Fame vote, I never really answered the question, "Who is the best player *not* in the Hall of Fame?" For one thing, I confess that I never really did a study on the subject. I just looked at the available candidates and determined, after closely studying Ashburn's career, that he was the best player outside Cooperstown.

I did say a few years ago that it was a "disgrace"—or some such hyperbole—that Gary Carter was not in the Hall of Fame, and off the top of my head that was probably the answer that I should have given Mr. Smith from the time when Carter first became eligible in 1999 and was ignored by the voters.

After Carter's election, though, I decided to take Smith's queries more seriously. Was there, perhaps, a player or several deserving players out there who the baseball writers had been ignoring for years? If we confine the discussion to twentieth century players, there's Joe Jackson and Pete Rose, of course, but to bring them into the discussion leads to endless sour, unwinnable arguments. (For the record, based solely on their statistics, *of course* Joe Jackson and Pete Rose belong in the Hall of Fame.) For that matter, Dick ("Don't Call Me Richie") Allen probably does, too, but I'm going to save his very special case for another time, and pitchers should be the subject of a separate study.

So then, who is the most deserving twentieth century non-pitcher not in the Hall of Fame? When I put the question to my friends and colleagues, one of them replied, "You already answered that in your last book." And so I had, sort of. In *Clearing the Bases* there is a chapter called "Minnie Minoso: The New Latin Dynasty" that more or less uses Minoso as a springboard for an essay on the unfortunate tendency by the baseball press to underrate or ignore Latin ballplayers.

For instance, after putting the query out to my friends, "Who was the first black Latin ballplayer in the major leagues?" or stated another way, "Who was the Latin Jackie Robinson?" none of them could answer. I didn't know the answer myself; I had to call the Hall of Fame to find out that it was Minoso.

The argument for Minoso is simple: He is credited in the

record books as having played for 17 seasons in the majors, though in the year of his big league debut, 1949, he played just 9 games, and in 1962 he played in only 39, in '64 just 30, in 1976 just 3 games, and in 1980 only 2 more. (He batted just 2 times in the '80 games.) In both '76 and '80, of course, he was brought back for a few at-bats to qualify for the Major League Ballplayers Association's new pension plan. That's the kind of guy Minnie Minoso was. He was good to people, and they remembered him for it.

Beyond his popularity, Minoso has excellent credentials for the Hall of Fame. He hit .298 for his career—if he had quit in l961 when he was thirty-eight he would have finished well over .300—including eight seasons over .300. He hit with pretty good power, 185 home runs including eleven seasons in double figures, and he lost more than a few in eight of his prime seasons with the White Sox trying to clear the fences in Comiskey Park.

He had a pretty good batting eye. For seven straight seasons, from 1951 through 1957, he had more than 70 walks, and he helped his team in a lot of small ways. For instance, from 1951 through 1961 he led the league in getting hit by pitches in every season but one.

In *Clearing The Bases* I compared him to two other outfielders who were, roughly, his contemporaries, one black and one white. Here are the basic career stats for Minnie Minoso, Larry Doby, and Enos Slaughter:

	Gms	HR	RBI	Runs	OBA	SlgAvg	SLOB
Minoso	1,796	185	1,013	1,122	.389	.459	17.9
Doby	1,533	253	970	960	.386	.490	18.9
Slaughter	2,380	169	1,304	1,247	.382	.463	17.7

If you didn't put names to those stats, you might conclude that the first guy on the list looks at least as worthy as the other two. Not only isn't he in the Hall of Fame, he got shafted worse than Doby, who lost prime time to segregation, and Slaughter, who lost it to the war. Minnie Minoso got to play in nine games at age twenty-seven, and then didn't get a chance to play a full major league season *until he was twenty-nine.*

It is ridiculous to argue that Minoso doesn't belong in the Hall of Fame because he had "only" 1,963 hits—he collected nearly 2,000 hits *after his twenty-eighth birthday.* How many players can you say that about? Minnie Minoso never had a chance at a prime in the major leagues; at least Larry Doby had a brilliant Negro League record to bolster his chances later, but who knows enough about baseball in World War II–era Cuba to tell us how good Minnie was in his early twenties? Minnie was said to be brilliant in brief stints in both the Negro National League and Pacific Coast League, but that's not going to help him get any votes on the Hall of Fame ballot.

It's absurd to argue that racism didn't cost Minnie Minoso at least two and probably three or four seasons that would have put him into the Hall of Fame, but the really unfair part of this is that there is no one around to make his case now. There were lots of ex–Negro Leaguers around to attest to Doby's greatness, and Slaughter had a lot of fans around from his great years with the Cardinals in the late '30s and '40s to remind the Hall voters that Enos missed his prime years in military service, but the players best able to plead Minoso's case are still living under Castro's rule.

I used to think that Minoso would never make the Hall of Fame, that Latin players as a group were almost invisible to the baseball establishment. It may not be long, however, before Latin players *become* the baseball establishment, and it may be just a matter of time before they become conscious of, and determined to honor, their own pioneer. I hope that it happens in Minnie's lifetime.

Meanwhile, there is one man I can think of who is more deserving of the Hall of Fame than Minoso, at least considered from the standpoint of what he accomplished on the field, another Chicago idol who was beginning his career just as Minnie's was winding down. That Ron Santo *isn't* in the Hall of Fame, and that no one makes much of a case for him year in, year out, is genuinely puzzling. Santo is still very popular in Chicago as a Cubs announcer and as a spokesperson for diabetes research—he lost the lower part of his right leg in 2001 to complications stemming from his diabetes. He certainly should have garnered enough sympathy and goodwill from the baseball public.

Santo's qualifications for the Hall of Fame are obvious: He hit 342 home runs in fifteen seasons, drove in 80 or more runs for eleven straight years, led the National League in walks four times, and was voted to nine All-Star teams and won five Gold Gloves at third base. He was unquestionably the NL's best third baseman all through the 1960s and was perhaps the best all-around player at the position in either league. Yes, that includes Brooks Robinson.

I'm not going to argue that Ron Santo was a better fielder than Brooks Robinson, but do you have to be a better fielder than Brooks Robinson to be in the Hall of Fame? Despite his diabetes, Santo played in 1,572 out of 1,595 games from 1961 (his first season of over 100 games played) to 1970. He set a major league record by leading the NL in total chances nine times and shares the league record for the most years leading in assists with seven and in double plays with six. His range factor of 3.14 was .22 better than the other NL third basemen of his time, and his career fielding average was 6 points better than the rest of the league's.

Put it this way, he was the best hitter and best fielder for a longer period at third base than any player in NL history except Mike Schmidt. Is that enough of an argument?

To be honest, Santo is one of those cases of a player not being quite as good as his basic stats indicate. Billy Williams, his sweet-swinging left field teammate, who *is* in the Hall of Fame, swore that Santo was the quickest infielder he ever saw; but then, Santo was one of the few he ever played behind, and the two men were friends. Some others who watched Santo play say he was steady and sure-handed, but not all that quick on his feet. No doubt some of those ground ball numbers were inflated by the fact that the Cubs, through most of those years, had a lousy pitching staff that allowed fielders plenty of opportunity to chase hard-hit balls.

For instance, in 1961, Santo's first full season, Cubs pitchers were next to last in the league in strikeouts (755), while Brooks Robinson's Orioles were second in the American League (926). In 1962 Cubs pitchers were ninth in a ten-team league in strikeouts (783) while the Orioles were third out of ten teams in the AL (898). In 1963 . . . well, you get the idea. The Cubs' pitching got better in '67–'69, but it was never on a level with the Orioles and their great, great Jim Palmer-led rotations from '66 through '69. Brooks Robinson, in comparison, had fewer chances for ground balls than Santo.

Santo's hitting statistics also benefited from playing in Wrigley Field, where he hit 212 of his 337 home runs as a Cub. But Ron Santo was a heck of a hitter anywhere, particularly in an era that was one of the worst for hitters in twentieth-century baseball. The marvelous Baseball-reference.com calculates "Special Batting" stats wherein the players' batting, on-base, and slugging average for each year and then for his entire career appear alongside those of a league-average hitter whose numbers have been "park adjusted" to simulate his performance in a neutral ball park. (The system is complex, but if you flip to their Web site you can find a detailed explanation.)

Let's compare Santo's career numbers to those of Brooks Robinson. (Baseball-reference.com uses "on-base percentage" rather than "on-base average," so here I'm doing it their way.)

	BA	LBA	OBP	LOBP	SA	LSA
Robinson (1955–77)	.267	.253	.322	.324	.401	.383
Santo (1960–74)	.277	.268	.362	.334	.464	.399

Wrigley or no Wrigley, Ron Santo was clearly a greater offensive force, in comparison to the average hitter in the league, than the other great third baseman of his time, Brooks Robinson. Robinson's supporters might point out that his numbers cover twenty-three seasons to Santo's fifteen—the relative shortness of Santo's career is sometimes cited as one of the reasons he isn't in the Hall of Fame—and so his averages suffered from his late career decline. Well, yes, some. But even at Robinson's best, Santo was much the superior hitter. In 1964, for instance, Robinson had his best season, hitting .317 with 28 home runs and a league-leading 118 RBIs. Santo had a slightly better one, batting .312 with 30 home runs and 114 RBIs. Robinson scored 82 runs, Santo scored 94; Robinson walked 51 times, Santo walked an NL-leading 94 times; Robinson grounded into 17 double plays, Santo just 11.

Moreover, in relation to the average hitters in their leagues, Santo's edge was even bigger. According to Baseball-reference. com, Robinson outhit the average AL batter by 61 points while Santo only outhit the average NL batter by 44 points, but Santo's

OBP was 72 points higher and his slugging average was 166 points higher than the NL's average hitter while Robinson's edges, respectively, were 34 and 124. Yes, Robinson was the superior fielder, but not superior enough to offset advantages like that at the plate.

Why, then, isn't Ron Santo in the Hall of Fame? Why, year after year, is there no clamor from fans and press for him the way there was for Phil Rizzuto and Bill Mazeroski (both, in my opinion, less worthy candidates than Santo)?

The answer is probably an accumulation of small reasons. First, as already mentioned, Santo's career wasn't especially long for a Hall of Fame player. In 1973, at age thirty-five and in his fourteenth major league season, Santo was still a productive player, appearing in 149 games, batting .267, hitting 20 home runs with 77 RBIs, and drawing 63 walks. By the next season, however, diabetes had taken its toll and he played in just 117 games, batting just .221. There's no use speculating on what might have been, but that's not necessary in any event, since Santo's credentials for the previous fourteen seasons more than suffice as Hall of Fame qualifications.

Another reason that Santo may not have made it is that his teammate Billy Williams did. Billy's stats are better than Santo's, though not by all that much. Playing in 223 more games than Ron, he had 84 more home runs, drove in 144 more runs, and outhit him by 13 points, .290 to .277. Santo's on-base average was a point higher, .362 to .361, and Williams's slugging average was 28 points higher, .492 to .464. Williams, however, was a poor fielder, averaging fewer chances in left field than the league average for the position, and for his career fielding an eye-opening 16 points lower than average for his position

In terms of all-around value, from 1960 through the early '70s, Santo and Williams were neck-and-neck just about every season, but Williams was more affable than Santo, who got into a couple of unfortunate controversies late in his career that stirred some bad blood with fans and press. For one thing—and this seems almost silly now, but much was made of it at the time—Santo angered opposing teams by jumping up in the air and clicking his heels after Cubs victories and, sometimes, important plays in the middle of a game. Even a few Chicago area sportswriters were displeased by this habit.

Second, in his final season, playing for the White Sox, Santo got into a spat or two with Dick Allen over who should have been the White Sox team leader. I don't want to go back and revisit that one now, but in retrospect we should all remember that Dick Allen was certainly involved in more of these kinds of controversies in his career than Ron Santo.

In any event, Billy Williams was around longer, and in 1972, when Santo was slowing down (he hit .302 but played in just 133 games and hit just 17 home runs, his lowest total in ten seasons), Williams was arguably the best hitter in the league, leading the NL in batting, slugging, and total bases, with 37 home runs. And so Santo became wedged in between the accomplishments of Ernie Banks, who preceded him, and Billy Williams, who outlasted him. Most voters probably couldn't see it clear to vote yet a third Cubs regular into the Hall of Fame from a franchise that was mostly mediocre to bad from the '50s to the early '70s.

In the final analysis, though, the real reason that neither Minnie Minoso nor Ron Santo are in the Hall of Fame is probably that there is no single outstanding reason why they should be. Both men were steady, all-around performers who contributed to their teams in subtle ways that weren't always noticed or appreciated during their careers. Who, for instance, gave Minnie Minoso full credit for leading the American League in getting hit by pitches ten times in eleven years? Hall of Famers, or at least the Hall of Famers who get in after the shortest waits, are usually the ones who lead their league in the high profile categories or are players who get to display their skills in the World Series, which leaves out these two guys from Chicago. (Poor Minnie. In 1954, when the Indians won the pennant, he was with the White Sox; in 1959, when the Sox finally won it, he was in Cleveland.)

I think Santo was probably the better player; over the last seventy years of the twentieth century, only Mike Schmidt, George Brett, and Eddie Mathews could be considered his superiors at third base. For the fourteen seasons before the diabetes wore him down, I'd take him over Brooks Robinson in a trade, even up. Minoso has been deserving for a longer time than Santo. Myself, I'd vote for either or both. But I don't have a vote. As for you Chicago fans, you've got pen and paper and Internet access, don't you?

5

Competitive Balance 2
or
Wrath of the Con

In November 2001, in front of the Senate Judiciary Committee's hearing on competitive balance, Commissioner Bud Selig was quoted as saying that "An increasing number of our clubs have become unable to successfully compete for their respective division championships . . . at the start of spring training, there no longer exists hope and faith for the fans of more than half of our thirty clubs."

This became the owners' dominant theme in the months that led up to the near-strike the following year. The sports press, taking their cue from Bud, sounded the refrain; as anyone who reads the sports pages of the *New York Times* or the *New York Daily News* can easily see, they haven't dropped it yet.

In the spring of 2002, as negotiations for the Basic Agreement between the owners and players were heating up, I wrote a column for the *Wall Street Journal* on the issue of competitive balance in baseball. Basically, what I wrote was that, one, by the standards of other professional sports, major league baseball was not only the most competitively balanced sport, *it was clearly the most competitively balanced sport,* and that, two, baseball had never been more competitively balanced in its history than it was by the year 2000.

To my surprise, I received a call from the MLB senior vice president of public relations, Rich Levin, and the following day from the commish himself. I was flattered until I found out later that every journalist who had written something on competitive balance that didn't quite jibe with the line put out by the commissioner's office had gotten similar calls.

I've never met Bud—which he insisted that I call him—but he seemed like a nice guy over the phone, concerned, responsible and sincere. He argued passionately against my conclusions, and as I politely attempted to counter, it occurred to me that I was in a ridiculous situation of advancing the argument that Selig should have been making. After all, wasn't it to the advantage of Major League Baseball for the public to see it as competitively balanced? Wasn't the news that it was more competitively balanced than ever before *good* news? Why was the man who is supposed to be the caretaker of the game not rejoicing at the fact that the playing field was more balanced than it had ever been?

Let me present my evidence and see if it makes more sense to you than it did to the Commissioner of Major League Baseball. As far as I can see, there are three basic yardsticks for measuring competitive balance. The first is by the number of teams that finish over .500, the second is by the number of different teams that make it to postseason play, and the third is by the number of teams that play for the championship. Let's compare Major League Baseball to the National Basketball Association and National Football League from 1981 through the end of

2002. (I'm updating my original comparison in the *Journal* to take in the results of the 2002 season.)

	Teams Over .500	Teams in Postseason	Teams in Championship Games
NFL	31	31	19
NBA	28	28	15
MLB	29	30	21

Baseball has taken quite a bit of hammering over the last few years from critics who want it to be more like pro football, at least in terms of revenue sharing and competition. I'll leave the issue of revenue sharing for later and confine myself right now to this observation: I don't see at all how baseball comes off poorly in *any* comparison of competitive balance with football and basketball over the last two decades.

For one thing, for several of the years included in this comparison the NFL has had twelve playoff spots to baseball's eight, thus providing pro football with many more opportunities for different teams to make the playoffs. For another, due to the 1994 strike, baseball had no postseason or World Series that year, and yet it still had more teams playing for the championship over the period than either football or basketball.

For yet a third, the NFL has an artificial means of both creating teams that can finish over .500 and of giving second level teams a greater chance of making the playoffs and the championships by *weighting* the schedules. That is, a team that plays for the championship one season can expect a tougher schedule the next. Or, stated another way, it means a team that finishes a season at, say, 7-9, might not improve at all the following year but be the beneficiary of a scheduling break that improves its record to 8-8 or even 9-7, which could easily be the difference between making or missing the playoffs.

Brushbacks and Knockdowns

It could be argued—and in fact was argued to me by Bud—that matters change too quickly in baseball for a twenty-two-year study to have any validity. Or as Bud phrased it to me, "Since the Yankees began this new period of domination, all previous comparisons went out the window." Well, let's look at this new era of Yankee domination. Here are the teams that have played in the World Series and in the Super Bowl from 1996 through 2002. Below them is the number of different teams that have won the leagues or conferences and then the number of different teams that won championships:

MLB

	AL	NL	WS Winner
1996	NYY	Atl	NYY
1997	Cle	Fla	Fla
1998	NYY	SD	NYY
1999	NYY	Atl	NYY
2000	NYY	NYM	NYY
2001	NYY	Arz	Arz
2002	Calif	SF	Calif
Diff Teams	3	6	4

NFL

	AFC	NFC	Super Bowl Winner
1996	NEng	Green Bay	Green Bay
1997	Den	Green Bay	Denver
1998	Den	Atl	Denver
1999	Tenn	St Louis	St Louis
2000	Balt	NY Giants	Balt

(continued)

	AFC	NFC	Super Bowl Winner
2001	NEng	St Louis	NE
2002	TBay	Oak	TBay
Diff Teams	5	5	6

During the period of Yankee domination that supposedly necessitated the owners' fight for competitive balance, nine different teams played in the World Series over seven seasons, with four different teams winning the Series. Over the same time frame, the NFL saw ten teams play for the championship with six different teams winning the Super Bowl. Has baseball really been competitively imbalanced over the past seven seasons compared to the NFL, or could the difference between ten and nine different champions be reasonably considered chance?

It could also be argued, of course, that the issue is not baseball's competitive balance as compared with other sports, but whether or not *baseball* is more or less competitively balanced than in times past.

Here's a list of fifteen seasons from the last century that are considered landmarks. I chose most of them for their easy historical recognition, such as 1909 for Honus Wagner's Pirates or '27 for the Ruth-Gehrig Yankees or '47 for Jackie Robinson's debut. I chose others, such as '69, because they have fond memories for me, but whatever the reason, I think these seasons are fairly representative of major league competition in the twentieth century. If you don't agree, try your own sampling and see if you get vastly different results than I did (but you won't).

The first column indicates the number of major league teams in existence, the second, the number of teams that finished with a won-lost percentage over .600, the third the number of teams that finished under .400. The final two columns indicate the teams with the best and worst won-lost percentages for that season.

Year	# Teams	Teams over .600	Teams Under .400	Best W-L%	Worst W-L%
1901	16	2	5	.647 (Pitt)	.358 (Milw)
1909	16	5	4	.724 (Pitt)	.276 (Wash)
1919	16	4	3	.686 (Cinn)	.257 (Phil-NL)
1927	16	3	3	.714 (NY-AL)	.331 (Phil-NL, Bos-AL)
1931	16	3	3	.704 (Phil-AL)	.366 (Chi-AL)
1936	16	1	3	.667 (NY-AL)	.346 (Phil-AL)
1941	16	3	1	.656 (NY-AL)	.279 (Phil-NL)
1947	16	2	1	.639 (NY-AL)	.383 (StL-AL)
1955	16	3	3	.641 (Bklyn)	.344 (Wash)
1961	18	3	3	.673 (NY-AL)	.305 (Phil)
1969	24	2	4	.673 (Balt)	.321 (Mon, SD)
1977	26	6	5	.630 (KC)	.335 (Tor)
1986	26	1	1	.667 (NY-NL)	.395 (Pitt)
1994	28	2	0	.649 (Mon)	.402 (SD)
2000	30	0	0	.599 (SF)	.401 (Chi-NL, Phil)

As I noted in *Clearing the Bases,* in the year 2000—for the first time ever—*not a single team in baseball finished above .600 or below .400.* That's out of *thirty teams,* nearly twice as many as there were in 1901, when seven out of sixteen teams finished above .600 or below .400, or 1919, the year of the Black Sox, when it was seven out of sixteen teams finishing above or below those marks, or 1961, the year I was first old enough to notice baseball, when the American League finally expanded and six of eighteen teams, one-third of them, finished above .600 or below .400, or 1977, the year after free agency, when eleven of twenty-six teams finished above .600 or below .400, or even 1986, when competition reached a never before achieved level as just one team in twenty-six finished above .600 and just one finished below .400.

Someone writing to *Sports Business Journal* took me to task for being "arbitrary" in my choice of .600 and .400; "Why not," he suggested, ".593 and .394 or any other pair of percentages?" Indeed, why not? Use any two percentages you care to. The point is that as the twentieth century went on, *the difference between the best teams in baseball and the worst teams narrowed, and by the year 2000 they were smaller than at any other time in baseball history.*

The average difference between the worst and best teams is 20 points, so 10 points plus and minus is all that's needed to close the gap between the best and worst teams. This is what the commissioner of baseball and the rest of the owners were willing to force a strike and possibly ruin the game over—*a difference of just 10 percentage points from top to bottom.* Think about that for a moment.

Think about that for a moment, and of course you'll see that it's bull manure. Of course that's not what the owners were willing to force a strike over. Competitive balance was never the issue in the first place. Indeed, as Andrew Zimbalist wrote in *May the Best Team Win—Baseball Economics and Public Policy,* "A league that seeks to maximize its revenue will not want each of its teams to have an equal chance to win the championship. Leagues want high television ratings. These are best achieved generally when teams from the largest media markets are playing in the championship series. Other things being the same, MLB would like to see the New York Yankees, the New York Mets, the Los Angeles Dodgers, the Anaheim Angels, the Chicago Cubs, and the Chicago White Sox appear in the World Series more frequently than the Milwaukee Brewers, the Cincinnati Reds, the Kansas City Royals, or the San Diego Padres. By the same token, MLB does not want to see the Yankees win or the Padres lose every year because that, too, engenders apathy in many cities."

In other words, Major League Baseball *wants* the Yankees to win frequently, just not as frequently as the Los Angeles Lakers win in basketball. And, happily, that's exactly the situation that baseball is in.

What, then, was the near strike of 2002 really about? As has been the case with every work stoppage or near work stoppage in the history of baseball labor negotiations, the issue has been about players' salaries.

I'm not denying that very rich teams have an advantage over the merely rich teams—though when you break it down it inevitably comes down to the Yankees and the Braves having an advantage over, say, Kansas City and Pittsburgh. (Exactly why the Yankees have such a big natural advantage in resources over the Mets or why the Braves have one over the Dodgers has never been adequately explained.)

I'm not saying that baseball's division of income is fair, or that it can't be drastically improved. I would, if you pressed me on the issue, ask why this isn't an issue to be resolved among the owners themselves rather than between the owners and the players. What I *am* saying is that the constant emphasis on competitive balance that came from the commissioner's office and the baseball press's naïve acceptance of MLB's propaganda was both misleading and irresponsible.

And I'm also saying, in no uncertain terms, that by any

TABLE 1: THE THREE MAJOR PROFESSIONAL SPORTS: NUMBER OF TEAMS WITH MULTIPLE CHAMPIONSHIP APPEARANCES (1981–2002)

	Teams with 2 Appearances	Teams with 3+ Appearances	Total Number of Teams With Multiple Appearances
MLB	8	4	21
NFL	5	7	19
NBA	5	6	15

traditional, objective, and reasonable yardstick, baseball is the most competitively balanced of this country's major sports. I've taken a lot of flack over the past year for insisting that Major League Baseball is as competitively balanced as its football and basketball counterparts. Take a look at the tables and decide for yourself.

Table 1 shows the number of different teams appearing in the World Series, Super Bowl, and NBA finals from 1981 to 2002. Note that baseball has had eight teams over the last twenty-two years that have made two championship appearances to the NFL's five different teams making it to the Super Bowl. But the NFL has had seven different teams that have appeared three or more times to baseball's four.

Some would argue that the NFL, after all, has had four different teams winning the Super Bowl in the last four seasons—four teams that never won the Super Bowl before—and this proves the NFL's system is more balanced. In response to that, (a) the NFL always gives the best teams tougher schedules the following year, so it's automatically harder for them to repeat—it's almost like starting the season one or two games behind where you finished last year. Also, we need a few more seasons to toss into the comparison before we'll really know if this is the result of a more balanced system or simply luck of the draw.

TABLE 2: WINNING SEASONS OF MLB TEAMS (1981–2002)

National League

HOU	81-83-85-86-88-89-92-93-94-95-96-97-98-99-01-02
LA	81-82-83-85-88-90-91-93-94-95-96-97-98-00-01-02
ATL	82-83-91-92-93-94-95-96-97-98-99-00-01-02
STL	81-82-84-85-87-89-91-92-93-96-98-00-01-02
SF	81-82-86-87-88-89-90-93-97-98-99-00-01-02
MON	81-82-83-85-87-88-89-90-92-93-94-96-02
NY	84-85-86-87-88-89-90-97-98-99-00-01
CIN	81-85-86-87-88-90-92-94-95-96-99-00
SD	82-83-84-85-88-89-91-92-96-98
MIL	81-82-83-87-88-89-91-92
PHI	81-82-83-84-86-93-01
CHI	84-89-93-95-98-01
PIT	82-83-88-90-91-92
COL	95-96-97-00
ARI	99-00-01-02
FLA	97

American League

NYY	81-83-84-85-86-87-88-93-94-95-96-97-98-99-00-01-02
BOS	81-82-84-85-86-88-89-90-91-95-96-98-99-00-01-02
TOR	83-84-85-86-87-88-89-90-91-92-93-98-99-00
CHI	82-83-85-90-91-92-93-94-96-00-01-02
OAK	81-87-88-89-90-91-92-99-00-01-02
ANA	82-84-85-86-89-91-95-97-98-00-02
BAL	81-82-83-84-85-89-92-93-94-96-97

(continued)

American League	
KC	81-82-84-85-87-88-89-91-93-94
CLE	86-94-95-96-97-98-99-00-01
TEX	86-89-90-91-93-95-96-98-99
DET	82-83-84-85-86-87-88-91-93
SEA	91-93-95-96-97-00-01-02
MIN	84-87-88-91-92-01-02

This one really surprised me. If you'd told me that the Houston Astros from 1981 to 2002 had two more winning seasons than the Braves and only one fewer than the Yankees, I'd have demanded a recount.

Again, once you get past the Yankees and Braves, it's hard to find a lot of evidence that winning and losing matches up with the size of the market. The Giants and A's, who we've been hearing for years can't be expected to compete because there isn't room for two teams in the Bay Area, have had twenty-five winning seasons between them from '81 to '02. Over the same time span, the White Sox and Cubs, two teams that share a much bigger market, have combined for only eighteen.

TABLE 3: MLB TEAMS APPEARING IN POSTSEASON (1981–2002)

National League	
ATL	82-91-92-93-95-96-97-98-99-00-01-02
STL	82-85-87-96-00-01-02
HOU	81-86-97-98-99-01
LA	81-83-85-88-95-96
SF	87-89-97-00-02
NYM	86-88-99-00

National League (continued)	
ARI	99-01-02
SD	84-96-98
CHI	84-89-98
PHI	81-83-93
PIT	90-91-92
CIN	90-95
FLA	97
COL	95
MON	81

Note: Each league expanded from four to eight playoff spots in 1995.

This is as good a time as any to bring up a fact that is seldom mentioned in discussions about baseball's so-called large- and small-market teams, namely that the Atlanta Braves, one of the two richest teams in baseball and the team with the most postseason appearances in baseball since 1981, *do not play in a particularly large market*. They do play to an absurdly large audience because of their TV network, which is a much different matter.

When I bring this up in a debate, I'm usually greeted with a response like "Why shouldn't the Braves have to share some of that revenue with teams that don't have their own TV channel?" And my response to that is: "They most certainly should." It's ridiculous for the Braves to have an advantage of this sort, particularly when it involves cutting into other teams' ratings (and therefore, revenues) in their own home markets. I know all the arguments to the contrary, and so do you, and they're all silly. The Braves don't earn that money on their own, they earn it because they're playing other teams. Nobody would pay to watch the Braves play *themselves*.

If you and your team can't make money without cooperation from me and my team, then you can't call it *your* money. It's *our* money, dammit, and before you play in my ballpark, you'd better be ready to discuss a more equitable way of sharing it. I can never understand why this isn't a bigger issue when it comes time to negotiate the Basic Agreement with the players. Well, on second thought, yes I can. The owners don't want to discuss it because it involves sharing an *owner's* revenues, whereas a salary cap, or a luxury tax that has the same effect, shares the *players'* money.

Anyway, it seems to me that the problem with the Braves and their unfair revenue share could be easily solved if the smaller-revenue owners put their minds to it.

There's no way that one can argue that being a small market team doesn't hurt Montreal's chances of making the playoffs, but look carefully at the order the rest of the National League finished in after Atlanta:

- St. Louis and Houston, second and third in the number of postseason appearances in the last twenty-two years, are generally regarded as mid- to small-market teams, while the Dodgers, who have done no better than the Astros when it comes to playoff appearances, may be the second-largest market team in baseball. I'm always skeptical when I see reports that neatly assign the Dodgers' domain to Los Angeles County and the Angels' to the Anaheim area. When I'm out there, I see plenty of Dodgers caps in the Mexican restaurants all over Orange County, and Angels caps in Beverly Hills are not unknown. However you divide it up, Los Angeles County is the largest geographic urban area in the United States, which gives them one heck of a TV market to draw from right there, so the

Dodgers' failure to at least equal the Cardinals in post-season appearances must be put off to management.

- The San Francisco Giants, a middle-market team at best, and one that has to share that market with the more successful Oakland A's, have made just one fewer playoff appearance since 1981 than the Dodgers (and that number will probably be even by the end of the 2003 season).

- The New York Mets. Ah, the New York Mets. Where to start when talking about the New York Mets? The Mets play in what is supposed to be the biggest market in the country, yet they have made just one more post-season appearance over the last twenty-two seasons than the San Diego Padres, who were in the World Series just five seasons ago and who were forced to sell all their players—remember?—because they couldn't pay their bills. And that's just the National League. The Mets have been in the World Series just one more time from 1981 to 2002 than the Minnesota Twins and Kansas City Royals.

  Let's phrase that a little differently: The New York Mets play in what is supposed to be the biggest market in baseball, with access to the same revenues as baseball's most successful team, the Yankees. Yet, eleven other teams from 1981 to 2002 made as many or more postseason appearances. I can never figure out why more sportswriters don't use the New York Mets as a counter to every argument that is made for the Yankees' advantages.

- The Chicago Cubs and the Philadelphia Phillies have both made just three postseason appearances from 1981 to 2002, exactly the same number as the San

Diego Padres, Pittsburgh Pirates, Minnesota Twins, and Kansas City Royals. Any argument about market imbalance automatically creating competitive imbalance must, it seems to me, deal with the ugly and obvious fact that the Cubs and the Phillies, for an entire century, seldom reached even a level of mediocrity.

Chicago may not be America's second city, but the Chicago-land area that the Cubs draw from is surely one of the three or four biggest markets in baseball. And while the Cubs' TV distribution isn't nearly equal to that of the Braves, it's a lot bigger than that of any other team in their division.

The Phillies are a case entirely unto themselves, a *huge*-market team whose revenues are vastly smaller than they should be. The Philadelphia tri-state basin is one of the largest population centers in the country, and

TABLE 3 (continued): MLB TEAMS APPEARING IN POSTSEASON (1981–2002)

American League	
NYY	81-95-96-97-98-99-00-01-02
OAK	81-88-89-90-92-00-01-02
CLE	95-96-97-98-99-01
BOS	86-88-90-95-98-99
TOR	85-89-91-92-93
SEA	95-97-00-01
MIN	87-91-02
CHI	83-93-00
TEX	96-98-99
BAL	83-96-97

American League (continued)	
KC	81-84-85
ANA	82-86-02
DET	84-87
MIL	81-82

Note: Each league expanded from four to eight playoff spots in 1995.

the Phillies don't have to share that market with any other American or National League team. And yet . . .

Some observations:

- Several people have asked me, "How can you argue that the Braves should share their TV revenue and not say the same thing about the Yankees? What does it matter if your games are telecast nationally or just in the northeast? Revenue is revenue, isn't it? I mean, the Yankees could no more make that TV money without the assistance of other teams than the Braves. Right?"

  To which I respond: "Right."

  Everything I've said about the Braves sharing their TV revenue applies to the Yankees as well. It's just that I don't think that it is going to happen in any meaningful sense until the smaller market teams demand it. All I'm trying to point out is that, while the Yankees' and Braves' TV revenues have given them far greater resources, those resources haven't necessarily or automatically translated into what is popularly referred to as competitive *im*balance.

  For instance, the Oakland A's are one of the smallest market, smallest revenue teams in the American

League, and they have made just one fewer postseason appearance from 1981 to 2002 than the Yankees. From 2000 to 2003 the A's record was comparable or better than the Yankees' every season.

- The Seattle Mariners have in the last nine seasons become kind of a reverse image of the Philadelphia Phillies. The Phillies are a large-market team with not particularly large revenues. The Mariners are a not-particularly-large-market team with huge revenues. Well, it's not exactly that simple, because no one knew how big the Mariners' market really could be until they went out and conquered it. Seattle used to be listed as one of baseball's small-market teams— let's not forget that the Seattle area had a bad reputation as a baseball town after losing the expansion Pilots after the 1969 season. (Readers of Jim Bouton's *Ball Four* will recall the author's complaint that Seattle was "too intellectual" to be a baseball town.)

    Now that they have established themselves as winners and big money makers, the owners want to group them with the "large-market" teams. The Seattle Mariners are the classic example of the shell game that baseball owners play with the terms "large market" and "large revenue."

- The Baltimore Orioles, you'll recall, were generally referred to as a large-market team after Camden Yards was built and the Birds were using crowbars to fit customers in. They became the major rationale for every mismanaged team as to why they, too, needed a new stadium. In 1995 George Steinbrenner, trying to bully New York taxpayers into building him a new stadium, actually cited the size of the crowds at Camden Yards and squealed, "How am I supposed to compete with that?" (I'm not making that up, by the way, I still have that interview on tape.)

• Does anyone now remember how, until they won the World Series in 2002, the Anaheim Angels managed to hide during discussions of large-market and large-revenue teams? What exactly were the Angels, large market or large revenue? Both?

Obviously they were not only a large-market team, but potentially a huge-market team, no matter what their revenues were, so any mention of their enormous fan base would automatically draw attention to the obvious fact that the franchise was atrociously mismanaged. Let's call the Angels the Philadelphia Phillies of the American League.

TABLE 4: MLB TEAMS APPEARING IN WORLD SERIES (1981–2002)

NYY	81-96-98-99-00-01
ATL	91-92-95-96-99
OAK	88-89-90
STL	82-85-87
SF	89-02
NYM	86-00
CLE	95-97
TOR	92-93
PHI	83-93
MIN	87-91
LA	81-88
SD	84-98

(continued)

ANA	02
ARI	01
FLA	97
CIN	90
BOS	86
KC	85
DET	84
BAL	83
MIL	82

After the Yankees and Braves, note that the teams appearing in the World Series from '81 to '02 don't break down at all along big market–small market lines.

The Oakland A's and San Francisco Giants, who are usually classified as small-market teams because they must split a middle-sized market between them, made five World Series appearances from 1988 to 2002. The Twins and Padres, both small-market teams, have as many World Series appearances as the Mets, Dodgers, and Phillies. Among the teams with just one World Series appearance, the Angels and Red Sox, both of whom play in undeniably large markets, have appeared in the World Series no more often than the Marlins, Reds, Royals, and Brewers.

TABLE 5: WINNING SEASONS OF NBA TEAMS (1981–2002)

Eastern Conference	
MIL	81-82-83-84-85-86-87-88-89-90-98-99-00-01-02
ATL	81-82-85-86-87-88-89-90-92-93-94-95-96-97-98
BOS	81-82-83-84-85-86-87-88-89-90-91-92-01-02
PHI	81-82-83-84-85-86-88-89-90-98-99-00-01-02

Brushbacks and Knockdowns

Eastern Conference (continued)

DET	83-84-86-87-88-89-90-91-95-96-98-99-01-02
NY	82-83-88-89-91-92-93-94-95-96-97-98-99-00
IND	86-89-90-92-93-94-95-97-98-99-00-01-02
ORL	92-93-94-95-96-97-98-99-00-01-02
CHAR-NO*	92-93-94-95-96-97-98-99-00-01-02
CHI	87-88-89-90-91-92-93-94-95-96-97
CLE	87-88-89-91-92-93-94-95-96-97
NJ	81-82-83-84-92-93-97-01-02
MIA	93-95-96-97-98-99-00
WAS	81-82-86-96-97
TOR	99-00-01

Western Conference

POR	81-82-83-84-86-87-89-90-91-92-93-94-95-96-97-98-99-00-01-02
UTAH	83-84-85-86-87-88-89-90-91-92-93-94-95-96-97-98-99-00-01-02
LAL	81-82-83-84-85-86-87-88-89-90-91-94-95-96-97-98-99-00-01-02
HOU	81-84-85-86-87-88-89-90-91-92-93-94-95-96-97-98-00-02
SEA	81-82-83-87-88-89-90-91-92-93-94-95-96-97-98-99-00-01
SAN	81-82-84-89-90-91-92-93-94-95-97-98-99-00-01-02
PHO	81-82-83-88-89-90-91-92-93-94-95-97-98-99-00-02
DAL	83-84-85-86-87-89-00-01-02
DEN	81-82-84-85-87-88-89-93-94
MIN	97-98-99-00-01-02
SAC	82-98-99-00-01-02
GST	81-86-88-90-91-93
LAC	91-92

*The Charlotte Hornets moved to New Orleans in 2002.

My only clear reaction from looking at Table 5 is that having a lot of winning seasons doesn't necessarily have to do with winning championships in the NBA. The Lakers are tied for the most winning seasons in the league over this period, twenty, but Portland and Utah have the same number, and neither of them has a single championship ring. Somebody could have slapped a twenty-dollar bill down on a bar and taken my money if they'd bet me that the two teams with the most winning seasons in the NBA's Eastern Conference from 1981 to 2002 were Milwaukee and Atlanta.

TABLE 6: NBA TEAMS APPEARING IN POSTSEASON (1981–2002)

Eastern Conference

NY	82-83-87-88-89-90-91-92-93-94-95-96-97-98-99-00
BOS	81-82-83-84-85-86-87-88-89-90-91-92-94-01-02
DET	83-84-85-86-87-88-89-90-91-95-96-98-99-01-02
ATL	81-82-83-85-86-87-88-90-92-93-94-95-96-97-98
PHI	81-82-83-84-85-86-88-89-90-98-99-00-01-02
IND	86-89-90-91-92-93-94-95-97-98-99-00-01-02
MIL	81-82-83-84-85-86-87-88-89-90-98-99-00-02
CHI	84-85-86-87-88-89-90-91-92-93-94-95-96-97
NJ	81-82-83-84-85-91-92-93-97-01-02
CLE	84-87-88-89-91-92-93-94-95-97
CHAR-NO*	92-94-96-97-99-00-01-02
ORL	93-94-95-96-98-00-01-02
MIA	91-93-95-96-97-98-99-00
WAS	81-83-84-85-86-87-96
TOR	99-00-01

Western Conference	
LAL	81-82-83-84-85-86-87-88-89-90-91-92-94-95-96-97-98-99-00-01-02
POR	82-83-84-85-86-87-88-89-90-91-92-93-94-95-96-97-98-99-00-01-02
UTAH	83-84-85-86-87-88-89-90-91-92-93-94-95-96-97-98-99-00-01-02
SAN	81-82-84-85-87-89-90-91-92-93-94-95-97-98-99-00-01-02
PHO	81-82-83-84-88-89-90-91-92-93-94-95-96-97-98-99-00-02
SEA	81-82-83-86-87-88-90-91-92-93-94-95-96-97-99-01
HOU	81-84-85-86-87-88-89-90-92-93-94-95-96-97-98
DEN	81-82-83-84-85-86-87-88-89-93-94
DAL	83-84-85-86-87-89-00-01-02
SAC	83-85-95-98-99-00-01-02
MIN	96-97-98-99-00-01-02
GST	86-88-90-91-93
LAC	91-92-96

Note: In 1983 the NBA went from twelve to sixteen playoff spots.
*The Charlotte Hornets moved to New Orleans in 2002.

Basketball, of course, kicks baseball's butt in a postseason comparison because of the far greater number of playoff spots available. One could begin to make a case that large market teams have an advantage in basketball because the leading teams are the teams in those conferences' largest markets, but then one would have to deal with Portland having made the playoffs as often as the L.A. Lakers.

And for that matter one would also have to deal with the sad phenomenon of the L.A. Clippers. The Clippers might be the most dismal franchise in the three professional sports, and though you certainly can't write off their miserable history to size of the market they play in, you have to ask if any system can be justified that produces a team that is so lousy over such a long period.

TABLE 7: NBA TEAMS APPEARING IN FINALS (1981–2002)

LAL	81-82-83-84-86-87-88-90-99-00-01
CHI	90-91-92-95-96-97
BOS	83-84-85-86
PHI	81-82-00
HOU	85-93-94
DET	87-88-89
NJ	01-02
SAN	98-02
NY	93-98
UTAH	96-97
POR	89-91
IND	99
SEA	95
ORL	94
PHO	92

I suppose it could be argued that the appearance of the L.A. Lakers, the Chicago Bulls, and the Boston Celtics in so many NBA finals since 1981 indicates an advantage for large-market teams. I would not make that argument. Instead, I suggest that it has more to do with the more restrictive free-agent market in the NBA, which allows teams to stay together longer.

But now that I think of it, maybe it does have something to do with the size of the market; after all, if Los Angeles wasn't more of a media hot spot than Orlando, Shaquille O'Neal would

Brushbacks and Knockdowns

still be in Florida. Anyway, of the forty-four available spots in the NBA finals from 1981 to 2002, half of them have been taken by three of the biggest cities. Only two of those spots, though, were taken up by the New York Knicks.

TABLE 8: WINNING SEASONS OF NFL TEAMS (1981–2002)

AFC

MIA	81-82-83-84-85-86-87-89-90-91-92-93-94-95-97-98-99-00-01-02
DEN	81-83-84-85-86-87-88-89-91-92-93-95-96-97-98-00-01-02
PIT	81-82-83-84-87-89-90-92-93-94-95-96-97-00-01-02
OAK	82-83-84-85-86-89-90-91-93-94-95-98-99-00-01-02
NEG	82-83-84-85-86-87-88-94-96-97-98-99-01-02
BUF	81-83-88-89-90-91-92-93-95-96-98-99-00-02
KC	81-84-86-89-90-91-92-93-94-95-96-97-99-02
NYJ	81-82-85-86-88-91-93-97-98-99-00-01-02
TEN	87-88-89-90-91-92-93-96-97-98-99-00-02
SEA	83-84-85-86-87-88-90-95-97-98-99-01
SD	81-82-85-87-92-93-94-95-96-99-02
IND	87-88-89-92-94-95-96-99-00-02
BAL	83-85-86-87-88-89-94-99-00-01
CIN	81-82-84-86-88-89-90-96
JAX	96-97-98-99
CLEV	02

NFC

SF	81-83-84-85-86-87-88-89-90-91-92-93-94-95-96-97-98-01-02
GBAY	81-82-83-84-85-89-92-93-94-95-96-97-98-99-00-01-02
WAS	81-82-83-84-85-86-87-89-90-91-92-96-97-99-00-01

NFC (continued)

MIN	82-83-86-87-88-89-91-92-93-94-95-96-97-98-99-00
NYG	81-84-85-86-88-89-90-91-93-94-97-98-00-02
DAL	81-82-83-84-85-91-92-93-94-95-96-98-99
PHI	81-88-89-90-91-92-93-95-96-00-01-02
NO	83-87-88-89-90-91-92-93-00-02
CHI	83-84-85-86-87-88-90-91-95-01
STL	83-84-85-86-88-89-99-00-01
DET	81-83-91-93-94-95-97-99-00
TBAY	81-82-97-98-99-00-01-02
ATL	82-91-95-98-02

TABLE 9: NFL TEAMS APPEARING IN POSTSEASON (1981–2002)

AFC

MIA	81-82-83-84-85-90-92-94-95-97-98-99-00-01
PIT	82-83-84-89-92-93-94-95-96-97-01-02
TEN	87-88-89-90-91-92-93-99-00-02
DEN	83-84-86-87-89-91-93-96-97-98-00
BUF	81-88-89-90-91-92-93-95-96-98-99
NENG	82-85-86-94-96-97-98-01-02
OAK	82-83-84-85-90-93-00-01-02
BAL	82-85-86-87-88-89-94-00-01
NYJ	81-82-85-86-91-98-01-02
KC	86-90-91-92-93-94-95-97
IND	87-95-96-99-00-02
SEA	83-84-87-88-99
SD	81-82-92-94-95

AFC (continued)	
JAX	96-97-98-99
CIN	81-82-88-90
CLE	02

NFC	
SF	81-83-84-85-86-87-88-89-90-92-93-94-95-96-97-98-01-02
MIN	82-87-88-89-92-93-94-96-97-98-99-00
DAL	81-82-83-85-91-92-93-94-95-96-98-99
PHI	81-88-89-90-92-95-96-00-01-02
NYG	81-84-85-86-89-90-93-97-00-02
GBAY	82-93-94-95-96-97-98-01-02
STL	83-84-85-86-88-89-99-00-01
CHI	84-85-86-87-88-90-91-94-01
WAS	82-83-84-86-87-90-91-92-99
DET	82-83-91-93-94-95-97-99
TBAY	81-82-97-99-00-01-02
ATL	82-91-95-98-02
NO	87-90-91-92-00
ARI	82-98
CAR	96

Note: The NFL went from ten playoff spots to twelve in 1990.

The two NFL teams that led their conferences in postseason appearances from 1981 to 2002 both play in what would be called small to middle markets in baseball. In fact, the '49ers have six more appearances than anyone in the NFC and four more than the leader of the AFC, Miami. By the way, the '49ers have one more postseason appearance over this stretch than the New York Yankees.

There is some evidence of competitive imbalance in the NFL; it's just not created by the market the team plays in but probably has more to do with a front office's inability to make deals to improve their teams.

TABLE 10: NFL TEAMS APPEARING IN SUPER BOWL (1981–2002)

DEN	86-87-89-97-98
SF	81-84-88-89-94
BUF	90-91-92-93
WAS	82-83-87-91
NYG	86-90-00
DAL	92-93-95
NENG	85-96-01
OAK	83-02
STL	99-01
GBAY	96-97
CIN	81-88
MIA	82-84
TBAY	02
BAL	00
TEN	99
ATL	98
PIT	95
SD	94
CHI	85

Brushbacks and Knockdowns

Let's sum it up this way: From 1981 to 2002, twelve NFL teams took up thirty-seven of the forty-four Super Bowl berths. In basketball, just six teams took up thirty-two of forty-four NBA finals. In MLB, twelve teams took up thirty-three of a possible forty-two World Series slots.

6

Where Have All the All-Stars Gone?

Seven years ago I wrote a story for the *New York Times Magazine* entitled "Baseball's Glory Days Are Now." The subtitle read "The 1996 season is the most spectacular season in the game's history, for a single reason: The players hit, field, run, and pitch better than ever." I meant it, too.

The story was partially written as a response to all the stories about baseball's woes in the wake of the 1994 strike. I simply got sick of reading about the health of baseball or any sport, but especially baseball, in terms of business and marketing, as if interest in sports was merely a question of trendiness, as if our allegiance to a sport should be expected to rise or wane simply because shoe sales or TV ratings or attendance is up or down by .6 percent. To pick up a paper or turn on a radio talk show program in the months that followed the 1994 baseball strike, you'd never have known that Major League Baseball was still in a boom market, that even with attendance down in '95 it was still well above almost any previous level and far greater than any of baseball's earlier so-called golden eras.

But that's not what I want to talk about. When callers on talk shows ask me how I can enjoy the game amidst all the talk about money, I have a simple answer: If you're sick of talking about money, don't talk about it, just pay attention to the game. *The game on the field.* And by the standards of the game itself, the '90s was a spectacular decade.

"For purists," I wrote in the *Times Magazine,* "baseball's greatness forever lies in its past. A recent article in *Sports Illustrated* contended that of the three main components of baseball—hitting, pitching, and fielding—only one, fielding, has improved since the good old days. The proof *Sports Illustrated* offered? Apparently a lot of old-timers think so.

"It's time to toss some chin music at the purists. Baseball's greatest season is *now.* The strike-shortened 1995 season and all of the 1996 season have been the most spectacular in baseball history, crammed with more accomplishments than any comparable span, and with records falling at a, well, record pace."

If, in retrospect, my argument seems overstated, consider the evidence:

- Mark McGwire threatened Roger Maris's record of 61 home runs throughout the '96 season and wound up with 52. Over a 162-game stretch from 1995 through 1996 McGwire hit 70 home runs.
- In 1996 the New York Mets' Todd Hundley hit 41 home runs, breaking Roy Campanella's single-season record for catchers, 40, in 1953.
- Mike Piazza threatened to become the first catcher since Boston's Ernie Lombardi in 1942 to win a batting

title. Piazza wound up hitting .336. (The following season he hit .362.)

- Ivan Rodriguez, the best catcher in the American League, set a new seasonal record for doubles by a catcher, 47.
- Three National League players—Gary Sheffield, Barry Bonds, and Jeff Bagwell—and five American League players—Mark McGwire, Edgar Martinez, Frank Thomas, Chuck Knoblauch, and Jim Thome—had on-base averages (OBA) over .450.
- Tony Gwynn and Ellis Burks in the NL and Alex Rodriguez, Frank Thomas, Paul Molitor, and Chuck Knoblauch in the AL all hit over .340.
- Four NL players—Eric Young, Lance Johnson, Delino DeShields, and Barry Bonds—and four AL players—Kenny Lofton, Tom Goodwin, Otis Nixon, and Chuck Knoblauch—stole more than 40 bases.
- Four NL players—Andres Galarraga, Gary Sheffield, Barry Bonds, and Todd Hundley—and five AL players—Mark McGwire, Brady Anderson, Ken Griffey Jr., Albert Belle, and Juan Gonzales—hit more than 40 home runs.
- Four pitchers—the Dodgers' Todd Worrell, the Reds' Jeff Brantley, the Padres' Trevor Hoffman, and the Yankees' John Wetteland—topped 40 saves.
- At a time when bats were booming, the Braves' John Smoltz won 24 games and had a 2.94 ERA while the Marlins' Kevin Brown posted an ERA of 1.89.

I could go on, and in fact I could go on about '97 and '98 as well. However, I think these few facts illustrate that there was some sensational play going on at all levels in baseball in the '90s. Note that none of the above includes such great performers from the decade as Roberto Alomar, Craig Biggio, Roger Clemens, Nomar Garciaparra, Tom Glavine, Derek Jeter, Randy Johnson, Chipper Jones, Greg Maddux, Pedro Martinez, Manny Ramirez, or Mariano Rivera—or Cal Ripken Jr., who would come to symbolize the excellence of baseball in the decade.

And that's just the top baker's dozen. No other decade has seen such diverse hitting and pitching performances, so much varied offense, and so many players at so many positions—including shortstop, second base, and catcher—who could hit and hit with power.

Now, seven years later, I find myself contemplating the 2003 All-Star Team and wondering where this golden era went. I've always been a now kind of guy when it came to baseball; I've always argued that baseball's golden era—by which I mean the game on the field, not the labor problems or money or scandals—is *now* and that the players, and thus the game itself, are constantly getting better. Now, in 2003, it seems to me that things have drastically and suddenly changed, and *not* for the better.

In 1933 the best players in the American and National Leagues faced each other for the first time. The American League All-Star roster featured twelve future Hall of Famers: Charlie Gehringer, Babe Ruth, Lou Gehrig, Al Simmons, Joe Cronin, Lefty Gomez, Lefty Grove, Bill Dickey, Jimmie Foxx, Earl Averill, Rick Ferrell, and Tony Lazzeri. The National League countered with eight future Hall of Famers: Frankie Frisch, Chuck Klein, Paul Waner, Chick Hafey, Bill Terry, Pie Traynor, Gabby Hartnett, and Carl Hubbell.

That's twenty Hall of Fame players in one game. The 2003 All-Star Teams feature perhaps two starters who seem a sure bet for Cooperstown, Barry Bonds and Alex Rodriguez, with perhaps

one or two others who seem definitely headed in that direction.
Am I being unfair? Let's look over the lineups:

National League

First Base—Todd Helton, Rockies.

Helton is a career .333 hitter, which makes him sound like Stan
Musial—except that Musial never got to hit at Coors Field. Last
year, for instance, Helton hit .378 at home with 18 home runs at
home, and .281 with 12 home runs in all other National League
ballparks. In 2001 and '02 he hit well enough on the road to
have seasons that could be called great by most standards, but
he's twenty-nine and I haven't seen anything from him yet that
indicates he's Hall of Fame material.

Second Base—Marcus Giles, Atlanta.

Giles is twenty-five years old and has yet to nudge his career batting average up to .270. At the winter meetings in '02 the Braves
were shopping him around; does that sound like a future Hall of
Famer?

Third Base—Scott Rolen, Cardinals.

Rolen is the best of an otherwise mediocre lot. Almost all the truly
great third basemen in baseball history came in the second half of
the century: Mike Schmidt and George Brett in the '70s and '80s,
Eddie Mathews in the '50s and early '60s, Wade Boggs in the '80s
and '90s were all better than any third baseman who played before
1950. So, probably, were Ron Santo, Brooks Robinson, and maybe
even Graig Nettles and Ken Boyer. It was reasonable to expect
that the new century would produce a new Schmidt or Brett, but

Chipper Jones never did bring his fielding up near the level of his hitting, and it looks as if Rolen is going to be the best on into his thirties. Okay, that's not entirely fair: He's twenty-eight years old, is an excellent fielder, and has pretty good power, but he's never hit over .300 in a season and has hit more than 31 home runs only once. Rolen will probably be the National League's All-Star third baseman for several years to come, but he's closer to being a young Robin Ventura than a young Mike Schmidt, who, by the age Rolen is now, had led the NL in home runs three times and driven in more than 100 runs three times.

Shortstop—Edgar Renteria, Cardinals.

Renteria is twenty-eight years old, a good fielder and base stealer, but in seven major league seasons before 2003 his career batting average was .283. Clearly '03 has been a career year for him, unless you think he's going to get better at age twenty-nine.

Catcher—Javy Lopez, Braves.

Lopez has been a good man for a long time at a tough position, a good catcher and decent power hitter. At age thirty-three, though, he is an All-Star this year only by virtue of Mike Piazza's injury—and Piazza turned thirty-five in '03. Anyway, a catcher who turns thirty-three without hitting his 200th home run isn't going to the Hall of Fame.

Outfield—Barry Bonds, Giants; Albert Pujols, Cardinals; Gary Sheffield, Braves.

Bonds is soon to be thirty-nine and Sheffield is thirty-four. Up until a couple of days before the voting closed, it looked as if Sammy Sosa, thirty-four going on thirty-five, was going to be the third outfielder; would that have made the 2003 NL outfield the oldest in All-Star Game history? Sosa was beaten out by Albert Pujols, who, at age twenty-three, looks to be a monster at the plate, but he's a slow runner with limited range in the outfield, not a real outfielder at all but a converted third baseman who wasn't a good enough fielder to hold on to his position. Where are the great young outfielders of previous decades—the guys who could hit for average and power as well as run, field and throw?

American League

First Base—Carlos Delgado, Blue Jays.

Delgado is a fine slugger, but at thirty-one no one has suggested that he is worthier of Cooperstown than a dozen other good-hit, no-field, no-run sluggers who make no contribution outside the batter's box and aren't in the Hall of Fame. He'd have to have at least two or three more seasons like 2003 before he could be spoken of as a candidate.

Second Base—Alfonso Soriano, Yankees.

I may be alone on this one, and if I'm wrong you can call me up in five years and Bronx cheer my answering machine. I don't see the greatness in Soriano that the New York sports press and even *Sports Illustrated* and *ESPN Magazine* go on about. He has tremendous power and great speed, but no discipline at bat (he averages better than one strikeout per game, and strikes out about six times more than he walks) or in the field (from 2000 to 2003 he made more errors than any second baseman in the league). And ask yourself this question: How many great hitters can you remember who averaged just 30-odd walks per season in their first three seasons?

Within five years the Yankees will be trying him out in left field. Then ask me if he's on track for the Hall of Fame.

Third Base—Troy Glaus, Angels.

Glaus can't hit for average (his career average hovers around .250), can't make consistent contact (he strikes out 27 percent of the time), and though he's not a bad fielder, at age twenty-six and weighing 245 pounds, he's not going to get any better. In four years he'll be in left field, and in seven he'll be DH-ing. I know a lot of knowledgeable baseball people who insist that Glaus is on the verge of superstardom, but I've never seen a right-handed-hitting superstar who, after more than 800 major league games, had to sometimes be platooned against right-handers.

Shortstop—Alex Rodriguez, Rangers.

At last, a legitimate young superstar on track for the Hall of Fame. *Is he the only multidimensional superstar in baseball under the age of thirty currently in the major leagues today?*

Catcher—Jorge Posada, Yankees.

A good catcher and hitter, nothing more. At age thirty-two he became the best catcher in the American League only because Pudge Rodriguez went to the National.

Outfield—Ichiro Suzuki, Mariners; Hideki Matsui, Yankees; Manny Ramirez, Red Sox.

Manny Ramirez has done nothing in the seven seasons since my '96 *New York Times Magazine* piece to indicate that he's not a great hitter, but he hasn't grown as a player and, in fact, his peripheral skills, to put it generously, have diminished. As a fielder he has no natural defensive position, and at thirty-one he's not going to get any faster. A Hall of Famer? Let's discuss it when he's thirty-five and lost some of his bat speed. As for Suzuki and Matsui, I'm a big fan of their attitude and all-around team skills, but they're simply not going to have enough good seasons in this country to make the Hall of Fame. The question as to whether they would rate as Hall of Famers based on their combined Japanese and American careers is an intriguing one, but not one I'm prepared to deal with now.

Why didn't anyone state the obvious? This is the most undistinguished group of flash-in-the-pans and career mediocrities having career-best years since the All-Star game was first played in 1933.

I'll ask the question again: Am I being unfair? A little. For the AL Nomar Garciaparra is in line for the HOF. How about Andruw Jones? Well, he's regarded as the best defensive center fielder in baseball, but he's twenty-six with a career BA of about .270 and has exactly two seasons with more than 100 RBIs.

What about the pitchers? Well, Oakland's Mark Mulder and Barry Zito appear to be the best of the lot, and the former is twenty-six with just 60 career wins while the latter is twenty-five and has 54 as I write this. Even with the scaled-down projections for starters in the era of five-man rotations, do you think these project to HOF numbers?

An obvious objection to examining current All-Stars in terms of the Hall of Fame is that we don't know what the rest of their careers are going to be like. "What about the careers of Frank Thomas and Roberto Alomar?" a friend asked me. "Just a few years ago they looked like they were dead on track for the Hall of Fame. Are you so sure about their chances now?"

That's a legitimate point, but it's not really the point I'm trying to make. If a player is going to the HOF, he certainly is going to show some signs of greatness before the age of thirty. Maybe three years ago Frank Thomas looked like a definite Hall of Famer and maybe now he doesn't, a question I'll deal with more later on, but years ago he definitely did look like one day he would have a plaque in Cooperstown. Where are the guys now who look like Frank Thomas three years ago?

I admit there are exceptions here and there, and that one or two or more of the players on this year's All-Star teams whose HOF credentials I've dissed could turn into a Barry Bonds and become a super-duper star after they turn thirty-five. My problem with that argument, though, is that Barry Bonds had demonstrated *before* he was thirty-five that he was an HOF player.

A stronger argument against comparing the number of HOFers on rosters from then and now is one voiced by my late friend, Leonard Koppett, who, a month or so before I wrote this, advised me, "Don't put too much stock in some of those Hall of Fame votes involving old guys. A lot of that was just nostalgia on the part of their friends on the committees. There's a lot of those guys in the Hall of Fame who couldn't make it in today's game."

Fair enough. There's little doubt in my mind that some of those old-timers weren't as good as their batting averages make them appear today. For instance, take Chick Hafey off the 1933 Reds and put him in an average hitter's ballpark today, and he'd probably hit .285 over his career instead of .317. Pie Traynor, though reputed to be a great fielder, wasn't much of a hitter in his own day (despite the career batting average of .320) and if he had to compete for Scott Rolen's job I doubt he'd get it. In fact, I seriously doubt if, under analysis, Traynor would show up better than several modern third basemen who aren't in the Hall of Fame, such as Ron Santo, Ken Boyer, and Graig Nettles. Rick

Ferrell was supposed to be a great defensive catcher, but he hit just .281 with just 28 career home runs in eighteen seasons, and no matter how you juggle the numbers I'm sure I could find at least a couple of catchers today who are at least his equal in value. (Frankly, even having a sub-par season, I'd take Pudge Rodriguez, who was not on this year's All-Star roster, over Ferrell or any other catcher on either the AL or NL rosters.)

For that matter, does Chuck Klein really belong in the HOF or did somebody just want to throw a bone to Phillies' fans? He did lead the NL in home runs four times, RBIs twice, and in slugging three times, but his numbers were greatly inflated by the ballpark he played in, the Baker Bowl, and by the hitting explosion that overtook the game from the late twenties to the early thirties, Klein's best years.

While I'm being skeptical, I may as well go all the way and say that Bill Terry's numbers are also better than they look, partly because his best seasons came at a time when hitting was booming—in 1930, when he hit .401, the last National Leaguer to hit over .400, the league's batting average was .303—and also because he only played fourteen seasons and his batting average (.341), on-base average (.393), and slugging average (.506) didn't have points shaved by middle age. (He played in more than 100 games in only ten seasons.)

If Bill Terry played in the '90s he might, if he was lucky, be as productive as two old guys who didn't make the 2003 All-Star team, Fred McGriff and Raphael Palmeiro, both of whom have been top-level players for more seasons than Terry. He definitely ranks below the level of Jeff Bagwell (whom I'll deal with in another chapter).

But that doesn't make today's players more distinguished or explain why there are so many one-dimensional players in today's game.

Brushbacks and Knockdowns

Just for the sake of argument—and the sake of argument is precisely why this book is written—let's compare the All-Star teams of 1933, '41, '48, '53, '58, '61, '69, '76, '86, '96, 2003—and for good measure, 1999—in the form of charts. I'm going to use the All-Star rosters from BaseballAlmanac.com, which includes all the players chosen for the game, whether they played or not.

There is, of course, the problem of the different methods used to select the all-stars over the years. In 1933 and '34 the teams were selected by the fans and the managers; from '35 through '46 the teams were selected just by managers; from '47 to '57 they were chosen by fan vote for the starters with manager selection for the pitchers and remaining players; from '58 to '69 managers, players, and coaches picked the players; and from 1970 on the fans chose the all-stars. I'm going to make an assumption here, namely that the truly great players who we are trying to identify here have, except for rare aberrations, made the All-Star teams regardless of who does the choosing.

If you think any of my evaluations are unfair, feel free to change them and add your own:

1933

American League

Player	Position	Legit HOFer	In HOF But Shouldn't Be	Not In HOF But Should Be
Earl Averill	OF	X		
Joe Cronin	SS	X		
Bill Dickey	C	X		
Rick Ferrell	C		X	
Jimmie Foxx	1b	X		
Lou Gehrig	1b	X		
Charlie Gehringer	2b	X		

American League (continued)

Player	Position	Legit HOFer	In HOF But Shouldn't Be	Not In HOF But Should Be
Lefty Gomez	P	X		
Lefty Grove	P	X		
Tony Lazzeri	2b	X		
Babe Ruth	OF	X		
Al Simmons	OF	X		

National League

Player	Position	Legit HOFer	In HOF But Shouldn't Be	Not In HOF But Should Be
Wally Berger	OF			X
Frankie Frisch	2b	X		
Chick Hafey	OF		X	
Gabby Hartnett	C	X		
Carl Hubbell	P	X		
Chuck Klein	OF		X	
Bill Terry	1b		X	
Pie Traynor	3b	X		
Paul Waner	OF	X		
Total		16	4	1

I know a lot of people are going to complain that I'm not being fair to Bill Terry. The truth is, I see many better players who aren't in the Hall, so I find it quite easy to put on the "In-HOF-But-Shouldn't-Be" category. If you want to include Terry as legitimate HOFers, be my guest.

I'm very close to putting Pie Traynor in this category, too, and only one thing stops me. Well, two things, actually. First,

Traynor's reputation as a great fielder, and second, if you don't put him in the HOF, the NL doesn't have an HOF third baseman for decades and decades, and somehow that doesn't seem quite fair.

Any way you look at it, the '33 team beats the '03 team by a wide margin in legitimately great players.

All right, so maybe 1933 was a fluke. Let's move ahead to 1941 and the next generation of baseball greats, the last one before the war:

1941

American League

Player	Position	Legit HOFer	In HOF But Shouldn't Be	Not In HOF But Should Be
Luke Appling	SS	X		
Lou Boudreau	SS	X		
Joe Cronin	SS	X		
Bill Dickey	C	X		
Joe DiMaggio	OF	X		
Bobby Doerr	2b	X		
Bob Feller	P	X		
Jimmie Foxx	1b	X		
Joe Gordon	2b			X
Red Ruffing	P		X	
Ted Williams	OF	X		

National League

Player	Position	Legit HOFer	In HOF But Shouldn't Be	Not In HOF But Should Be
Stan Hack	3b			X
Billy Herman	2b	X		

National League (continued)

Player	Position	Legit HOFer	In HOF But Shouldn't Be	Not In HOF But Should Be
Carl Hubbell	P	X		
Johnny Mize	1b	X		
Mel Ott	OF	X		
Enos Slaughter	OF	X		
Arky Vaughan	SS	X		
Totals		15	1	2

To my eye, there was more first-rate talent on the '41 team than on the '33 squad (and more great shortstops near or close to their prime than in any other year ever).

Joe Gordon, I think, has been unjustly neglected by a generation of Yankee fans that forgot him when he was traded to Cleveland in 1947. He was a great player, greater, I think, than Phil Rizzuto, who hung around the Yankees till the end of his career and then put in several decades in the broadcast booth, while Gordon died in Los Angeles in 1978. He played for just eleven seasons, missing, like Rizzuto, the '44 and '45 seasons to the war (though Gordon played in '43). He couldn't pick up his game right away when he came out of the service in '46 and had his worst season, only hitting .210 with just 11 home runs. Actually, '46 was his only bad season. Gordon's career batting average was just .268, but he could draw walks—never less than 50 in a season—and hit with excellent power, especially for a middle infielder, with 253 home runs, including two seasons with 30 or more and seven with 20 or more. He drove in more than 80 runs eight times and more than 100 four times.

As a power-hitting second baseman the recent player he most resembles is Jeff Kent, but unlike Kent, Gordon could hit

Brushbacks and Knockdowns

1948

American League

Player	Position	Legit HOFer	In HOF But Shouldn't Be	Not In HOF But Should Be
Yogi Berra	C	X		
Lou Boudreau	SS	X		
Joe DiMaggio	OF	X		
Bobby Doerr	2b	X		
Bob Feller	P	X		
Joe Gordon	2b			X
George Kell	3b		X	
Bob Lemon	P	X		
Hal Newhouser	P	X		
Vern Stephens	SS			X
Ted Williams	OF	X		

National League

Player	Position	Legit HOFer	In HOF But Shouldn't Be	Not In HOF But Should Be
Richie Ashburn	OF	X		
Ralph Kiner	OF	X		
Johnny Mize	1b	X		
Stan Musial	OF	X		
Pee Wee Reese	SS	X		
Red Schoendienst	2b	X		
Enos Slaughter	OF	X		
Totals		15	1	2

and still excel at second base. He led the American League in assists four times, double plays three times, and range factor twice. This is a Hall of Fame–level career without excuses, and if it hadn't been for the war it would be obvious to everyone how good Joe Gordon was.

Stan Hack is a closer call. He was better than many players, including a couple of third basemen who are in the Hall. Maybe I'm being a tad too hard on Red Ruffing, but his won-lost percentage of .548 isn't very good for a guy who spent fifteen of his twenty-two seasons with the Yankees. I'd vote Luis Tiant in before him.

Next I'm choosing 1948. The war years are not an accurate gauge of how much talent was available to the big leagues, and by 1948 things had settled down a bit, with most major stars who were still young enough having returned to the game.

Before I looked at the rosters for the '48 teams I assumed that the talent level would be low because the interruption of World War II would have both ended some promising careers and kept some others from blossoming. But the '48 teams don't appear much different from the '33 and '41 teams in terms of Hall of Fame candidates, and I've always thought Vern Stephens (who also starred during the war, but who had some great seasons out of it, such as 1948, '49, and '50 when he hit 98 home runs and drove in 352 runs) should have been given more consideration. Whether you agree or not about Newhouser and Stephens, you must admit that in 1948 there was no drop in talent from the previous All-Star teams.

Now, I choose 1953 for two reasons: One, because by '53 integration was starting to have a strong effect on baseball. Two, since we can't do every season, 1953 is a convenient stopping place, being half a century from the time when I wrote this essay.

Brushbacks and Knockdowns

1953

American League

Player	Position	Legit HOFer	In HOF But Shouldn't Be	Not In HOF But Should Be
Yogi Berra	C	X		
Larry Doby	OF	X		
Nellie Fox	2b	X		
George Kell	3b		X	
Bob Lemon	P	X		
Mickey Mantle	OF	X		
Minnie Minoso	OF			X
Johnny Mize	1b	X		
Satchel Paige	P	X		
Phil Rizzuto	SS	X		
Ted Williams	OF	X		

National League

Player	Position	Legit HOFer	In HOF But Shouldn't Be	Not In HOF But Should Be
Richie Ashburn	OF	X		
Roy Campanella	C	X		
Ralph Kiner	OF	X		
Eddie Mathews	3b	X		
Stan Musial	OF	X		
Pee Wee Reese	OF	X		
Robin Roberts	P	X		
Jackie Robinson	3b	X		
Red Schoendienst	2b	X		

National League (continued)

Player	Position	Legit HOFer	In HOF But Shouldn't Be	Not In HOF But Should Be
Enos Slaughter	OF	X		
Duke Snider	OF	X		
Warren Spahn	P	X		
Hoyt Wilhelm	P	X		
Totals		22	1	1

I never thought about it before, but the early '50s may have had the greatest number of talented players ever. Think about it: Between the integration of black and Latin players and improved transportation, which brought in more players from California and other distant spots, not to mention that there would be no expansion until 1961, the amount of talent available to just sixteen major league teams was enormous.

Keep in mind that those twenty-two Hall of Famers *do not* include arguably the best players of the decade, Willie Mays, who was in the army, and Whitey Ford, the AL's best pitcher of the decade, who was just coming out of the army. The number also doesn't include Al Rosen, who, from 1950 to 1954, until he sustained a back injury, was the best third baseman in the game.

1958

American League

Player	Position	Legit HOFer	In HOF But Shouldn't Be	Not In HOF But Should Be
Luis Aparicio	SS	X		
Yogi Berra	C	X		
Whitey Ford	P	X		
Nellie Fox	2b	X		

Brushbacks and Knockdowns

American League (continued)

Player	Position	Legit HOFer	In HOF But Shouldn't Be	Not In HOF But Should Be
Elston Howard	C			X
Al Kaline	OF	X		
Mickey Mantle	OF	X		
Ted Williams	OF	X		
Early Wynn	P	X		

National League

Player	Position	Legit HOFer	In HOF But Shouldn't Be	Not In HOF But Should Be
Hank Aaron	OF	X		
Richie Ashburn	OF	X		
Ernie Banks	SS	X		
Eddie Mathews	3b	X		
Willie Mays	OF	X		
Bill Mazeroski	2b	X		
Stan Musial	1b	X		
Warren Spahn	P	X		
Totals		16	0	1

Let's jump ahead to 1958. Why '58? No particular reason except the major leagues were, by then, more fully integrated and more completely national, having expanded farther south (to Baltimore) and farther west (Milwaukee, Kansas City, and, of course, Los Angeles and San Francisco).

My selection of Elston Howard as "Should Be In The HOF" will be eye-opening to many, and I admit that I'm bending the definition a bit. What I really mean is "Would Have Been In the HOF Had He Gotten a Break." Elston Howard played fourteen years in the big leagues, hit .274 with very good power, and was a great defensive catcher. He won an MVP award in 1963 and was voted to nine consecutive All-Star teams.

Regrettably, he didn't get a crack at the majors till he was twenty-six years old, a rather advanced age for any ballplayer, but very advanced for someone whose primary position was catcher (1,138 of 1,605 games were spent behind the plate). Even after he broke in he had to contend with being Yogi Berra's backup, until he began assuming the regular catching duties in 1960 when he was thirty-one years old. From '60 to '64 he was the AL's All-Star catcher. I submit that a man good enough to be the league's best player at the game's toughest position from age thirty-one through thirty-five could have made several other All-Star starts had he been given the chance he deserved several years earlier. I further submit that a man who could have done so should be in the Hall of Fame.

Whether you agree with my argument for Howard or not, there were sixteen legitimate HOFers on the 1958 All-Star Team, which—though down a bit from five years earlier—is still an impressive number.

Now, move ahead to the 1961 All-Star Game—or perhaps I should say the two 1961 All-Star games. Why '61? Well, it's the first year of expansion, but even more important, it was the year when I first became conscious of baseball.

I think that Don Drysdale was a very good pitcher for perhaps eight or nine years. He led the National League in wins one time and never in won-lost percentage or earned run average. In 1956, '59, '63, '65, and '66 his teams won pennants. In one of those pennant-winning seasons, 1965, he was terrific, going 23-12. In the other four he was a good pitcher whose won-lost record, 54-51,

Brushbacks and Knockdowns

1961

American League

Player	Position	Legit HOFer	In HOF But Shouldn't Be	Not In HOF But Should Be
Yogi Berra	OF-C	X		
Jim Bunning	P	X		
Whitey Ford	P	X		
Nellie Fox	2b	X		
Elston Howard	C			X
Al Kaline	OF	X		
Harmon Killebrew	3b	X		
Mickey Mantle	OF	X		
Brooks Robinson	3B	X		
Hoyt Wilhelm	P	X		

National League

Player	Position	Legit HOFer	In HOF But Shouldn't Be	Not In HOF But Should Be
Hank Aaron	OF	X		
Ernie Banks	SS	X		
Orlando Cepeda	OF	X		
Roberto Clemente	OF	X		
Don Drysdale	P		X	
Sandy Koufax	P	X		
Eddie Mathews	3b	X		
Willie Mays	OF	X		
Stan Musial	OF	X		
Frank Robinson	OF	X		
Warren Spahn	P	X		
Totals		19	1	1

probably doesn't reflect quite how good he was. But, with four pennant-winning teams, he should have been better than 54-51.

Two things strike me about the best players from the 1961 All-Star teams. First, how many terrific all-around players there were. Al Kaline, Mickey Mantle, Hank Aaron, Roberto Clemente, Willie Mays, and Frank Robinson excelled in every area of the game. Have there ever been six outfielders so close to their prime who could do so many things so well on a baseball field? Before moving on, look at that list and check it against the 2003 All-Stars, both starters and subs.

Second, I'm impressed, looking back on the '61 All-Stars, at how many near greats there were. Over the years there have been many all-star cases made for Roger Maris, Ken Boyer, and Maury Wills; I think Boyer is the worthiest of the three (I'd rate him ahead of Pie Traynor and George Kell). I've already made my case for Elston Howard. Very good cases could be made, too, for Norm Cash and Rocky Calavito. I wouldn't make them, but others with good judgment have, and neither one of them rates far behind any of the players just mentioned.

The next year I'm going to examine is 1969, for no particular reason except that it was the year of the Miracle Mets and because the major leagues had expanded by four more teams to 24.

If you go by what he did on the playing field there should be no controversy about Pete Rose, and I've already written a chapter on Ron Santo, so as far as I'm concerned that's twenty legitimate Hall of Famers. By the way, the American League pitching staff of Mel Stottlemyre, Blue Moon Odom, Darold Knowles, Denny McLain, Dave McNally, Sam McDowell, and Ray Culp failed to produce an HOFer, though McNally—who pitched for just twelve full seasons and won 20 or more games for four straight seasons from '68 through '71—was pretty good, and Denny McLain . . .

Well, we all know about Denny McLain. Still, most people

Brushbacks and Knockdowns

1969

American League

Player	Position	Legit HOFer	In HOF But Shouldn't Be	Not In HOF But Should Be
Rod Carew	2b	X		
Reggie Jackson	OF	X		
Harmon Killebrew	1b	X		
Brooks Robinson	3b	X		
Frank Robinson	OF	X		
Carl Yastremski	OF	X		

National League

Player	Position	Legit HOFer	In HOF But Shouldn't Be	Not In HOF But Should Be
Hank Aaron	OF	X		
Ernie Banks	1b	X		
Johnny Bench	C	X		
Steve Carlton	P	X		
Roberto Clemente	OF	X		
Bob Gibson	P	X		
Juan Marichal	P	X		
Willie Mays	OF	X		
Willie McCovey	1b	X		
Phil Niekro	P	X		
Tony Perez	3b	X		
Pete Rose	OF			X
Ron Santo	3b			X
Tom Seaver	P	X		
Totals		18	0	2

forget that he was 16-6 in '65, 20-14 the following year, and the year after his 31-6 season, 1968, he went 24-9. From 1965 through 1969 he was 108-51 for a won-lost percentage of 68 percent. His off-the-field shenanigans notwithstanding, McLain's credentials over that five-year stretch weren't counterfeit.

I'm going to leap ahead to 1976, the first year of free agency and the year in which *Sports Illustrated* proclaimed a "Baseball Boom." Here's the tally:

1976

American League

Player	Position	Legit HOFer	In HOF But Shouldn't Be	Not In HOF But Should Be
George Brett	3b	X		
Rod Carew	1b	X		
Rollie Fingers	P	X		
Carlton Fisk	C	X		
Rich Gossage	P			X
Catfish Hunter	P	X		
Carl Yastrzemski	OF	X		

National League

Player	Position	Legit HOFer	In HOF But Shouldn't Be	Not In HOF But Should Be
Johnny Bench	C	X		
Joe Morgan	2b	X		
Tony Perez	1b	X		
Pete Rose	3b			X
Mike Schmidt	3b	X		
Tom Seaver	P	X		
Totals		11	0	2

(Just a thought, but I wonder why *Baseball Almanac* chose to list Jim Hunter as Catfish Hunter, but identifies Goose Gossage as Rich Gossage?)

This All-Star Team has less HOF fodder of any up to this time, even with Pete Rose and Rich-Goose Gossage under the heading of "Should-Bes." Catfish-Jim is borderline in my book; I'm not sure that Gossage isn't more deserving. If I had to, I'd take Gossage over several pitchers now in the HOF, including Rube Waddell, Red Ruffing, and probably Hunter.

Some good HOF arguments have been made for Thurman Munson and Dave Conception. I would not endorse those arguments, though I don't see any significant difference between Conception's credentials and Phil Rizzuto's.

I'm skipping to 1986, again for no particular reason except it was the last time the Mets won the World Series. By now, there were twenty-six big league teams, and we are going to change our categories to "Legit HOFer," "On Track for HOF," and "Iffy."

All of the players from the 1986 All-Star Game who are in the Hall of Fame deserve to be, and I think I'm justified in saying that all the ones who I chose as will-bes will be consensus picks, even if, like Ryne Sandberg, they get shafted in their first year of eligibility. (This will probably also happen to Tim Raines, who might have been the most underrated player of his time.) Still, though, that leaves just thirteen legitimate (in my view) Hall of Famers from the 1986 All-Star Game, and considering that there were two more teams than in '76, you have to wonder if the talent level hadn't declined a bit in the ten years since '76, when we had eleven Legits and two should-bes.

And what you really have to wonder is why after '69 the number of immortals has dropped off so drastically.

What's going on here? Was there really less talent in the game in the '70 and '80s than in previous decades? Or are we losing

1986

American League

Player	Position	Legit HOFer	On Track For HOF	Iffy
Wade Boggs	3b		X	
George Brett	3b	X		
Roger Clemens	P		X	
Rickey Henderson	OF		X	
Don Mattingly	1b			X
Eddie Murray	1b		X	
Kirby Puckett	OF		X	
Jim Rice	OF			X
Cal Ripken Jr.	SS		X	
Dave Winfield	OF	X		

National League

Player	Position	Legit HOFer	On Track For HOF	Iffy
Gary Carter	C	X		
Keith Hernandez	1b			X
Dale Murphy	OF			X
Dave Parker				X
Tim Raines	OF		X	
Ryne Sandberg	2b		X	
Mike Schmidt	3b	X		
Ozzie Smith	SS	X		
Lou Whitaker	2b			X
Totals		5	8	6

perspective? Perhaps the answer is to be found in the "Iffy" column. I wouldn't vote for any of the six for the Hall of Fame, though I wouldn't argue too vociferously to keep Mattingly out. Not that all of them weren't fine players and haven't had their fans make Hall of Fame arguments for them over the years, but are they really good enough for Cooperstown?

Don Mattingly was probably the best of the bunch, so let's look at his credentials. Donnie Baseball played in the majors for fourteen seasons, thirteen of them full, and hit .307, with 222 home runs and a whopping 442 doubles. He had more than 100 RBIs five times, led the AL in hits twice, batting once, total bases twice and doubles three years in a row, from '84 through '86. He was a superb fielder; I covered both the Yankees and Mets for three years for the *Village Voice* and watched him and Keith Hernandez both every day—well, every other day—and I can assure you they were both as good as their reputations. New York fans used to argue constantly about who was the better fielder, but I could never see that one was better than the other, though the local press almost always sided with Hernandez.

Whoever was better, Mattingly was very, very good. He won nine Gold Gloves and led the league in fielding average seven times, including four straight, from '84 through '87. (He had such good hands that for three games in 1986 he actually played third base, one of the few left-handers in the entire century to do so. For what it's worth, he had eleven assists and one error and participated in two double plays.)

Mattingly wasn't fast, but he was a smart and savvy base runner, and as far as intangibles count, Donnie had the admiration and respect of all his teammates, managers, coaches, and colleagues. He may have been the most respected player in the game during the '80s, if not for Kirby Puckett. In 1986, the year after he won the Most Valuable Player award, the *New York Times* conducted a poll of major league players, asking them who the best player in the game was. Mattingly won by a large margin.

I mention this not to argue that Don Mattingly was the best ballplayer in the league in '85 and '86—he probably wasn't, though he was close. I point this out as an example of how well-respected Mattingly was during his playing days.

The problem with Mattingly's Hall of Fame candidacy is essentially that he had only six good seasons in baseball—as my friend, the great novelist Kevin Baker, phrases it, "He was Stan Musial for the first six years of his career and Jim Spencer for the last six."

That's not entirely true regarding either Musial or Spencer, but Kevin's point survives his exaggeration. Before Mattingly injured his back in 1990, an injury that deprived him of most of his power, he was definitely on track for the Hall. After that, he was perilously close to ordinary.

Mattingly is the best of the '86 Iffys, and if I can't make a strong enough case for him I'm not even going to try with the others. Let's start with Mattingly's career numbers and put them in the context of their time and place. When you do that, he doesn't seem a great deal less worthy than several first basemen who are in the Hall of Fame, including Bill Terry, George Sisler, and Orlando Cepeda. For that matter, his hitting stats compare quite favorably with a near contemporary who played center field. Look at these:

	AB	R	H	HR	RBI	OBA	SA	BA
Player A	7,003	1,007	2,153	222	1099	.363	.471	.307
Player B	7,244	1,071	2,304	211	1085	.363	.477	.318

Player B is Kirby Puckett. I not only don't know anyone who thought his election to Cooperstown wasn't justified, I don't know anyone who didn't assume that in the last couple years of Puckett's career that he was going to the Hall of Fame. Puckett was a great center fielder; Mattingly was a great first baseman. In the field a great center fielder is more valuable than a great first baseman, but when their hitting stats are almost identical, does the center fielder merit the Hall of Fame while the first baseman doesn't, simply on the basis of center field being a more important defensive position?

Of course not. The reason why Kirby Puckett merits the Hall of Fame and Don Mattingly does not, or at least the reason that Puckett deserves it more than Mattingly is—well, to be honest, after examining this issue up close, I'm really not sure why. I feel that Puckett *does* deserve a plaque more than Mattingly, but I'm not sure how to articulate it.

Usually, when Hall of Fame arguments are made for players, career totals are cited: So-and-so had x number of hits and this guy had so many seasons of 100 or more RBIs. Most fans and writers are satisfied that, if a player achieves a certain level of success in these basic numbers as compared to past greats, there is a consensus that the player is worthy of the Hall of Fame. People who use such arguments are generally right. When for some reason the player doesn't have a long career—in Mattingly's case because of the back injury, in Puckett's glaucoma, which caused irreparable damage to his right eye—people are willing to cut them some slack if their averages are good. Puckett fits neatly into the first category: His career averages are great, his career was cut short, and his greatness is unquestioned. He walked, unquestioned, into the Hall of Fame.

Puckett played in 241 more games than Mattingly, about the equivalent of one and a half more seasons, and drove in 15 fewer runs. Both were popular, respected players. Yet Puckett is a consensus Hall of Famer and Mattingly is not. Why, exactly?

The difference between them is one that isn't instantly perceivable to someone who doesn't look at their year-by-year record. Essentially, it comes down to this: Mattingly had six very good seasons and six average ones, while Puckett, after two unimpressive seasons in 1984 and '85, had ten straight good to very good ones. It's hard to make the HOF with just six very good seasons, unless you're Sandy Koufax, and your very good seasons are six great ones.

There is a perception among baseball fans, whether correct or incorrect, that if two players have roughly identical stats, the one that delivers the longest record of good service is the most deserving. I think that perception is valid, although I've always been more concerned with peak performance (as in "Who was a better player at his peak, Mickey Mantle or Willie Mays?"). I can't deny the value of length of service when it comes to Hall of Fame selection.

But—and here's the point—is it likely that, say, ten or twelve or twenty years from now, if Don Mattingly becomes the manager of the Yankees and proves to be as popular in that capacity as he was during his playing career, that a movement to vote him into the Hall will gain some momentum? And if that happens, will the memory of the shortness of Mattingly's period of greatness still be a factor? Or is it more likely that his boosters will just do what most boosters do when they boost someone for the Hall of Fame and simply compare his career totals with other players of his period, like, say, Kirby Puckett? By that standard, how could Don Mattingly not make it into the Hall of Fame?

And even though Mattingly is the best of the six players among the 1986 Iffys, why couldn't advocates of some or all of the other Iffys get their guys elected the same way? Might not this factor account for some of the disparity between the number of players voted to the Hall of Fame before the '70s and afterwards?

Stated another way, if we searched back through the records of some of the players elected by old friends and teammates on the Veterans Committee—not immediately after their careers were over, but years later—might some of the players I listed (and possibly you agreed with) as Legit seem less legit?

1996

American League

Player	Position	Legit HOFer	On Track For HOF	Iffy
Roberto Alomar	2b			X
Albert Belle	OF			X
Wade Boggs	3b	X		
Ken Griffey Jr.	OF	X		
Mark McGwire	1b	X		
Cal Ripken Jr.	SS	X		
Alex Rodriguez	SS	X		
Ivan Rodriguez	C	X		
Frank Thomas	1b			X

National League

Player	Position	Legit HOFer	On Track For HOF	Iffy
Jeff Bagwell	1b	X		
Craig Biggio	2b	X		
Barry Bonds	OF	X		
Tony Gwynn	OF	X		
Chipper Jones	3b			X
Barry Larkin	SS	X		
Greg Maddux	P	X		
Pedro Martinez	P			X

National League (continued)

Player	Position	Legit HOFer	On Track For HOF	Iffy
Fred McGriff	1b			X
Mike Piazza	C		X	
Ozzie Smith		X		
John Smoltz	P			X
Totals		1	13	6

Maybe a look at the '96 team will clarify things. Except for Ozzie Smith, we are now dealing in Hall of Fame projections, so I suppose I should justify my ranking for each player on those rosters.

Roberto Alomar

Alomar, I would argue, was probably the best American League second baseman since Charlie Gehringer, which, if I'm correct, makes him the best man at his position in the league for more than half a century and for nearly six decades.

How about Rod Carew? Carew was a better hitter; his career SLOB was 16.86 to Alomar's 16.73, which doesn't sound like much, except that it includes Carew's declining years and doesn't take into account that Alomar played at a time when it was much easier to compile impressive hitting stats. Alomar has been a much better fielder and a better base-stealer. (Carew stole 353 bases in 540 tries for a 65 percent success rate, while Alomar, as of July 13, 2003, had stolen 468 of 579 for 80.1 percent.)

Well, maybe it's a toss-up, but you really can't argue that Alomar wasn't one of the two best AL second baseman of the last sixty years and one of the three best since Eddie Collins in the late 1920s. That's a pretty strong Hall of Fame argument right there.

For all that, I'd say his HOF chances right now are iffy. For one thing, there's the spitting incident, which could hurt him the way Juan Marichal's attacking John Roseboro hurt Marichal for three years when he became eligible. More serious, though, has been Alomar's dramatic fade over the last two seasons, and the fact that it happened while the New York press was watching.

Seldom in the last couple of decades has a great player declined so swiftly for no perceptible reason as Roberto Alomar; Dale Murphy comes to mind, but few others. In 1983 Murphy won his second consecutive MVP award, the youngest player (at age twenty-seven) ever to do so, then proceeded to win consecutive home run titles. In 1987 he rebounded from a sub-par season to hit .295 with 44 home runs. At this point in his career there was no question that Murphy was headed for the Hall of Fame, but in 1988, at age thirty-two, he hit just .226 with 24 home runs. He never had another good season. The reason for Murphy's swift decline can be traced to knee problems; he had arthroscopic surgery on his right knee late in 1988.

To date, nothing comparable has been found to explain Roberto Alomar's decline. He was a good player from the year he broke in, at age twenty in 1988, hitting .266, scoring 84 runs, and stealing 24 bases. He hit over .300 for the first time four years later and then did it nine times in the next ten seasons. Six times he scored over 100 runs; twice he drove in more than 100, a rare achievement for a middle infielder. He was second in stolen bases four times, won nine Gold Gloves, and made the All-Star team twelve straight years from 1990 through 2001. Then he came to the Mets in 2002 and hit .266. It wasn't a fluke; in 73 games in 2003 before the Mets dealt him to the White Sox, he hit just .262. What happened?

Many Mets fans I know have been quick to blame Shea

Stadium, where many a fine hitter has gone to grow old quickly. But Shea, notorious among National League hitters as a pitcher's park, might take a career .305 hitter and pull his average down to .285 or .280, not all the way down to .266 and .262, not all by itself. It certainly doesn't seem possible that it could take Roberto Alomar all the way from his best season, 2001, when he hit .336, to his worst, the following year, when his batting average dropped 70 points. Besides, *everything* got worse for Alomar: His home runs went from 20 to 11, his walks from 80 to 57, his stolen bases from 30 of 36 to 16 of 20, and his range factor from 4.71 chances per game to 4.42. And for the first 73 games of '03, his slide was continuing: His projected numbers for 2003 with the Mets were .258, 3 home runs, 59 walks, and 10 stolen bases.

Every aspect of Alomar's game, his batting eye, his range in the field, his base running ability, dropped off sharply. *Very sharply—and from a career-best season the previous year.*

The pressure of playing in New York? C'mon, a twelve-time All-Star with two World Series rings doesn't suddenly fold up because he is playing in front of a New York crowd.

I don't know what happened to Roberto. Perhaps he suddenly got old, though players with his all-around ability almost never get *that* old *that* quickly. I'm not going to speculate. Instead, I'm going to focus on how good Alomar *was*.

Most baseball analysts, I'm sure, would rank Roberto Alomar and Craig Biggio as the best second basemen in the American and National Leagues during the '90s. With the possible exception of Ryne Sandberg, whose career was winding down as theirs were heating up, they were probably the best second basemen in baseball since Joe Morgan. Let's do a quick career comparison through July 13, 2003:

	Yrs	G	AB	R	H	HR	RBI	W	SO	SB-CS
Alomar	16	2,265	8,684	1,451	2,623	203	1,095	993	1,078	468-111
Biggio	16	2,187	8,328	1,459	2,395	204	902	992	1,322	386-115

	BA	OBA	SA	SLOB	FA	LFA	RngFac	L RngFac	DP
Alomar	.302	.373	.446	16.64	.984	.981	4.78	4.53	1,297
Biggio	.288	.376	.433	16.28	.984	.981	4.85	4.52	937

That's pretty amazing; I doubt if you'll find any two players in baseball history who broke into the big leagues the same year and played for sixteen seasons who had such nearly identical numbers. Biggio has one more home run; Alomar has one more walk. Biggio has 8 more runs scored, and an on-base average 3 points higher; Alomar has a slugging average 13 points higher and a range factor one-hundredth of a point higher. Their fielding averages are identical. Alomar has 360 more double plays, but he has played more games at second base (Biggio spent most of his first four years as a catcher).

Who's been the greater player? I don't know, but that's not to the point right now. They've both been great players, great all-around players, and for a long time. Judging from the evidence of their career statistics at bat, in the field, and on the bases, there isn't enough evidence to argue that one should be in the Hall of Fame and the other shouldn't.

But one of them, Biggio, will probably be in the Hall of Fame, and Alomar's chances, as of the All-Star break in 2003, seem dubious. Biggio, who is three years older, is a better player right now than Alomar—as I write this he is hitting .273 with 9 home runs and 58 runs scored—and may outlast him (Biggio has moved to left field, which may add a couple of years to his career). And, of course, Biggio never spit at an umpire.

Albert Belle

Most fans who remember Albert Belle years from now will, I'm sure, be surprised to find that anyone ever considered him a HOF candidate. But foul though his personality may have been, there were times when he was a terrific, almost a great player. Or at least, a great hitter. His career batting average was .295, and in twelve seasons, just ten of them full, he collected 381 home runs and 1,239 RBIs, and led the AL in RBIs and total bases three times each. For nine straight years he never had less than 28 home runs and for eight straight never fewer than 101 RBIs per season, numbers that were difficult to ignore, even in an era when runs were cheap.

If he had been a little nicer, its possible that some misty-eyed teammates or sportswriters would trot out his credentials in a few years and make his HOF case, but somehow I don't see many people who knew him getting misty-eyed about Albert Belle.

Wade Boggs

I shouldn't have to argue a case for a man who won five batting titles and led the league six times in on-base average. He led AL third basemen in DPs four times, too.

Ken Griffey Jr.

As I write this in the summer of '03 the perceptions of Ken Griffey Jr. as a sure HOFer and as a disappointment seem to be running concurrently. No doubt the group that holds the first opinion is larger and he'll get in, probably on the first ballot, but I'd like to give some voice to the minority. As I write this, the man many regard as the best player in baseball during the past decade is headed for age thirty-four and, with injuries limiting him to just 49 games, is batting .245 with 11 home runs and just 23 RBIs. Last year injuries limited him to just 70 games, in which he batted .264 with 8 home runs and 23 RBIs. The season before injuries limited him to 111 games in which he hit .286 with 22 home runs and 65 RBIs. Neither Mickey Mantle nor Ted Williams ever had a three-year stretch with injuries like this.

Junior's problems, though, can't be written off entirely to injuries. In 1998, at age twenty-nine, he had the second of his consecutive 56-home-run seasons, driving in 146 runs. Great numbers, but they disguised the fact that his peripheral skills were swiftly eroding. He batted just .284, his lowest full-season average since his rookie year of 1989. His .365 on base average was his lowest in five seasons. The following season he again hit under .300 at .285, and while his OBA jumped 19 points to .384, his slugging average dipped 35 points to .576. From there, after turning thirty, his production in nearly every area dropped off sharply. In 2000 he hit just .271, his lowest average since his first year, and his slugging average of .556 was the lowest in his previous seven full seasons. Perhaps more telling, he stole just six bases in ten attempts, the first time ever he had failed to steal in double figures, except for 1995 when he played just 72 games. From 1989 through 1999 he stole 167 bases; from 2000 till the All-Star Break of '03 he stole 10.

Sure, much of Griffey's decline can be written off to injuries. But how much? Since 2001 to the day I write this (two days before the 2003 All-Star break) he has played in just 230 games, several as a pinch hitter, and batted just 716 times, for a batting average of only .271. His on-base average has also continued to decline; in fact, it has declined not simply during his period of injury but since 1994, the last time he was over .400.

The last time his slugging percentage was over .600 was 1998; it was also the last time it was over .576.

In the field his range has declined drastically. Over the last 230 games he has averaged about 2.2 chances per 9 innings, well below the 2.7 he had averaged up to the 2000 season. Again, this can't be ascribed entirely to injury. In 1996 he had his best range factor, 2.95; he played full seasons in both '97, '98, and '99, but never approached 3.0 again.

As a point of comparison, let's take Mickey Mantle, who had as much difficulty with injuries late in his career and who surely played with as much pain as Griffey or anyone else.

In 1961, at age thirty, Mantle recorded the third highest on-base average of his career (.448) and his second-highest slugging average (.687). This despite spending most of the last two weeks of the season in a hospital bed watching Roger Maris break Babe Ruth's single-season home run record. On the bases, he stole 12 in 13 attempts, and in the field, despite those absurdly bandaged knees, he averaged 2.44 fly balls per 9 defensive innings, compared to the league average of 2.25. The following season his knees limited him to just 117 games, but at age thirty-one he still managed to hit .321 (the third-highest batting average of his career) and have an on-base average of .486 (the second-highest of his career) with a slugging percentage of .605. Almost unbelievably, *he stole 9 bases in 9 attempts.* He was voted his third Most Valuable Player Award—it really should have been his fifth or sixth—though 377 at-bats were the fewest of any player ever to win the award.

Perhaps his '63 and '64 seasons, during which Mantle played with so much pain that his teammates couldn't look at him without grimacing, offer a more striking comparison with Griffey. At age thirty-three injuries cut Mantle's playing time to just 65 games. Yet he was able to hit .314 with an excellent on-base average of .441 and a slugging average of .622, actually 17 points higher than the previous season. In 1964, hobbling all season and missing 19 games, he still hit .303, led the league with a .423 OBA and even stole 6 bases in 9 attempts. From '62 through '64 his range factor declined, but only by .2 of a percent below the league average.

Over Mantle's last four seasons, 1965–68, his quality numbers did drop, though he was still able to draw walks—an amazing 107 at age thirty-six in '67, and an equally amazing 106 the following season. Here's a little number to chew on: In Mantle's last four seasons, when he was on the serious downside of his career, his OBA was over .380, higher than Ken Griffey Jr.'s career OBA *right now*.

Okay, you may well reply, Ken Griffey Jr. is not Mickey Mantle. To which I would reply: You got that right. Even though many people have been quick to compare the two over the years, particularly when the discussion comes around to great power hitters who are also great all-around players. And why, I'm entitled to ask, is the comparison unfair, if, as so many contend, Ken Griffey Jr. was supposed to be the best ballplayer of his generation? Griffey has had a lot of injuries; so did Mantle. Griffey did not play well when coming back from these injuries; Mantle was sensational coming back from his injuries. Griffey's peripheral skills, his quality stats such as batting, on-base, and slugging averages, his fielding range and his stolen base average, leveled off or began to decline sharply *before* he turned thirty. Mantle's peripheral skills and his quality stats were sensational, even when he was playing with pain or returning from injuries.

Those who contend that Ken Griffey has a lock on the Hall of Fame should consider the possibility that from here on in he may be finished as a top-flight ballplayer. Should this prove to be the case, I must ask how they are going to justify voting a player into the Hall of Fame who didn't have a great season after the age of thirty. His totals, of course, are imposing; no matter how much he has slipped he is bound to pass the 500 home run mark, probably around May 2004, and if he escapes another serious injury he will almost certainly pass the 1,500 RBI mark before September 2005. But will it be remembered that those fabulous numbers were compiled at a time when runs were cheap and scoring records were falling everywhere? And will it be remembered that once he passed the age of thirty he practically ceased to have any value to his team except as a long-ball hitter?

I'm not saying Ken Griffey Jr. won't make the Hall of Fame, or that at his best he wasn't a great player. I'm saying that he is not one now and hasn't been one for quite a while. But that probably won't affect his Hall of Fame status.

Hold the presses—the day after I wrote the above Griffey injured his ankle—running the bases after hitting a home run!—and may be out for the rest of the season. I am tempted to say that his HOF chances depend very much on what he does with the rest of his career, but I don't want to risk putting any more bad luck on the guy.

Mark McGwire

There are a few people out there who doubt Mark McGwire's HOF credentials. I understand their point of view: It's hard for some people to get passionate about a player whose only great skills were hitting home runs and collecting walks. But in terms of how much those two things could do to help win ball games, look at this comparison between Big Mac and Ken Griffey Jr. (Griffey's numbers include games up to July 11, 2003):

	G	AB	HR	RBI	BA	OBA	SA
Junior	1,910	7,068	479	1,381	.294	.378	.561
Big Mac	1,874	6,187	583	1,414	.263	.394	.588

I wonder how many people who lament Ken Griffey Jr.'s lost playing time know that as of the midway point in 2003 he had played more games than Mark McGwire did in his entire career? Griffey's batting average is 31 points higher than McGwire's, but what of it? McGwire's on-base average is 26 points higher and his slugging average 27 points higher.

You really have to see a comparison like this to understand how great a run producer McGwire was.

Cal Ripken Jr. and Alex Rodriguez

I don't suppose there could be anyone reading this who doesn't know that Cal Ripken Jr. is a legitimate Hall of Fame shortstop or who doesn't understand why Alex Rodriguez is definitely on track for the Hall. If A-Rod is to continue performing at his accustomed level for another three seasons, he'll almost certainly be regarded as the second-best shortstop of all time behind Honus Wagner.

Ivan Rodriguez

Pudge Rodriquez is one of the ten best catchers in baseball history. Probably, he's better than that. At his best, he has been better than Carlton Fisk, and he's certainly a better all-around catcher than Mike Piazza, though whether or not that makes him more valuable than Piazza is another matter. (I don't think so, but it's close.) Anyway, after Berra, Bench, Campanella,

Cochrane, and Dickey I'm hard put to come up with anyone else who has been better.

That's at his peak, of course. He's thirty-one, headed towards thirty-two as I write this, and not having a bad season, though having moved to the National League and the Florida Marlins, it almost seems as if he's dropped off the face of the earth. His career totals are pretty impressive for a catcher: .305 BA, 228 HRs (including the 13 he has so far in the '03 season), and .489 slugging average.

There are, however, complications. Pudge has a herniated disc in his lower back that put a crimp in his 2002 workload, causing him to miss 47 games. He has just passed the 1,500-game mark, which is a danger zone for all catchers, even the relatively young. (He threw out just 33 percent of attempted base runners last year and his career average is slightly over 46 percent.) Staying in the American League, where he could have caught and DHed, might have been a wise move.

If he remains in the NL, don't be surprised to see him change positions sometime soon. What this will do to his HOF chances isn't certain. It might help his batting totals over the next couple years, but Hall of Fame voters expect more production from a first baseman or left fielder than they do from a catcher. I think his chances are very good, though, no matter what happens. He will be in his eleventh good season in a row at baseball's most grueling position in 2003. He's a ten-time All-Star with ten Gold Gloves and an MVP award, and it's hard to think that any catcher with credentials like that wouldn't be going to the Hall of Fame.

Frank Thomas

This is a tough call. Let's start out with a reminder of how good a hitter Frank Thomas was. My friends and I like to argue about who was the best hitter of the '90s, Thomas or Edgar Martinez. I always argue for Thomas.

Frank Thomas broke into the majors in 1990 playing 60 games and batting .330. For some reason, Edgar Martinez played only 92 games from 1987, his first season in the majors, to 1989. 1990 was his first full season, 144 games, and he hit .302 with 11 home runs. After that he was a regular and had full seasons every year except '93, when injuries held him to 42 games, and the strike year of '94, when he played in just 89 games. So Thomas and Martinez are almost contemporaries.

Here are their basic career numbers through the 2002 season:

	G	AB	HR	RBI	BA	OBA	SA
Martinez	1,769	6,230	273	1,100	.317	.424	.528
Thomas	1,698	6,065	376	1,285	.314	.432	.568

Martinez was (and is) a great hitter. Thomas was a greater one. If you calculate their value as hitters by SLOB, it comes out to 22.4 runs per 100 at-bats for Edgar and 24.5 for Frank. That's not a big difference, but it all comes down on Thomas's side. Martinez has led the league once in runs scored, twice in doubles, twice in batting, and twice in OBA. Thomas has led the league once in runs scored, once in doubles, four times in walks, once in batting, four times in OBA, and once in slugging. Essentially, the difference between them is that Thomas has a bit more power; in 71 fewer games, Thomas, up to 2002, had 103 more homers, though Martinez had 73 more doubles.

Earlier I quoted my friend Kevin Baker saying that Don Mattingly, for the first six years of his career, was Stan Musial, while for the next six he was Jim Spencer. I also said that that was an exaggeration, that at his best Mattingly wasn't quite as good as Musial or at his worst as bad as Jim Spencer. With Frank Thomas the case is more extreme. For the first seven years of his career he was *better* than Musial, and from 2001 through 2002 he was *worse* than Jim Spencer.

Okay, that's not true; I just said it for effect. But in 2001 and 2002 Thomas batted .249, a point below Jim Spencer's lifetime batting average. Of course, he also drew 98 walks over those 597 at-bats, which is more than Jim Spencer ever had in any two full seasons, and Thomas's 28 home runs in 2002 were 5 more than Spencer ever hit in any season. (On the other hand, Spencer could *field*. He led the AL in fielding average four times at first base.)

Frank Thomas was once a *fabulous* hitter, probably, for most of the '90s, the best in either league. He can still produce runs—on the day I write this, July 12, 2003, he is hitting .271 with 20 home runs and a .411 OBA. At age thirty-five he is no longer a great hitter, and it's doubtful he'll ever be a great hitter again. Part of the problem was a torn right triceps that kept him out of all but 68 games in 2001, but big Frank was in sharp decline before that. Some say it was an acrimonious divorce that unfocused him in 1998 and brought his batting average down 81 points and his slugging average down 131 points from the previous season. Just about everyone agrees that he has a problem with conditioning. On opening day he was listed at 275, which is at least 30 pounds too heavy for a guy who thinks he's justified in complaining when he's left off an All-Star team.

Though a lot of baseball writers don't see it that way right now, Thomas's HOF chances are shaky. Unlike Ken Griffey Jr., he has never made a contribution to his team outside the batter's box. No, let me rephrase that: He's a bad base runner and a terrible fielder, maybe the worst first baseman I've ever seen. Put as simply as possible, Frank Thomas has not merely failed to make a contribution outside of the batter's box, he's been a total liability.

Frank Thomas sulked when the White Sox, finally acting on what was obvious to everyone else, exercised the "diminished skills" clause in his contract. He showed up late for workouts, he reported for spring training woefully out of shape, his team didn't want to keep him, and no one else in either league was eager to make a deal for him. And despite all this, there really are people who think Frank Thomas will be a shoo-in for the Hall of Fame, all because he has such a high OBA and has driven in more than 100 runs so many times. And many of these same people are quick to tell *me* that *I'm* too focused on statistics.

Jeff Bagwell

He's been in the major leagues for thirteen seasons now, and six or seven of those seasons were truly great (especially his MVP season of '94, in which he hit .368 with a .750 slugging average, one of the greatest seasons ever by a National League hitter) and the rest very good. He's been a fine fielder, a fine base runner, particularly for a first baseman (quick, can you name another first baseman who in thirteen seasons was closing in on 200 stolen bases? I can't), and a great hitter. He will finish the 2003 season with a career batting average a little over .300, about 410 home runs, and nearly as many RBIs in thirteen years as Mark McGwire had in sixteen (though Bagwell will have played in a few more games).

Here's an oddity: He's the only major league player ever to have six straight seasons with at least 30 HRs, 100 RBIs, 100 runs scored, and 100 walks, and he just missed making that seven straight seasons in '02, falling short by just 2 RBIs and 6 runs scored. I mean odd in the sense that from Babe Ruth though the end of the twentieth century you'd have thought *somebody* else would have done that.

With the possible exception of Stan Musial, whose best years were spent in the outfield, Bagwell is probably the best first baseman in NL history. *Of course* Jeff Bagwell is going to the Hall of Fame.

Craig Biggio

See Roberto Alomar.

Barry Bonds

Bonds, of course, is a first-ballot Hall of Famer and probably was well before his home runs explosion of the 2000s. He gets his own chapter.

Tony Gwynn

I don't think there's any dispute that Tony Gwynn will score a Hall of Fame vote standing up.

Chipper Jones

Now here's an interesting case. A couple of seasons ago when Chipper was playing third base, few people doubted that the pace he was on would, if he maintained it, take him to the Hall of Fame. From 1995 through 2001 Chipper collected an MVP award, a World Series ring, six All-Star souvenir shirts, six straight seasons of 100 or more runs scored, seven straight seasons of 100 or more RBIs, and the future looked rosy. Then he turned thirty, moved to left field, hit "just" 26 home runs and drove in "only" 100 runs and failed to score 100 for the first time since 1995, and suddenly the future seemed a little less rosy.

Well, left fielders are supposed to hit better than third base-men, and Chipper was never more than an average third base-man anyway. But that hardly seems reason to give up on his Cooperstown chances. At the All-Star Break in 2003 he had a pretty good shot at reaching 100 RBIs for the eighth straight year, but he was hitting under .300 (if he misses it will be for the first time since 1997). He was once a pretty good base stealer—114 out of 152 through '02—but with just a single stolen base through the first half of '03 he's apparently abandoned that part of his game. Nobody is writing him off, but he's going to have to hit better to get back on the HOF path.

Barry Larkin

Larkin is going to be a hard sell when it comes to the Hall of Fame because he has never done anything, well, spectacular. He did hit .342 in 97 games back in 1989, but that was a bit of an aberration, as he has never hit higher than .317 in any other season. He did hit 33 home runs in 1996, but in no other season has he hit more than 20. He did steal 51 bases in 1995, but in only one other season has he stolen as many as 40. He has never driven in 100 runs and has scored more than 100 only twice.

Larkin did win the MVP award in 1995, but looking at his career record you wonder why they picked that one and not any of three or four others. He hit .319 in '95, his second-best mark, but one he has come within 4 points of in three other years. He hit 15 home runs, a mark he bettered three other times. He drove in 66 runs, a total he has surpassed in six other seasons. His range in the field was .13-chances-per-nine-defensive-innings better than the rest of the NL shortstops, but he had several seasons when he was better than that in the field.

Perhaps they gave him the MVP award in 1995 for simple

all-around excellence over a long period. If so, let's hope the same logic will win out when he becomes eligible for the Hall of Fame. I'd rate him at least on a par with Ozzie Smith and ahead of five or six shortstops already in the Hall.

Greg Maddux

He probably won't make 300 wins, but he has been the best starting pitcher in the National League from 1988 to 2002. If he had pitched in the '60s he'd have won 20 or more games ten times

Pedro Martinez

Alone among my friends who follow baseball, I don't see Pedro Martinez as a lock for the Hall of Fame. I'm not arguing that at his best he isn't the most effective pitcher in baseball, but he's also one of the most brittle. Martinez is going to be thirty-four early next season with fewer than 170 wins and five consecutive seasons of having pitched fewer than 220 innings. How many pitchers go to the Hall of Fame with numbers like that? He's had six outstanding seasons before 2003 and a lot of people say, well, that's as many as Sandy Koufax had, which is true, but Sandy quit while he was on top. If Pedro has a couple of subpar seasons— well, Dizzy Dean parlayed 150 wins into Cooperstown and a career as a broadcaster. And his English wasn't as good as Pedro's.

Fred McGriff

When Rafael Palmeiro hit his 500th home run early in the 2003 season he immediately jumped into Hall of Fame contention in the eyes of many people who hadn't given him serious consideration before. Palmeiro was thirty-nine in September of '03; Fred

McGriff was forty last October. Let's look at their career numbers as of the 2003 All-Star Break.

	G	AB	R	HR	RBI	BA	OBA	SA	SLOB
Palmeiro	2,501	9,305	1,509	511	1,630	.291	.373	.521	19.43
McGriff	2,414	8,625	1,329	488	1,538	.285	.378	.511	19.32

Who do you like? There's a slight edge in the numbers for Palmeiro, though he gets a bit of a boost from having played nine years in Texas in a hitters' ballpark. On the whole, it looks like a jump ball to me. Palmeiro was a little better fielder, but if just one of them is going to make it, my money is on Palmeiro because he reached the 500 mark earlier. Also, midway through the 2003 season he looks like he has a little more gas left in his tank.

By the way, in his autobiography, Whitey Herzog criticized McGriff as "a guy who hit thirty-plus homers for seven straight years, but in three of those years he didn't have hundred RBIs. That's not very good clutch hitting." I refer Mr. Herzog to Branch Rickey: "Surely it is valid evidence of thoughtlessness to overstress the value of RBIs and thereby give the press and television a full right to spread the most misleading column of figures in baseball today."

Mike Piazza

Even allowing for the inflated hitting numbers of recent seasons, Piazza looks to be the best hitting catcher of all time, and by a fairly substantial margin.

Fans always fantasize over what their favorite player's numbers might look like if he had played his home games in a ballpark favorable to his talents. In Piazza's case, the possibilities are *really* interesting, considering that he has played almost his entire career—actually, all but five games with the Florida Marlins—for the Dodgers and Mets, playing his home games in what are probably the two worst hitters' parks in the National League.

Here is his career home-road breakdown as of the All-Star break, 2003:

	G	AB	R	HR	RBI	BA	OBA	SA	SLOB
Home	693	2,479	386	160	499	.302	.371	.539	20.00
Away	732	2,748	486	194	589	.338	.405	.611	24.74

That's a pretty big gap: The road Mike Piazza is worth about 4.7 runs per 100 at bats more than the home Piazza.

Let's look at it from a different perspective: Piazza's career numbers compared to his road numbers times two (to simulate what life would have been like for Mike had he played all his home games in something like a neutral park).

	G	AB	R	HR	RBI	BA	OBA	SA	SLOB
Actual Career	1,425	5,227	827	354	1,088	.321	.389	.576	22.41
Road Stats × 2	1,464	5,496	972	388	1,178	.338	.405	.611	24.74

One can only imagine what Piazza's career numbers would look like if he had played his home games in a good hitters' park, or if he had played first base or left field instead of catcher, or both.

Ozzie Smith

In addition to being probably the best defensive shortstop in baseball since Honus Wagner, Smith created a few runs for his teams by drawing walks (twelve times in sixteen seasons of 380 or more at-bats he had more than 50 walks, nine times more than 60, and five times more than 70), stealing bases (580 of 728 for an excellent 80 percent success rate with eleven seasons stealing 30 or more), and not hitting into double plays (just 167 for nineteen seasons, with thirteen seasons of 10 or less).

As for Ozzie's fielding, it may be true, as Branch Rickey said, that "There's nothing you can do with fielding statistics," at least in a year-to-year or short-term comparison. But when a guy excels in something season after season for more than fifteen years, you have to believe there's something to his fielding statistics. In sixteen seasons of playing 90 or more games at shortstop Ozzie Smith led National League shortstops in assists in half of those seasons. He led the NL in double plays five times, in fielding average eight times, and in range factor seven times.

For his career, his career fielding average was 12 points higher than the league average and his range factor was .44 higher than the league. In comparison, Omar Vizquel, considered by many to be the best defensive shortstop of the '90s, was just 9 points better than AL shortstops during his peak years in the '90s and just .07 better than AL shortstops in range factor.

John Smoltz

Maybe I'm being overly generous here, but many think Dennis Eckersley belongs in the Hall of Fame for his combined starting and relieving, and I say Smoltz was a better starter than Eckersley. He hasn't yet proved to be as good a reliever as Eck, but posting an earned run average of about one run per nine innings is a heck of a year. He has 99 career saves going into the 2003 All-Star Break; if he can notch perhaps 200 to 250 career saves, he has a very good shot.

So that's my projection for the 1996 All-Star Team: One man in, thirteen to go, six with a decent shot. Of the Iffys, I figure that two or three will get in, giving the '96 All-Stars at least sixteen Hall of Famers.

Now I'm going to squeeze one more in. Here's the 1999 All-Star Team:

1999

American League

Player	Position	On Track For HOF	Iffy
Roberto Alomar	2b		X
Nomar Garciaparra	SS	X	
Ken Griffey Jr.	OF	X	
Derek Jeter	SS		X
Pedro Martinez	P		X
Raphael Palmeiro	DH		X
Manny Ramirez	OF		X
Cal Ripken Jr.	SS	X	
Mariano Rivera	P	X	
Ivan Rodriguez	C	X	
Jim Thome	1b		X

National League

Player	Position	On Track For HOF	Iffy
Jeff Bagwell	1b	X	
Tony Gwynn	OF	X	
Trevor Hoffman	P		X
Randy Johnson	P	X	

National League (continued)

Player	Position	On Track For HOF	Iffy
Barry Larkin	SS	X	
Mark McGwire	1b	X	
Mike Piazza	C	X	
Sammy Sosa	OF	X	
Totals		12	7

I don't think that most fans would argue with most of my picks, but let me justify two choices about whom most fans might feel uneasy. First, Mariano Rivera: It isn't that most people who have seen him deny that he's great; the arguments for or against any relief pitchers are more along the lines of "How exactly can you rank relief pitchers?" and "How are you going to prove that he deserves it and not Trevor Hoffman or Troy Percival or Robb Nenn?"

Maybe they *all* deserve it. For now, I'll just make the assumption that for the most part what a statistic means for one man will pretty much mean the same for another. Here's how Rivera, Percival, Hoffman, and Nenn stack up as of July 21, 2003:

	Age	IP	W-L	Svd-Blown	Pct.	ERA
Rivera	33	618.1	42-27	261-39	87.0%	2.53
Percival	33	518.2	27-32	271-42	86.6%	2.92
Nenn	33	715.0	45-42	314-54	85.3%	2.98
Hoffman	35	701.0	45-44	352-44	88.9%	2.79

Hoffman's "save" percentage is the best of the bunch, but it certainly is close. Also, his ERA would be substantially higher if one assumes that most of the difference between the two leagues is caused by the DH and adjusts accordingly. So would Robb Nenn's.

One quick way to measure the relative effectiveness of relief pitchers is to combine their saves and wins with their blowns and losses. Tabulated that way, their percentages rank this way:

Rivera	82.1%
Hoffman	81.9%
Percival	80.1%
Nenn	78.9%

Of course, to get an absolutely accurate gauge you'd have to measure wins and losses vs. team wins and losses—but we're starting to split hairs. The point is that they're all great and they're all dominating, but no matter how you cut it, none of them has a genuine statistical edge over Mariano Rivera. But that's not the reason why, if most voters had to choose one of the four for the HOF, they'd pick Rivera. They'd pick him because of his playoff and World Series performances. There are those who would say that this is unfair, that the other three haven't had that kind of opportunity, and that Rivera's postseason record shouldn't be a consideration. But what great pitchers ever get considered for the Hall of Fame when their playoff and World Series achievements aren't part of the package? I wonder if any HOF voter could honestly say he didn't consider Bob Gibson's World Series performance when evaluating him for the Hall.

As I write this, Hoffman and Nenn have not pitched this year and their status is not certain, while Rivera, who missed time earlier in the season, is back strong as ever. It's likely that 2003 will put an even greater distance between Mariano and the

National League relief aces, and in quality stats, at least, he already has a substantial lead over Percival.

The case for Jim Thome isn't as strong as the case for Rivera, but it's much simpler. On the day I write this, Jim Thome is approaching his thirty-third birthday, and he has 360 home runs and 1,000 RBIs. If he continues at this pace or even slows down a bit, by the time he reaches his thirty-fifth birthday he'll have maybe 440 home runs and perhaps 1,220 RBIs. Would anyone deny that he has the same chance at the Hall of Fame as Raphael Palmeiro?

I can't chart the 2003 All-Stars the way I have those of previous years, since most of them haven't been around for very long; but let's look through the rosters and see if we have some possible future ringers (I'm not going to list their teams, by the way; if you don't know what teams they play for then you shouldn't be arguing that they're legitimate All-Stars):

- **Garret Anderson.** A fine player, age thirty, just coming into his own after winning his first World Series ring. No chance for the Hall of Fame.
- **Hank Blalock.** He won the 2003 All-Star Game with a home run. He's twenty-two, and I really have no idea at all what kind of player he'll develop into. He hit just .211 in 49 games the previous year, but The Sporting News-STATS, Inc.'s *The Scouting Notebook, 2003* labels him a Top Prospect. However, they also cautioned that "defense is not his calling card" and that "he has below-average speed."
- **Bret Boone.** He's thirty-four years old, with a batting average of around .270 and an on-base average a bit above .320. I have no idea how he became a slugger after turning thirty, but he's not HOF fodder.

- **Carl Everett.** If there's ever a Hall of Fame for Yankee haters, he's a first-ballot. But not Cooperstown.
- **Nomar Garciaparra.** Yup, he's on track.

By the way, if I don't mention it here, it'll probably never get mentioned anywhere, but in *The New Yorker*, December 1998, Roger Angell, in his last year-end Christmas poem, linked my name and Nomar's:

> Ah, there, Nomar Garciaparra,
> Karen Allen, Allen Barra.

- **Jason Giambi.** Hmmm, let me think about this one. He'll be thirty-three when the 2004 season starts, but he'll have about 270 home runs, a .308 batting average, an MVP award, and a history of several playoff teams to recommend him. If he has a great 2004 and maybe wins another MVP award, I might be ready to concede him a shot.
- **Ramon Hernandez.** No way.
- **Melvin Mora.** Melvin Mora is, as I write this, on the downside of thirty-two, is in his fifth major league season, has a career average of .250 for just under 600 games, and happens to be having a good year in 2003. I can't think of another player who better typifies the mediocrity of the 2003 All-Stars.
- **Magglio Ordoñez.** Fine ballplayer; heading for age thirty with a career batting average over .300 and about 180 home runs. Not an immortal.
- **Mike Sweeney.** Good hitter; at age twenty-nine, after more than 900 games, he has an average of over .300. But I've never heard anyone use the word "great"

when talking about him who didn't smell of Kansas wheat.

- **Jason Varitek.** You don't have to be over thirty to be an All-Star catcher anymore, but it seems to help.
- **Vernon Wells.** At age twenty-four he might prove to be the young all-around superstar that the AL needs. But it's early, and besides, he needs to learn to walk more (so far fewer than 60 in nearly 1,000 big league at-bats). The great ones usually show discipline early.
- **Dmitri Young.** Can't run, can't field (next stop, first base, in a couple of years DH), and can't hit for much power. This is what you get for an All-Star when the worst team in baseball has to be represented.
- **Lance Carter.** Rated a "C" prospect by *The Scouting Notebook* before the 2003 season. He's twenty-eight as I write this.
- **Roger Clemens.** Of course he's going to the Hall of Fame; he's the greatest starting pitcher in baseball history.
- **Brendan Donnelly.** It isn't enough to say that he's having his best major league season ever; he's thirty-two as I write this and had 49 innings pitched in the bigs before this year. Forget the World Series ring. How lucky is this guy to even be in professional baseball? A few years ago Tampa Bay released him to make roster space for a rookie. The rookie was Jim Morris, played by Dennis Quaid in the Disney movie *The Rookie.*
- **Keith Foulke.** Getting close to age thirty-one. Had a career record of 19-24 before this All-Star season.

- **Eddie Guardado.** He's close to thirty-three as I write this, and his career record before his All-Star season was 33-42. Hey, didn't I just write this about someone?
- **Roy Halladay.** Now here's a real prospect. As I write this Halladay is twenty-five, has a 14-2 record so far in 2003, and was 19-7 last year. *And* he beats the *Yankees.* One of the best young pitchers in baseball. We'll see what happens.

Okay, let's cut this off. I listed the AL reserves to illustrate how thin the talent is right now and how old most of the players are who are being called the game's best. I'm not going to do the National League reserves because there's no point. The NL squad has perhaps three first-rate players I haven't mentioned: Luis Gonzalez (who is thirty-five), Jim Edmunds (thirty-three), and Andruw Jones, a fine power hitter and terrific defensive center fielder who, at the end of the season, barring injury, will be just twenty-five with around 220 career home runs and, probably, three 100-plus RBI seasons. But I find it very hard to say that anyone with more than 1,000 big league games who has a batting average of .270 and an on-base average of .344 is on track for the Hall of Fame.

Before I come to a final judgment I want to give the 2003 teams every possible chance. I'm going to cast aside my reservations about Alphonso Soriano, Manny Ramirez, and Albert Pujols and call them future Hall of Famers. I'm also going to give the 2003 team credit for at least one Hall of Fame pitcher, either Mark Mulder or Roy Halladay. So, then, if you lined up the totals of all the Hall of Fame players on the eight All-Star teams I've examined from 1933 to 1976 they'd total out like this:

Brushbacks and Knockdowns

Year	Legit HOFer	In HOF But Shouldn't Be	Not In HOF But Should Be	PDG
1933	16	4	1	21
1941	15	1	2	18
1948	15	1	2	18
1953	22	1	1	24
1958	16	0	1	17
1961	19	1	1	21
1969	18	0	2	20
1976	11	0	2	13
Totals	132	8	12	152
Avg/Yr	16.5			19

PDG stands for Pretty Darned Good, a category that includes all the players in the Hall of Fame, whether I think they should be there or not, and all of the very, very good players who are better than many players who are in the HOF.

So that's how I see it: In the eleven All-Star Game rosters I examined from 1933–99 there were 132 players I call legitimate Hall of Famers and twenty more that were very, very good—all in all 152 "A" category ballplayers. The average number of legits in each of those eleven seasons is 16½, the average number of A-listers is 19. If you don't agree entirely, I'll bet your numbers aren't too different from mine. So, then, how can we compare the number of A players from the earlier All-Star teams to those from the teams of 1986, 1999, and 2003? Obviously we can't say for certain who the legitimate Hall of Famers are among current players, nor can we judge precisely how future voters will regard players we might now consider Iffy. What we can say with some certainty is that several players, judged by the standards of past performers, are performing at a level which, if maintained, would put them in the Hall of Fame—or at the least put them on a level of many players who are already there.

So what percentage of our "On Tracks" won't die in plane crashes or get involved with drugs or blow their knees out? And how many Iffys, if they make it through long careers and still maintain a high level of play, will have their talents fully recognized years after their retirements? I'd say two-thirds sounds about right for both categories, and that may be a little high. So if we add the five legit Hall of Famers from the '86 team and give them two-thirds credit for the eight still-active players who are on track and six others who are Iffy we get—well, I'm lousy with fractions, and who wants a fraction of a player, anyway, so we'll round it out to fifteen.

And if we take the twelve who are On Track from the 1999 team and add the seven who are Iffy and give them two-thirds credit we get—well, let's round it off to thirteen. And neither fifteen nor thirteen is anywhere close to the nineteen that we figured for the previous eleven combined American and National League rosters. And if you accept my line of reasoning up to now, get ready for worse news: There are maybe eight future legitimate Hall of Fame candidates on the 2003 teams. And at that I'm being generous.

Here's the way it looks on a chart:

	Legit HOFer	On Track for HOF	Iffy	Future HOFer?
1986	5	8	6	15?
1999		12	7	13?
2003		4	7	8?

I'm sure many of you can find fault with some aspect of my study. Some of you will object that using the Hall of Fame as a primary yardstick is unfair, since undeserving players from earlier eras are often voted in by former pals or teammates on the Veterans Committee, while equally deserving modern players get ignored. I agree, but that's why I devised categories to include deserving players and single out undeserving ones.

You might say, "But what about the number of really good players, people like Derek Jeter, Jeff Bagwell, Craig Biggio, Mike Piazza, Randy Johnson, Greg Maddux, and Sammy Sosa, that because of injury or corked bats or whatever didn't make the All-Star Team this year?" Good point—except that really good players fail to make the All-Star Team *every* year for one reason or another. Remember that the '53 team, perhaps the most talent-rich in the game's history, didn't include Willie Mays, the National League's best player in the decade, or Whitey Ford, the American League's best pitcher. Besides—and here's the real point—with the exception of Jeter, who turned twenty-six while I was writing this, all of the above are in their mid or late thirties. Where are the great young stars that should be coming along behind them?

Whether you agree with all my choices or not, can you really argue that the last few seasons have produced as many great players as earlier ones?

What exactly is happening? Are we suddenly entering an era when the seemingly vast well of baseball talent is drying up? Or is this some kind of illusion caused by our lack of perspective? The latter, I hope; but I don't know how to make that argument. I have always said publicly and loudly that the other major sports were *not* siphoning talent from baseball, that the American population was growing, and besides, there was a vast wealth of talent coming into the big leagues from Latin America and, in recent years, from Asia.

It is entirely possible that, say, Ichiro Suzuki and Hideki Matsui are legitimate Hall of Famers who simply didn't grow up in our big leagues and so we can only guess at how great they would have been. That's a legitimate point. But the major leagues were producing around nineteen grade-A players per All-Star Game for years without counting the great Japanese stars; now they can't produce that many *with* them.

Is it somehow possible that Major League Baseball's problem isn't too little talent but too much? Don Sutton, who saw most of the previous generation of players from the pitcher's mound before retiring in 1988 and who has seen most of the new ones from the Atlanta Braves broadcast booth, suggests to me that "With so many good Latin and now Oriental players in the big leagues, the talent level might have been raised to a point in the last few years that it's harder than ever for anyone to rise above the pack. We might not know who the real greats are until we can look back on them ten years from now."

Sutton may well be right, and I very much hope he is. What worries me is that in recent years when older players have faded or been injured, there doesn't seem to be enough hot young studs stepping into the All-Star ranks to take their places.

Jim Bouton recently offered me another possible explanation. "I'm afraid that the kind of baseball we've been seeing in the last few years is the result of having stressed the home run too much in the '90s. About the only complete players with sound fundamentals I'm seeing in the major leagues these days are coming out of Japan." There might be something to what Bouton says; so many of the biggest stars in recent years are big, slow sluggers like Manny Ramirez (and, I fear, Albert Pujols) who hit a ton but can't do anything else on a baseball field to help you win.

Or maybe, in some weird way, Sutton's and Bouton's points *both* have some validity. No, I'm not going to go there, it's starting to make me dizzy. One thing I'm fairly certain of is that this problem extends to all American sports and isn't confined to baseball. Every basketball fan I know acknowledges that the athletes have never been better and that the quality of the play has never been poorer—though foreign-born players seem to be better schooled on the whole than American players.

In pro football specialization has taken over the game to such a degree that it's difficult to say that the players are better or worse than those of previous generations. One obvious difference between the NFL of today and the NFL of my youth is that today more than 50 percent of the players are black. Now, clearly I'm stepping into a minefield in forcing a discussion in this area. Whenever I bring it up in front of my liberal friends, the quick reply is "Well, why does that matter to you?" My immediate rejoinder is that it no more matters to me that most pro football players are black than that an increasing number of baseball players are Latin and Japanese.

The point I'm getting at is that if there is no real physical difference between the races, nothing in the way of heredity would make black men better football players or Latin men better baseball players, then doesn't that imply that there are some sociological or cultural reasons why there are fewer and fewer white kids in American sports? Look, even if in some way black athletes were physically superior to white athletes, what would explain the fact that there are *fewer* white athletes in American professional sports than twenty or even ten years ago?

Clearly the answer is—isn't it?—that fewer white kids are trying out for team sports, particularly baseball. The statistics are irrefutable: According to the Little League's own records, there were 2.46 million kids playing Little League ball in 1997, and by 2003 the number had dropped alarmingly to 2.3 million. You know that most of those kids are white, and you also know that the ones who drop out or simply don't try out for Little League at all aren't learning the fundamentals of baseball somewhere else. And if white kids are dropping out of team sports at an increasing rate, doesn't that suggest that college and professional team sports are drawing from a shallower talent pool?

But it's not even as simple as that. In truth, black kids are dropping out of the baseball talent pool faster than white kids. In 1975, black players comprised 27 percent of major leaguers; by 2003, the number was down to 10 percent. That couldn't possibly mean anything but that fewer black kids are playing organized baseball.

I'm not going to use any charts in making this point because I don't know where to find accurate information. But I have a very strong suspicion that the sudden and dramatic decline in top-flight baseball talent has much to do with the equally sudden increase in the number of kids—and by no means all of them white, as can be seen in a quick drive through my affluent, integrated neighborhood of South Orange New Jersey—on skateboards. Or by the empty baseball fields, basketball and tennis courts that were once filled by young teens who are now sitting at home playing video games. Yes, of course, baseball has done a poor job of promoting itself in the inner cities. But not all black kids in this country live in inner cities, and the ones who live in the suburbs aren't playing much baseball either.

I wish I could end this chapter on a more optimistic note, but until American parents start pulling the plug on the TVs and computers and learn the patience to get their kids involved again with baseball, all of us baseball fans had better be ending the day on our knees muttering the words "Thank God for the Dominican Republic."

Postscript: Editing this chapter in early November 2003, I find little reason to change most of the opinions I formed midway through the season. The 2003 season definitely confirmed that Mariano Rivera is a legitimate Hall of Famer as well as Pudge Rodriguez. (I thought about cutting the line about Pudge having "dropped off the face of the earth" when he joined the Marlins, but the joke on me is too good to cut.) During the World Series it was announced that Jason Giambi would undergo knee surgery after the season and that his knee had been plaguing him most of the year.

7

Don't Blame the Yankees
or
Yankees Town, Red Sox Press

This morning, Wednesday, October 8, 2003, I woke up to this editorial in the *New York Times:* "The Boston Red Sox' nail-biting victory over the Oakland Athletics on Monday night moves professional baseball one step closer to the Dream Series: the Red Sox vs. the Chicago Cubs. With all due respect to our New York readership—Yankee fans among them—to George Steinbrenner, and to the Yankees themselves, we find it hard to resist the emotional tug and symmetrical possibilities of a series between teams that seem to have been put on earth to tantalize and then crush their zealous fans . . . Cold reality favors the Yankees. Warm sentiment, which is at the heart of baseball and to which we are always susceptible, favors one or the other of baseball's most reliable losers."

At this point I could only wonder if I had taken too large a dose of that prescription for the sinus infection. A New York paper—the *New York Times,* for Gawd's sake—actually *endorsing* the Boston Red Sox for the World Series? Why on earth would anyone not born and raised in New England want such a thing? Why would any *New York* paper call for it?

"Dream Series"? Whose dream? Is it possible that the *New York Times*—which, it ought to be mentioned, at least in passing, is a partial owner of the Red Sox—really thinks that the rest of the country would prefer to see the Red Sox in the World Series rather than the Yankees? To most baseball fans I know the Yankees are the team they love to beat. To most fans in other parts of the country, the Red Sox are—well, just another team that gets beaten.

"Emotional tug"? For whom, exactly? Certainly not for the overwhelming majority of *Times* readers. For the rest of the country? Well, the Cubs do have national appeal, as their games have been broadcast for many years through the Midwest and the South. My mother in Birmingham, Alabama, roots for the Cubs much harder than she does for the Braves, who live less than three hours away. But the Red Sox? Does the *Times* seriously think that the Red Sox evoke some sort of emotional tug on the heartland?

The *Times* couldn't pull for the Florida Marlins because the Marlins are "a team for which it is hard to muster much enthusiasm if you're a baseball traditionalist." But what if you're a "baseball traditionalist" who happens to live in Florida? Isn't it possible that you could invest as much psychic energy in your team as a Red Sox fan?

The answer, of course, from a Northeastern perspective, is no, because no one else could want to win as much as a Red Sox fan. No one could agonize as much as a Red Sox fan. Pick up almost any baseball anthology and you'll find a chapter from some well-known baseball writer, a Red Sox fan, more full of self-pity than a celebrity-child memoir. If you don't trust me on this, try stopping into a Barnes & Noble or a Borders in Charlotte, North Carolina, or Nashville, Tennessee, or Tucson, Arizona, as I have recently, and look at the number of books available on the Boston Red Sox. Has any team in all of sports with so few victories generated so much ink?

No one's misery could ever be as deep as a Red Sox fan's. It never seems to occur to sportswriters outside a handful of Northeastern states that fans in Kansas City or Houston or Oakland or Philadelphia or possibly even Anaheim—which, lest we forget, had never won a postseason series before 2002—could have as much "warm sentiment" for their team as Red Sox fans have for theirs. (One might question whether *any* sentiment a Red Sox fan had was warm, but let that pass.)

To me, there is no stranger phenomenon in the field of sportswriting than the amount of gushy nonsense that gets written about the Boston Red Sox. No, there is one other even stranger: that so many in the New York sports media have bought into it.

Who, I want to know, was it that placed the Boston Red Sox "at the heart of baseball"? Black fans, perhaps, who have tended to avoid the warm sentiment of Fenway Park with about the same regularity as the Red Sox have avoided black players? "Curse of The Bambino," my butt. This is the team that passed up a chance to sign Jackie Robinson *and* Willie Mays. Ted Williams on the same team with either or both of those guys? Do you think if that had happened anyone would be whining now about selling Babe Ruth to the Yankees?

Just what is it that so many writers in the Northeast think is so lovable about the Red Sox? More to the point, which is perfectly illustrated by the *Times* editorial, is why the New York media is so indifferent to their own team, particularly at a time when it has played some of the greatest baseball ever seen. New York has become a Yankees town with a Red Sox press.

Any day now I expect to see a brown envelope with a review copy of a book with a title like *How The Yankees Ruined Baseball.* I don't know who the author will be, but I'm positive the book will be written. In fact, I wouldn't be surprised to see several books out soon with that or similar titles. That the Yankees are ruining the game has, after all, been the dominant theme in baseball writing since Luis Gonzalez hit that wounded duck off Mariano Rivera in the ninth inning of the 2001 World Series. Along with "Pitching is 75 percent of the game" and "It ain't over till it's over," one of baseball's primary axioms has now become "What's wrong with baseball is the Yankees."

The idea that the Yankees are bad for baseball dates back at least to the 1920s, when John McGraw, manager of the old-school New York Giants, would tell any reporter within earshot that the new power style of the Babe Ruth Yankees would destroy the "scientific" game he had helped create. More than a few baseball writers, out of step with the vast new crowds the Yankees were bringing to baseball, bought into McGraw's line. Their spiritual descendants are with us still, only they take their lead not from John McGraw but from Bud Selig.

Attendance at Yankee Stadium will probably reach an all-time high in 2003—which is to say, up from last year's all-time high—threatening to exceed a staggering 3.6 million. More impressive still, coming at a time of recession when attendance around the rest of baseball is down about 5 percent. Yankee caps, whether the traditional navy blue with classic white NY insignia or one of its garish rainbow variants, dominate the streets of New York. No, dominate doesn't even begin to say it: Yankee insignias seem to outnumber other sports logos—the Mets, Knicks, Giants, Jets, Rangers, Notre Dame, St. John's, Brooklyn Dodgers, Brooklyn Cyclones and everybody else—by a *combined* ratio of at least ten to one. Immigrants to the metropolitan area from Latin countries, Eastern Europe, and the Caribbean all wear the Yankees logo as a badge of assimilation.

Never has New York's love affair with the Yankees been more passionate than now, and never has the press that covers the Yankees been so negative. Every night Yankee fans go to sleep with the warm memory of an upper deck Jason Giambi home run or a spectacular throw from deep in the hole by Derek Jeter, and every morning they rise to a sports media relentlessly telling them to curb their enthusiasm.

From September 11 to the end of the 2001 World Series, the Yankees were, for a brief shining moment, America's team, a symbol of New York's indomitable will and resilience. As negotiations with the players became heated in the winter of 2002, the Yankees were transformed into what hostile Interneters (a good many of them Mets fans, I'm sure) were calling "Satan's team."

If you followed New York baseball from the fall of 2001 and all through 2002, you heard a virtual chorus of anti-Yankee sentiment screamed at you by radio talk show hosts. One day on ESPN there'd be an interview with Larry Dolan, owner of the Cleveland Indians—the same Cleveland Indians that went to the World Series in 1995 and '97 and that went to the playoffs in 2001—in which George Steinbrenner and the Yankees are blasted for being "a big part of what's wrong with baseball."

The next day the Boston Red Sox president and CEO, Larry Lucchino, would be heard on WFAN calling the Yankees "The Evil Empire"—a phrase that several in the New York sports media were quick to jump on. Dumping on Steinbrenner—*that* we can live with. Yankee fans accept the stigma of Steinbrenner; it's the luxury tax, as it were, that we pay for winning. But since when do we have to take garbage from the president of the *Boston Red Sox,* a man with the resources to buy and sell George Steinbrenner several times over? Since when did Boston become a small market and the Red Sox an object of sympathy in New York? *Pity* I can understand, but *sympathy?*

If you picked up a *New York Daily News,* you read Mike Lupica (a Boston refugee, by the way), writing at the top of his lungs, telling us that "Baseball is dying because there is too much cable television money for the Yankees and not enough money everywhere else." Not enough for who, exactly? The Oakland A's and Seattle Mariners, who have had the best records in the American League during this young century? For the New York Mets, who compete in the same town as the Yankees?

If you flipped to the sports pages of the *New York Times,* instead of reading about the latest Yankee victory you were likely to see a half-page color photo of a Pittsburgh Pirates fan holding a banner that said "Stop Yankee Oppression." *Yankee Oppression?* In *Pittsburgh?* The Pirates are in the *National* League. How, exactly, were the Yankees oppressing the Pirates? The last time the Yankees played the Pirates was 1960, and the Pirates won the game on Bill Mazeroski's home run.

Now, please don't try to tell me that the Pirates fan who made up that banner thought of the idea on his own. Of course not; no one in Pittsburgh ever thought to use the word "oppressed" to describe his own condition, even when it applied to what U.S. Steel was trying to do to the steelworkers back in the 1950s. He heard it on TV or read it in his local paper, probably in a column referring to something written in the New York press.

If you picked up the *New York Post* on your Amtrak ride into the city, you read about a Kansas City Royals fan in a restaurant yelling at Derek Jeter "You're what's wrong with baseball!" *Derek Jeter is what's wrong with baseball?* That's enough to make any reasonable person hop on a plane to Kansas City, find that guy, grab him by the collar, and yell something like "You ungrateful jerk, you ought to feel privileged to be able to buy a ticket and see him play!" But then, what would be the point? An attitude like that obnoxious fan's didn't originate in Kansas City.

The day before the 2002 season opener in an op-ed in the *New York Times,* Nicholas Dawidoff, author of a superb biography of catcher-turned-spy Mo Berg, chastised the Yankees' new free agent acquisition Jason Giambi as "a shameless mercenary." "The Yankees already had a perfectly good first baseman in Tino Martinez," he wrote, so why did they need Giambi?

Without the slightest intention of knocking Tino Martinez, I want to make three points. First of all, Jason Giambi was the first free agent slugger the Yankees had signed since Dave Winfield back in 1981. Aren't the Yankees entitled to go out and get a big hitter once every twenty years or so? Second, at the time the 2002 season began, Tino was thirty-three years old. Giambi was four years younger and a far better hitter than Tino ever was. Why shouldn't the Yankees make a move to acquire a younger, better player? And, third, why shouldn't Jason Giambi be able to choose the team he plays for? Did Nick Dawidoff sell the rights to his next book (which I'm sure will be as good as everything else I've read by him) to the first bidder, or did he choose the publishing house whose offer he was most satisfied with?

How times have changed. Just a quarter of a century earlier, two years after the advent of free agency, the New York area press went into a state of euphoria when another Oakland A's slugger, Reggie Jackson, was signed by the Yankees. Who called Reggie a shameless mercenary?

Dawidoff's piece set the tone for the 2002 season. After the Yankees swept the Tampa Bay Devil Rays in the season's first home stand, the headline for Murray Chass's column in the *New York Times* read, "NY Goliaths Too Rich For Tampa Bay Davids" (apparently the *Times*'s crack fact checkers neglected to check the Old Testament and see who won that fight). On June 23, after a furious chase of nearly three months, the Yankees overtook the Boston Red Sox. In the past, such an occurrence was always greeted with front-page headlines; this year, the *Times* relegated the news to page five status.

On July 2, the Yankees beat the Cleveland Indians 10-5; the *Times'* sports page headlines read "Free Spenders Clobber Cost-Cutters." Forgotten was that just a few years earlier, when Cleveland was winning two pennants in three years, it was the Indians who were signing superstars to long-term contracts while the Yankees were being castigated for failure to keep up.

On July 1, the Yankees attempted to address a weakness in right field by acquiring a thirty-one-year-old journeyman outfielder named Raul Mondesi from Toronto. Mondesi was hitting .224 at the time and had not batted over .300 in the previous five seasons; but to read Mike Lupica the next day, you'd have thought the Yankees had picked someone's pocket for another Babe Ruth. (As Yankees announcer John Stirling quipped during a broadcast, "Since the Yankees signed him, Mondesi seems to have gone from journeyman to Hall of Famer.")

The Yanks got Mondesi because they were willing to pay the $5.5 million remaining on his salary for 2002 and $7 million for 2003, a deal that prompted Lupica to write, "Money is never an object around the Yankees anyway . . . the Yankees are why everybody else wants to change the business of baseball." Lupica might have added: nor should money be an object with the Yankees, since they have it because their fans are happy to give it to them. (Was money an object for Lupica when he jumped from *Newsday* to the *Daily News*?)

It was left to a player for the enemy, Boston's Nomar Garciaparra, to best put the Yankees' penchant for deal making in perspective. "What's the fuss about?" he remarked before a Yankees-Red Sox game after New York traded lefthander Ted Lilly for righthander Jeff Weaver. "There isn't a team in baseball that couldn't have made those deals if they wanted to."

You might have thought that with the Yankees losing to the Angels in the first round of the 2002 playoffs—thus apparently helping to save baseball by paving the way for a World Series that drew lower ratings and less national interest—things would have lightened up in 2003. Not a bit.

The Yankees weren't far into the season when it became apparent that there was a lot of deadwood among the position players, including veteran infielder Todd Zeile, left fielder Rondell White, and right fielder Raul Mondesi—the same guy whose acquisition the year before, you'll recall, was supposed to practically guarantee a Yankees pennant. The bullpen wasn't just bleeding runs, it was hemorrhaging them.

In the space of a month, the Yanks made several dazzling deals that plugged the holes and turned the season around. General Manager Brian Cashman quickly dispatched White and Mondesi, added thirty-three-year-old journeyman outfielder Karim Garcia, traded to the Mets for Armando Benitez, sent Benitez to Seattle in a deal that brought Jeff Nelson back to New York, and also added reliever Gabe White in the Aaron Boone deal. Brilliant! In the space of a couple of weeks the Yankees improved their hitting, fielding, relief pitching, and morale, but to read the local press, you'd have thought the Yankees had dumped a corpse on New York's doorstep.

A typical response was that of Mike Francesa on WFAN:

"With all the flesh peddling in the Bronx, this is a radically different team than the one they opened the season with. How can these Yankees possibly have any team chemistry now?" This was nonsense. Chemistry is exactly what the Yankees *didn't* have *before* the deals were made. Chemistry is an exact science; you combine element A and element B in the correct amounts and you get C. What Francesa meant when he said chemistry was really something closer to alchemy, the medieval form of chemistry wherein lead was supposed to be transformed into gold. In baseball, you can't turn lead into gold. When the lead proves to be lead, your only solution is to get the lead out and try to mine some gold.

In baseball chemistry, consistency, power, and fundamentals are transferred into runs and the prevention of runs. Mondesi and White were not reaching base, were eating up outs, and were playing unfocused, indifferent defense in the outfield, and when they were benched in favor of players with more desire, they had the gall to distract the team by complaining to the press. How in the world the Yankees could have hurt their "team chemistry" by getting rid of a pair of disruptive and unproductive players who weren't content to play for a potential World Series winner is difficult to understand.

To the critics who accused the Yankees of radically changing their roster from the one fielded on opening day—true, by the way, mostly because players had to be shuttled in and out to fill gaps created by injuries to Derek Jeter, Nick Johnson, Bernie Williams, and Mariano Rivera—the reply should have been, "And thank God for that!"

The crown jewel of Brian Cashman's summer deals was the one that brought Boone and White to New York without the loss of a single key player. The Yanks sent to the Los Angeles Dodgers a thirty-seven-year-old former All-Star third baseman, Robin Ventura, and replaced him with a thirty-year-old *current*

All-Star third baseman. The Ventura trade and Boone acquisition was one of those rare moves that pleased all parties involved. The Yankees upgraded their team while lowering its age, Ventura got to spend his last playing days near his home in Los Angeles, Boone got to leave the Cincinnati Reds, with whom he was angry for firing his manager and father Bob, while the Reds, for their part, gained an opportunity to whine and plead poverty as an excuse for leaving one of their best players out on the doorstep. As Nomar said the year before, "Any team in baseball could have made those deals if they'd really wanted to."

The New York press seemed to wish some other team had. "New 3B Can't Carry Yanks" read the headline in the *New York Post*. Dumbfounded Yankee fans might have replied, "Well, who said that he would? Was *Ventura* carrying the Yanks?" A *Daily News* headline read "The Yanks Will Miss Robin In the Clubhouse," implying that at postseason time Ventura's calming influence would be sorely missed. I hate to point this out, but it was exactly the year Ventura was with the Yankees that they *lost* in the first round of the playoffs. There's no reason to pin that on Ventura, but I don't know what the evidence is for claiming that the Yankees would have missed him in the 2003 playoffs.

The shrillest reaction was from Mike Lupica in the *Daily News*. The Yankees, he wrote, were simply out to "win at any cost. It is the real business of the Yankees, and it sucks the joy out of the season." Out of *whose* season, exactly? The New York Mets, who made bad expensive deals while the Yankees made economical good ones? Out of the Cincinnati Reds, who claimed they weren't giving up on the season one day and then ushered Boone out of the clubhouse the next?

And why, exactly, shouldn't Steinbrenner and Cashman be out to "win at any cost"? If the fans are willing to pay the price for the tickets and beer, what is Steinbrenner supposed to do with the money? Pocket it as profit, as so many of those teams getting that fat luxury tax from the Yankees do?

All of a sudden, within the space of little more than two years the New York baseball press has become socialist in its bent. Not as regards any other aspect of American life, and certainly not regarding distribution of income or medical care or anything that actually *matters*, just *baseball*, as in New York Yankees baseball. For instance, an article in the August 5, 2003, issue of the *New York Times* that stated, "Certainly the new system of revenue sharing and luxury taxes has not been a panacea to small-market teams everywhere." No it hasn't. Nor could any system of any kind ever be a panacea for such ills. When you have thirty teams you're going to have a lot of losers, and it's a pretty safe bet that at least half of those losers are going to be from small-market cities. Neither did the system help the Los Angeles Dodgers, Chicago Cubs, Philadelphia Phillies, or even the New York Mets all that much. Or at least no more or less than it's helped or hurt the San Francisco Giants, Oakland A's, Minnesota Twins, or Houston Astros. In fact, the Yankees are the *only* team that will be paying the luxury tax for surpassing the $117 million threshold. As Doug Pappas wrote in the Society for American Baseball Research newsletter, *Outside The Lines*, "The Yankees are almost certainly the only club which will *ever* owe the luxury tax."

But, a reasonable person might ask at this point: *How can you deny that the Yankees' enormous TV contracts give them an advantage over other American League teams?* The answer is that the charge can't be denied.

Now that I've said that, let me restate it with some reservations. First, the Yankees' revenue advantage hasn't mattered that much in the area of signing free agents, since the Yankees simply don't sign many high-priced free agents. As I mentioned earlier, Jason Giambi was the first big free agent slugger the Yankees signed in more than two decades. The core of the Yankees since 1996, the first World Series in this recent run, has been the same through 2003: Derek Jeter, Bernie Williams, Andy Pettitte, and Mariano Rivera, all players produced within the Yankees' system and, since his first year as a regular in 1998, Jorge Posada as well. It can be argued, I suppose, that the Yankees' revenue allows them to keep such players by signing them to long-term contracts, where other teams would probably lose them to free agency. This is true, but isn't there a difference between signing expensive players and rewarding very good players with big contracts *after* they have produced world championships? Isn't there a difference between paying someone to win and rewarding them for having won?

Second, money without smarts doesn't produce pennant winners, it produces the 2003 New York Mets. For that matter, it produces the New York Yankees from 1982 through 1994 when the New York press continually hammered Steinbrenner and the Yankees' front office for their inability to produce a winner in spite of the biggest TV contracts in baseball.

Third, the notion that having a dominant team is bad for baseball is a crock. The recent Yankees are only the most extreme example of the kind of domination that American sports fans have always loved. The old saying used to be, "There's three institutions in sports that aren't supposed to lose: Joe Louis, Notre Dame, and the New York Yankees." Joe Louis died and Notre Dame is now just another private school with a catchy fight song, but the Yankees remain.

The rise of all professional sports leagues has always centered around flagship teams. In football, the popularity of the

NFL in the 1960s was sparked by the public's fascination with Vince Lombardi's Green Bay Packers, which played in six championship games in eight seasons, winning five. After that the NFL flourished, despite—or perhaps because of—the domination of a handful of teams—the San Francisco 49ers, the Pittsburgh Steelers, and the Dallas Cowboys, who won fifteen of the thirty-two championships between 1970 and 2002. When the NBA took off in the '80s, it wasn't "competitive balance" that ignited the league but great teams, first the Boston Celtics' and Los Angeles Lakers' Bird and Magic and then the Michael Jordan-led Chicago Bulls.

As every baseball fan knows, for forty-five years, from the coming of Babe Ruth in 1920 to the last Yankee pennant under the old regime in 1964, the Yankees were the biggest winners in American sports. During all that time no one took the notion seriously that the Yankees were bad for baseball, though in fact fans of the Kansas City A's—who were often referred to derisively as the Yankees' farm team for dealing them so many key players—might have had a very good case. After the old Yankee dynasty faded in '65, baseball went into its deepest slump since the Great Depression, suffering a large drop in attendance and national TV revenues. Exactly how much of that decline can be written off to the Yankees' collapse is problematic, but it's doubtful that baseball's big comeback in 1976—"The Baseball Boom Is On!" proclaimed a *Sports Illustrated* cover—owed nothing to those twin devils, free agency (which became a part of the game following arbitrators' decisions on the Catfish Hunter and, later, the Andy Messersmith and Dave McNally cases) and the New York Yankees (who won their first pennant in eleven seasons).

You might reasonably reply, "Well, if dominant teams are good for sports, then why does the dominant team in baseball have to be the Yankees?" The obvious answer, of course, is that this is the way that God intended it to be. But even if it wasn't, or if God were to change His or Her mind tomorrow, it wouldn't make any difference—the essential points would remain the same regardless of *who* the dominant team was. Major League Baseball has a great many problems, but it isn't in any kind of economic trouble, and there is no evidence that any other team would be in better economic shape if the Yankees didn't exist.

You might further reply, "Okay, but wouldn't baseball be a more interesting game if all teams had the same resources? Wouldn't it be *fairer?*" I would reply that there is no reason to believe baseball would be any more interesting without a dominant team, since it is already every bit as competitive as NFL football and NBA basketball, but instead I'll answer by saying *of course* it would be fairer. But we are getting into dangerous waters here.

All sports would be fairer if revenues and resources were equally distributed among all competing teams. But the NFL doesn't do that. It doesn't distribute revenues equally, so much as it prevents any team from spending any more than any other. In other words, the money the NFL is credited with "sharing" is the money that would, without a salary cap, be paid to the players. I suppose some call that fair.

That, I admit, doesn't answer the question as to whether or not baseball would be fairer with more revenue sharing. I must concede that it would. What I don't understand is why this is such an issue in baseball.

NASCAR would be fairer if fledgling racers had access to the same men and machines as the top drivers, but I never heard fans of Dale Earnhardt complain. College football would be a great deal fairer if the perennial doormats in every conference had the same recruiting power as the conference bullies, but Vanderbilt, Northwestern, and Stanford don't have the clout to slug it out with the great football powers from year to year and never will, and I have never heard anyone argue that that fact is hurting college football.

If we make the argument for equal allocation of revenue and resources for baseball in the name of fairness, I don't see how we can stop before we've applied it to all other sports. And from there, I don't see how we can stop until we've applied it to every area outside of sports as well, and then we will all be socialists and we won't be devoting all this time and money to something as trivial as sports.

Now, I don't want socialism, I'll bet you don't want socialism, and I'm damned sure Bud Selig and the Major League Baseball owners don't want socialism. Every baseball fan ought to know what the near work stoppage of 2002 and in fact every work stoppage since the start of the Players Association has been about. It hasn't been about the owners' desire to force socialism on the players—it's been about the owners' desire to hold down players' salaries.

If it were about more revenue sharing in the name of competitive balance, then the so-called smaller-market teams would revolt against the few large-market teams and force them to a more equitable distribution of TV money. Simply put, the struggle would be, as it should have been all along, between smaller-market and bigger-market owners, rather than a senseless war in which the commissioner, backed by a handful of powerful owners, tries to strong-arm the players.

If the work stoppages were about competitive balance, then there would be ironclad rules that all the money the other teams make from the Yankees' luxury tax payments would have to be earmarked for players' salaries. (Since, if you don't get better players, how can you produce a better team?) There are no such rules. The smaller-market teams are allowed to take that money and do what they want with it.

But this chapter isn't about socialism or fairness or even competitive balance. It's first about how the press bought into the line put out by Bud Selig in preparation for the Basic Agreement negotiations with the players, and second, how the perception of Yankee dominance that resulted from that propaganda has unfairly tainted perhaps the greatest run of clutch play in baseball history. I've already said everything I want to say about the first, now I'll deal with the second.

Let's see, year by year, exactly how the Yankees "dominated" from 1996 through 2001:

1996

Some would start with the 1995 season, since that's when the Yankees' resurgence seemed to begin; but there are several reasons why I'm skipping '95, beginning with the fact that in many ways it was an aberration, really the close of an era rather than the beginning of another.

It was Buck Showalter's last season as Yankee manager—Joe Torre, in a daring and controversial selection by Steinbrenner and his front office, would take over the next year. With the exception of Bernie Williams, who played 144 games and hit .307 with 18 home runs, and Paul O'Neill, who hit .300 with 22 home runs, the roster featured practically none of the names that would come to be associated with the new Yankee era. Mariano Rivera appeared in just 19 games with an unpromising 5.51 ERA, Andy Pettitte finished 12-9, and Derek Jeter, playing in just 15 games, hit .250. The spiritual leader of the '95 Yankees was Don Mattingly, playing his last season. The Yankees failed to win the division, finishing 7 full games behind the Red Sox, and they lost in a brutally tough playoff to Seattle. Since nobody complains about Yankee dominance when they lose, we'll start with 1996.

In '96 the Yankees won their first American League pennant in 16 years and went on to win their first World Series in 18. That was a fine team, but probably not the best team in baseball or even in the AL. At 92-70, they finished 4 games ahead of the Orioles in the AL East, but won 7 fewer games than the defending AL champion Cleveland Indians, who won the Central Division by 14½ games. The Yankees led the AL in not a single primary statistic either at bat, on the mound, or in the field. It was a solid, well-balanced team from top to bottom, batting .288 with a .364 on-base average, 5 points behind the Indians in batting and 8 points behind them in OBA. (The Indians led the league in both categories.)

But there were no superstars on the '96 Yankees, at least no players that had as yet developed into superstars. Derek Jeter led the regular players with a .314 batting average. But in the Year of The Home Run—a new mark would be set with 4,962 of them—no one had as many as 30 home runs and, in fact, Bernie Williams, with 29, was the only hitter with more than 25. Andy Pettitte was sensational as the staff ace, going 21-8 with an ERA of 3.87, a pretty impressive number in a year when the league was just a fraction under 5 runs per nine innings. No other starter won as many as 13 games; Kenny Rogers, Jimmy Key, and Dwight Gooden were a combined 35-26, just a handful of bloopers and bleeders away from mediocrity. The starters' numbers, though, were slightly deceptive: David Cone, probably the best starter on the team, was limited to just 11 starts by physical ailments, but he had won 7 of 9 decisions with a really terrific ERA of 2.88, and he was fit and ready for the playoffs.

The bullpen was the team's hidden strength, hidden largely because Mariano Rivera was still pretty much an unknown quantity in '96. John Wetteland was the closer, and a good one, with an ERA of 2.83—not nearly so good as his league-leading 43 saves would indicate. Rivera was primarily used as a setup man for Wetteland and thus had no gaudy save stats, but his other numbers (an 8-3 record, a 2.09 ERA, 130 strikeouts in 108 innings) were sensational. Rivera and Wetteland in '96 just might have been the best setup-closer combo ever. When the Yankees had the lead after seven innings, or even six when Rivera would work longer, it was lights out—the game, in effect, was shortened to seven and sometimes six innings.

It was the Indians that had the superstars. Cleveland led the AL in lowest ERA at 4.34, paced by Charlie Nagy and Orel Hershiser, who were a combined 32-14. With such hitters as Jim Thome (.311 with 38 home runs), Manny Ramirez (.309, 33 HRs), and Albert Belle (.311, 48 HRs), the Indians had top-level sluggers that the Yankees couldn't come close to matching. Actually, the Orioles—with Rafael Palmeiro (.289, 39 HRs), Roberto Alomar (.328, 22 HRs), Cal Ripken Jr. (.276, 26 HRs), and Brady Anderson (.297, 50 HRs)—had even more power than the Indians, shattering all existing records for home runs with 257. Baltimore's only outstanding pitcher, though, was Mike Mussina at 19-11. Still, the Indians contrived to lose the division series to the Orioles, 3 games to 1, allowing 25 runs in the 4 games.

At first glance the Yankees drew the easiest possible match in the first round of the playoffs, the Texas Rangers, whose 90 wins was the least of the league's four playoff teams. Looked at a little closer, though, the Rangers were the equal of the Yankees. In fact, they outscored the Yankees by 58 runs during the regular season, hitting 59 more home runs with a 33-point edge in slugging. The Yankees were assumed to have the better pitching, but in fact the Rangers' 4.65 ERA was precisely the same as the Yankees, and the Rangers staff led the AL with 19 complete games. The Rangers fielded at just about the same level of efficiency as the Yankees, leading the league in average with .986, a point better than the Yanks, and they also led the league in fewest errors, 87.

In other words, there was no compelling reason why the Rangers couldn't have beaten the Yankees in that best of five, particularly after winning the first game in a rout, 8-2, at Yankee Stadium. The Yankees then came back to win three games by a total of just 4 runs, the last two wins coming in Texas. But to simply to say that the Yanks won three games by 4 runs doesn't convey the true drama: All three wins were come-from-behinds, including last-at-bat wins in the final two. In the second game, Jeter scored the winning run on Dean Palmer's throwing error in the tenth inning—that is, the Yankees won the game on an error by the team that committed the fewest errors in the major leagues that season.

The Yankees then proceeded to roll over the Orioles four games to one in the championship series, winning all three games played in Baltimore with the big hitting punch delivered by Darryl Strawberry with 5 hits, 3 of them home runs. Darryl, you may recall, started the 1996 season playing in the Northern League. I wonder, will George Steinbrenner get time off in purgatory for giving Strawberry a break?

The first game will always be remembered for a twelve-year-old fan named Jeffrey Maier, who caught Derek Jeter's double about eight inches below Yankee Stadium's right field wall, turning it, in the umpire's eyes, into a home run. The play and the ump's bad call are often pointed to as evidence that God and umpires, in tight situations, tend to favor the Yankees. Maybe it would have been a double anyway, not an out. Trust me on this, or replay it yourself and see.

It's true that if the Orioles had won the game, they would have been up two-zip with the series headed for Baltimore, but as the Yankees were to show twice in the 1996 season, a 2-0 deficit was far from a lock. Anyway, even after being given a break, the Yankees still had to go out and win the game, and that's what the Yankees did, winning in the eleventh inning on Bernie Williams's home run.

So, having won seven of nine playoff games, *five of them on the road,* against two teams that matched up with them well in most important categories, the Yankees prepared to take on the best team in baseball, the defending World Champion Atlanta Braves.

That's what the Braves were.

Let's review the evidence for that statement.

- The Yankees finished the regular season 92-70 for a won-lost percentage of .568. The Braves finished 96-66 for .593.
- The Yankees were ninth in the American League in runs scored. The Braves were fourth in the National League.
- The Yankees were tied for fifth in the AL in team ERA. The Braves were second in ERA in the NL to the Dodgers, who play home games in the best pitcher's park in the league.

The American League's ERA was .78-of-a-run-per-game higher than the National's, most or probably all of it being the difference between what designated hitters and pitchers (buffered by late-innings pinch hitters) produced at the plate. But no matter how you juggle the numbers, the Braves were a better hitting club than the Yankees. No matter how you juggle them back again, the Braves had better pitching—not by a lot, but enough to give them a fine edge. And, of course, they were the defending World Series champs.

In the division series the Braves had dispensed with the Dodgers in three games, the first two of them tense, tight, one-run affairs—as would be expected between two teams with great pitching, playing in a ballpark where runs are hard to come by. If there was an ominous note in the Braves' postseason performance, it was the difficulty they had in the second round with St. Louis, the NL's weakest playoff team. After winning the first game in Atlanta behind Andy Benes, the Braves, in a puzzling pattern they were to repeat several times over the next few years, failed to win with either of their two best starters, Greg Maddux and Tom Glavine. When the Cardinals won game four, Atlanta was on the verge of elimination; the Braves rebounded to take the next three games by a total of 31 runs, allowing them to go into the World Series on a triumphant note as a slight betting favorite.

The 1996 World Series was a classic of some kind—I'm not sure what, but of some kind. I've been following the World Series since 1962, and I've never seen so many improbabilities and dramatic turnarounds as the one in '96. The record book doesn't begin to indicate how strange it was.

With hindsight, it is possible to see a kind of pattern in the Yankees' play: As they did in the division series against Texas, the Yankees lost the first game big; as they did against Baltimore in the AL championship, they lost the second game; in all three series, after game two they never lost again. How improbable is that? I don't know, but I've never seen anything in the history of postseason play quite like it.

In game one of the World Series, Andy Pettitte, the Yankees' twenty-one-game winner, pitching in Yankee Stadium where lefthanders have an advantage because of the deep left-center field fence, was creamed. He gave up two towering home runs to Andruw Jones, who, a day younger than Mickey Mantle in the 1952 Series against the Brooklyn Dodgers, became the youngest man ever to hit a home run in the World Series. John Smoltz, the Braves' twenty-four-game winner, with help from three relievers, shut the Yankees down on 4 hits.

In game two the Braves scored a run in the first inning, and that was it. Greg Maddux pitched 8 shutout innings, Mark Wohlers pitched a shutout ninth, and the Yankees had had the stuffing beat out of them in two consecutive games at Yankee Stadium: out-hit 23-11, outscored 16-1, and committing 2 errors to the Braves' none.

Consider some of the oddities. The Braves, with a 40-41 record on the road, won two games at Yankees Stadium, traditionally the toughest park in baseball for visitors. In Atlanta, the Braves compiled the best home record in the major leagues, 56-25. What are the odds that the better team, up two games to none and headed for its home field, where it compiled the best record in the game that season, would lose *three straight games* to a team supposedly demoralized by two crushing defeats in their own home park? I don't know what those odds would be—ten to one? fifteen to one? What kind of odds would you have given?

The Yankees, though, slipped a ringer into game three in the slender form of David Cone, who probably would have started game one had he been injury-free in the second half of the season. Cone shut down the Braves till the seventh, when a combination of Rivera and Australian lefty Graeme Lloyd took over. (Lloyd came in because Torre didn't yet realize how effective Rivera was against lefthanders.) Wetteland got the save.

Game four is the one everybody remembers because of Jim Leyritz's dramatic three-run homer in the eighth inning off Mark Wohlers that tied the game at 6-6.

Prior to that, the Braves had slapped the ineffectual Kenny Rogers all over the place in the first two innings, building up a 4-0 lead after two innings and taking a 6-0 lead into the sixth before the Yankees scratched back.

And I mean scratched. Forget the sixth game of the 1975 World Series: *This* was the classic. In the sixth inning, a three-run Yankee rally was kept alive when third baseman Charlie Hayes squibbed a ground ball down the third base line that Chipper Jones allowed to roll foul, only after rolling to the left halfway down the line, it suddenly reversed itself and rolled right. I've never seen anything like it.

In the tenth inning, Bobby Cox ordered Bernie Williams walked intentionally to load the bases in order to pitch to Wade Boggs. Boggs, thirty-eight in 1996, had hit .311 during the season but was wearing down in the postseason, hitting just .111 (3 for 27) in the playoffs. (He would finish the entire postseason at only .158.) But in the tenth inning of the fourth game of the 1996 World Series, Boggs put on a performance that Margo Adams would have applauded, working his way from an 0-2 count, fouling off pitch after pitch, and finally drawing the walk that brought in the winning run. The Yankees had tied up the series at 2-2. What are the odds?

In game five, the Yankees were outhit 5-4, but Pettitte, with help in the ninth inning from Wetteland, outdueled the Braves' best starter, Smoltz, and won 1-0.

Before we move on to the final game, let's take note of a truly amazing fact. At this point, the Yankees had now won *eight consecutive games against three of the best teams in base-*

ball on their own home fields—four of them late-innings comebacks. Do we write this off to clutch performance, or to some other intangible that can't be quantified, or to something easier to believe in, such as Divine Intervention? Whatever you call it, it was a team effort, because the Yankees had no superstars to step forward and take over. It was a question of the entire team, even the so-called role players, stepping forward at crunch time.

Well, not everybody: Joe Girardi hadn't yet been heard from. Girardi was a light hitter (.294 in 1996, but with just 2 home runs and 23 doubles in 422 at-bats) with an inflated reputation as a defensive catcher. In the playoffs, he had gone just 5 for 21 with one extra-base hit and one RBI. But in the third inning of game six he belted a triple off Greg Maddux and subsequently scored, helping the Yankees to build a 3-0 lead, to which they hung onto for a 3-2 win. Jimmy Key, who had beaten the Braves twice in the 1992 World Series while with Toronto, went $5\frac{1}{3}$ shutout innings for the win.

So that was it. The Yankees had won eleven of fifteen postseason games, eight of them decided by either one or two runs.

Tell me it was luck, or tell me that, as Branch Rickey once put it, luck is the residue of design. But whatever you tell me, do not tell me the Yankees dominated their way to a world championship in 1996.

1997

The Yankees lost in the playoffs to Cleveland, three games to two. They didn't win, so nobody can say they dominated. Let's move on.

1998

They dominated. The 1998 Yankees were the greatest team in baseball history. They should have dominated that year. They beat the Rangers three games to none in the first round, the Indians four games to two in the second round, and swept San Diego by four games in the World Series. That made eleven wins in the last thirteen postseason games.

1999

Such was the aura of invincibility that surrounded the Yankees after 1998 that they were clear favorites to win the 1999 World Series, even though there was no evidence that they were any better than the Braves. Atlanta was 103-59 to the Yankees' 98-64 during the regular season. The Yanks scored 900 runs to the Braves' 840, not the size bulge you'd expect to see from a team that used a DH. The difference in ERA (the Braves' 3.63 was the NL's top mark, by the way, while the Yankees' 4.13 was second in the AL) indicated that the pitching was pretty close to even.

The Yankees didn't exactly dominate the American League. New York won just four more games than Boston in the East, just one more game than Cleveland in the Central, and just three more than Texas in the West. But the Yanks crushed Texas in three games in the division series and Boston four games to one for the AL Pennant. In game three of the Red Sox series, Pedro Martinez gave up three hits, the Sox pounded out 21, and Boston won in a rout, 13-1. It was the only blip on the Yankees' '99 postseason.

The Braves were pretty good, too, beating Houston in the

first round three games to one and the Mets four out of six for the NL Pennant. It should have been a very close World Series. In fact, it was.

It's often said that football is a game of inches. Baseball is a game of inches too—they just don't measure them with sticks.

The New York Yankees won the 1999 World Series in four games and did it by an accumulated score (21-9) that made it seem easy. Bob Costas, who is as astute a baseball observer as I know, summed it up afterwards by saying, "It wasn't a close series." Well, that's what the final numbers said, but I was there, and on the field the games looked a lot closer.

Game One

Clearly the strategy of both teams' pitching staffs was to stop their opponent's biggest run producers, Derek Jeter for the Yankees and Chipper Jones for the Braves. This was an easier task for the Yankees than for the Braves, since Chipper, who batted third, could be pitched around, while Jeter, who batted second in the order, was "protected" in the Yankees lineup by the presence of Paul O'Neill (who drove in 100 runs during the season) batting third and Bernie Williams (115 runs batted in) batting cleanup. In the second inning of game one, the Braves' Greg Maddux, probably the best control pitcher in baseball, took advantage of Jeter's one real weakness as a hitter: a tendency to go for low-and-away breaking pitches out of the strike zone. Maddux set him up with an inside fastball, then came back with a slider low and away—just off the plate—getting Jeter to slap it harmlessly to second base.

Orlando "El Duque" Hernandez, meanwhile, elected to

pitch to Jones with the bases empty and missed his low-and-away setup by perhaps an inch. Chipper hit it around the right field foul pole, fair by perhaps five or six inches, for a home run. In the seventh, El Duque went with the game plan and did what other Braves opponents have done to Jones in recent big games—he walked him. Again, the Braves had no one to pick up the sticks, and the Braves failed to score.

Then, in one of the game's crucial but unheralded moments, Jeter, with bases loaded, got behind the count 1-2, but layed off Maddux's slider, which missed the outside corner by an inch maybe. Jeter then got the pitch he wanted, a high fastball, and singled to tie the game. Later, against the lefty John Rocker, O'Neill showed patience by taking a sharp breaking ball that missed the strike zone by one or two inches; on the next pitch, he singled to right, barely underneath the outstretched glove of the Atlanta second baseman, Bret Boone. The Yankees led by 2 runs.

In the ninth, Mariano Rivera pitched so carefully to Jones that it almost seemed like an unintentional walk. The free pass brought the tying run to the plate. Again, the Braves couldn't follow up, and the game ended on Ryan Klesko's pop-up. The Yankees won 4-1.

By the way, game one featured two outrageous statistical improbabilities. The first was Yankee third baseman Scott Brosius, who hit just .263 off right-handers in 1999, getting 3 hits—half the Yankees' total—off Greg Maddux, against whom right-handed batters hit just .229 during the regular season.

The second was Paul O'Neill, who hit just .190 off left-handers during the season, getting the game-winning hit against John Rocker, against whom left-handers hit just .163 all year. It seemed like almost every time the Yankees had a statistical improbability like this in postseason they somehow prevailed.

Game Two

After the Yankees scored 3 runs in the first inning, the Braves nearly got most of it back. With a runner on base, Brian Jordan caught a David Cone breaking pitch that hung maybe an inch in the strike zone and drove it to deep left field for what looked off the bat like a two-run homer. But the ball died perhaps five feet short of the fence in the cold Atlanta night air. Later, in the clubhouse, Cone said, "On a warm day, that ball is five rows deep."

The third and fourth innings proved to be the Braves' worst nightmare. With a runner on third, Cone hit a wiffle ball to shortstop Ozzie Guillen, a former Gold Glove winner . . . *who dropped it!* The error lead to a Yankee run. In the fourth inning, on a routine double play, Braves second baseman Keith Lockhart couldn't get the ball out of the webbing of his glove and threw wild to first, costing the Braves another run. The Yankees won 7-2, but for want of five feet on Jordan's drive and perhaps two inches in the field, the game could have been tied 5-5 after nine.

Derek Jeter was 2 for 5 and scored 2 key runs; Jones reached base twice with a single and a walk, but never got to bat with a runner on base. Later, watching the game, I heard Costas comment that Jones hadn't "really gotten untracked in the Series." Well, yes and no. In the first two games, the Braves had scored just three runs, of which Jones drove in one and scored another. Up to that point in the entire postseason, he had batted just .270, which doesn't sound like much, but in 54 postseason plate appearances he had reached base an amazing 27 times—an OBA of .500. Through the playoffs and into the Series he had driven in just three runs, but he had only seven base runners in twelve games to deliver.

Game Three

The third and probably decisive game of the Series came down to two plays in right field, both by the ill-fated Brian Jordan. In the first inning, after the Braves gained a psychological edge by scoring first at Yankee Stadium, they lost it when Jordan ran after Chuck Knoblauch's long fly ball to right center only to have it pop out of the heel of his glove. O'Neill then singled to score Knoblauch. In the eighth, Jordan mistimed his jump on Knoblauch's drive to the short right field wall and dropped the ball. Later, Jordan would say that if he had grabbed perhaps a half-inch more ball on each play, he'd have had them both. If it had happened that way, the Braves would have saved 3 runs in a game they lost by a score of 6-5.

Game Four

This game typified the Series. In the third inning, Braves shortstop Walt Weiss muffed a ground ball hit deep in the hole by Knoblauch. Though it spilled out of Weiss's glove and was scored a hit, the play could certainly have been made. Four batters later Tino Martinez hit a hard grounder to Ryan Klesko at first base. This play could have had any number of results—a force-out at second, an out at first, or even a double play. The Braves got none of these; instead the ball skipped off Klesko's body and for the second time in the inning a bad fielding play by a Braves infielder was scored a hit. For want of a few inches, the Braves, on these two third inning plays, gave the Yankees the opportunities to score the 3 runs that proved to be the difference in the 4-1 game.

How did Chipper Jones end up doing? In the sixth inning of game four, batting left-handed, he smashed a hard grounder down the third-base line that would surely have been a double if not for a spectacular play by Scott Brosius who speared it, recovered, and threw him out. Then, in the eighth, with the Braves down 3-1 and facing Rivera, Jones, batting left-handed with the tying runs on base, hit a screaming liner down the right field line that would probably have tied the game—but went foul by maybe three inches. Two pitches later he laced a ground ball by Tino Martinez at first base that was grabbed by Yankees second baseman Luis Sojo at the outfield grass, where he proceeded to throw Jones out by half a step to complete the four-game sweep.

The Yankees in 1996 and '99 won five straight World Series games against the Braves, the team with the best home-field record in baseball for those two seasons.

So, in the record books it is an easy Series victory for the Yankees, but in truth it was perhaps six or seven or maybe eight plays in the field and perhaps four or five key pitches that made all the difference. If you calculated it in terms of the number of inches that could have turned things around, what would that come to? Well, there was Brian Jordan's shot off Cone in game two that died just past the warning track, so that's about five feet right there. As for all the remaining plays and pitches the Braves failed to make, ten inches or less could have turned the World Series completely around.

Any of those plays, even several of them, could be written off to chance, luck, or coincidence. What couldn't be written off as luck is that *all of them went the Yankees' way.*

Of course there's such a thing as luck in baseball—how could anyone who has followed the game for years deny it? It was good luck for the Yankees that Chad Curtis, who went into the Series with a career total of 90 home runs in nearly 3,600 major league at-bats, had two home runs to Chipper Jones's one. It was bad luck for the Braves that their second- and third-best players, Andres Galarraga and Javy Lopez, were unavailable for the Series. But the Braves compounded their bad luck with bad play. The Yankees were the best-schooled, best-managed, and most fundamentally sound team in baseball. This was a Branch Rickey World Series—luck was the residue of design.

2000

If baseball teams were seeded playoff berths according to their won-lost records, here's what the top ten—let's make it the top thirteen—would have looked like after the 2000 season:

Team	W-L	Pct.
1. San Francisco	97-65	.599
2. Chicago (AL)	95-67	.586
3. Atlanta	95-67	.586
4. St. Louis	95-67	.586
5. New York (NL)	94-68	.580
6. Oakland	91-70	.565
7. Seattle	91-71	.562
8. Cleveland	90-72	.556
9. New York (AL)	87-74	.540
10. Los Angeles	86-76	.531
11. Boston	85-77	.525
12. Arizona	85-77	.525
13. Cincinnati	85-77	.525

That's thirteen of thirty teams, all in contention for most of the season for a chance to win it all. I don't know what Bud Selig calls "competitive balance," but that's what I call it. In fact, as I had occasion to mention in the "Competitive Balance" chapter, in the year 2000, for the first time ever, every team in the major leagues finished with a won-lost percentage lower than .600 and better than .400.

Now, I defy you, or rather, I would defy you if you didn't know anything about baseball, which can't be true of you since you're reading this, but if you didn't know anything about baseball, I would defy you to pick from that list the team that was going to go all the way.

The 2000 Yankees didn't "stumble" into the playoffs as everyone said. They didn't even crawl into the playoffs. They just sort of fell in the dirt during the last three weeks of the season and lay there while the playoffs overtook them. The Yankees lost their last seven games and fifteen of their last eighteen in one of the worst regular season stretches in team history. They went into the postseason with the worst record of any team in the playoffs.

The Yanks lost the first game of the series, Gil Heredia outpitching Roger Clemens in Oakland. You win the first game in your home ballpark, you're supposed to win the series, but Pettitte and Rivera combined for a shutout in game two to tie it up. Then, in game three El Duque and Rivera teamed up for a 4-2 gem, out-dueling the A's ace, twenty-game winner Tim Hudson. Game four saw the hungry young A's come back in a big way behind Barry Zito, pounding Clemens and winning 11-1. At this point, the A's had outscored the Yankees 22-12 through four games.

After this demoralizing loss, the Yankees had to board a plane early on Sunday morning and fly to Oakland for the deciding game. Well, the loss on Saturday *should* have been demoralizing.

Instead, it seemed as if the A's were the team who were demoralized, or at least emotionally exhausted from the effort. The Yankees scored 6 runs in the first inning, the big blow coming on Tino Martinez's long drive to center field that was misplayed by Oakland center fielder Terrence Long. (To be fair, Tino drove the ball all the way to the center field wall; I won't say the ball *should* have been caught, but it *could* have been caught.) Pettitte got the win, El Duque pitched some relief, and Mariano pitched the last of the eighth and all of the ninth to seal a 7-5 win. Here's a stat for you: In the fifth and final game, Dave Justice hit the only Yankee home run of the series. What are the odds of the winning team going five games with one home run?

The Seattle Mariners were the wild card team that year, but they had won four more games than the Yankees during the regular season and whipped the Chicago White Sox (who had won four more games than they did and eight more than the Yankees) soundly in three games, limiting them to just 17 hits. There was every reason to believe that Seattle could take the Yankees, even without the extra home-field advantage.

In the first game, Freddy Garcia and three Mariner relievers combined for a 6-hit shutout. At this point the Yankees had scored only *18 runs in fifty-three playoff innings*. Excepting the 6-run outburst in the fifth game with Oakland, they had scored just *12 runs in fifty-two innings*.

In game two, Seattle starter John Halama tacked on seven more scoreless innings, making the Yankees' drought just *18 runs over sixty innings*. Then, down 1-0 in the eighth, the Yanks erupted for 7 runs and the Series turned around. Andy Pettitte beat Aaron Sele 6-2 in game three; Clemens, suddenly revitalized, pitched a complete-game shutout in game four; Garcia came back again to beat Denny Nagle in game five; and then, in game six, down 4-3 in the seventh, the Yanks came back again to score 6 runs (capped by David Justice's 3-run homer off lefty Arthur Rhodes), and the Yankees were in their third World Series in four years.

Mets fans weren't sure that the Mets could win the 2000 Series, which means that deep in their hearts they didn't think they would. And Yankee fans—well, Yankee fans always think they're going to win. It was all summed up by two T-shirts worn by friends for game three at Shea Stadium. The Mets' fan on the left had "Mets Fans Believe" across his chest. His friend on the right wore one that said "Yankees Fans Know."

Not that there was any great difference between the two teams. In fact, most edges seemed to go to the Mets. Their regular-season numbers stacked up like this (the number under each column denotes league rank. I used league ranks, rather than the actual numbers, to avoid the question of how much the DH affects run scoring).

	BA	OBA	SA	HR	ERA	W-L	Playoffs W-L
Yankees	(6)	(5)	(6)	(6)	(6)	87-74	7-4
Mets	(7)	(8)	(8)	(6)	(3)	94-68	7-2

If you didn't know which team was the Yankees and which team was the Mets you couldn't tell by looking at those numbers which was supposed to be the *dominant* team. Derek Jeter said afterwards that the Mets were "The best team I've seen [in the postseason] in the five years that I've been here," and though he was probably being a bit generous, he wasn't too far from being right. The Mets' ERA got a boost from Shea Stadium, which is primarily a pitcher's park, but conversely, the Mets' hitters were better than they looked for the same reason. In any event, the Mets not only had a better record than the Yanks during the regular season, but in the postseason as well.

The record book will show that the Yankees won in five games, which makes it sound easy. Those who saw the games know that they were tighter and tougher even than the Yankees '99 sweep of the Braves.

How tough and tight? Consider . . .

- Three of the five games, all Yankees victories, were decided by a single run; the others were decided by two runs.
- Three of the games were decided in the last at-bat for the winning team; in the other two the game ended with the tying run at the plate.
- The Yankees won both the first and final games of the Series on two-out singles by backup infielders.
- Both teams hit 4 home runs; the Yankees outscored the Mets by just 3 runs in forty-seven innings.

Even those facts don't suggest how close this Series was. Let's recall two key at-bats from game one that summed it up:

The first occurred with two outs in the Mets' sixth with Timo Perez on first base. Todd Zeile got under an Andy Pettitte pitch and sent a drive towards the short-left field corner of Yankee Stadium. I was in the press section about twenty rows back in the left field corner, so I had a perfect view. The ball certainly seemed to be headed for the seats, then, as if it hit turbulence, it began to drop, drop, drop until it hit on the very top of the blue padding on the backfield wall, falling back onto the field as if pulled by the collective will of nearly 55,000 Yankee fans. Most of the people in the stands thought it was a home run.

Andy Pettitte said later he thought it was a home run, everyone in the Mets dugout thought it was a home run, and, most unfortunately for the Mets, Timo Perez also thought it was home run, raising a fist in the air as he loped towards second base.

I did not see Perez loping; Jennifer Lopez was seated about about five rows in front of me, wearing some kind of gold halter top contraption. She stood and cheered wildly, though whether for the Mets or Yankees I could not tell. I'm going to be honest: I was distracted. Wally Matthews of the *New York Post,* who was seated next to me, was far more professional. As he rounded second Perez began to accelerate. Matthews began to shout, "He slowed down! Perez thought it was a home run! He slowed down!"

David Justice, not fast, but a fundamentally sound outfielder, kept his eye on the ball, picked it up and fired a perfect relay throw to Derek Jeter, who caught the ball on the run, spun like a ballet dancer and threw while in full stride—think Joe Montana throwing to Dwight Clarke in the 1981 NFC championship game against Dallas—as third baseman Scott Brosius wisely ducked so as not to obstruct Jeter's throw to Jorge Posada. Perez was out by a good seven or eight feet.

I have never in my life seen a batted baseball strike the top of the outfield fence and bounce back in the direction it came. I don't imagine I shall ever see it again. Like Charlie Hayes's ground ball in the '96 series against the Braves, the laws of physics suddenly seemed to be reversed for the Yankees.

On the Subway Series videotape, a Yankees fan named Jack Nelson, who had the seat directly in front of Zeile's shot in the short left field corner, put his finger on what he thought was the exact spot the ball hit. Apparently he could have simply reached out and caught it in his hands, but not wishing to risk a possible reversal of the Jeffrey Maier decision against Baltimore in '96, he let it go. If he had touched it, the Mets would have had runners at second and third with two out. By letting it go, he gave the Yankees the chance to make the play that ended the Mets' threat. Maier and Nelson are living proof that Yankee fans are the smartest, most disciplined in baseball. They know when to touch the ball and when to let it bounce.

Was it sheer luck that made Zeile's fly ball bounce back onto the field? Probably, though Yankee fans generally see providence where others see luck. But even if God took a hand on that long fly, Dave Justice still has to focus and still has to make a perfect relay to Jeter, Jeter has to make a perfect throw home, Brosius has to duck, and Posada has to catch the ball and make the tag. None of this would have mattered, of course, if Perez had simply kept on running. By failing to do so, like Jack Nelson, he gave the Yankees the opportunity to make the play. So it would seem that God is on the side of the team that keeps its eye on the ball.

The second key at-bat in the game came in the ninth, with the Mets leading 3-2, when Paul O'Neill faced Mets' closer, Armando Benitez, one out and nobody on. Battling back from an 0-2 count, O'Neill proceeded to foul off six pitches, wore Benitez down, worked the count full, and then drew a walk that resulted in the tying run after Luis Polonia, of all people, singled, and Jose Vizcaino, of all other people, followed with another single, and Chuck Knoblauch hit a sacrifice fly. The game went into extra innings, and the Yankees won in the eleventh on yet another clutch single by Jose Vizcaino.

I'm tempted to say that O'Neill's at-bat was the one that best symbolized the Yankees' tenacity over this incredible six-year span, but the truth is that there were so many moments like this that it's impossible to single one out. And there were more to come in this Series.

In game two Roger Clemens made perhaps his most over-powering start ever in postseason, shutting down the Mets on 2 hits over eight innings and striking out nine with no walks. Considering that the Yankees led 6-0, Joe Torre might have been overly cautious for taking him out and putting in Jeff Nelson to start the ninth. It was about time for the Yankees bullpen to falter in the postseason, and it did. First Nelson, then Rivera proceeded to give up 5 hits and 5 runs—but the Yankees held on to win a 6-5 thriller.

(You'll note I haven't said a word about the famous Clemens-Piazza bat-throwing incident. That's because it was the most over-hyped non-incident of the series. What happened was that Mike Piazza broke his bat on a hard slider, the barrel skipped towards the mound, Clemens picked it up, and tossed it to his left, to the bat boy. What was he supposed to do with it? Stick it in his pocket? Clemens would later say that he thought he had caught the ball, and skeptical reporters would ask, "How could you mistake a bat for a ball?" But Clemens didn't say he thought he was *throwing* a ball off the field, he merely said he thought he had caught the ball Piazza hit.

Later, most Mets players shrugged to reporters' questions and said they thought there was "no intent" in Clemens' gesture, or something like that; but the press, apparently not having enough to write about with the game itself, chose to blow the incident out of all rational proportion. If anyone lost his temper, it was Piazza, who stopped about a third of the way down first base yelling "What's your problem?" at Clemens. Piazza yelled that and something else, undecipherable at least to me, apparently trying to get Clemens to at least admit that the tossed bat was an accident. Clemens stubbornly refused to do anything but ask umpire Charlie Reliford for a new ball. What made everything look worse than it was was the emptying of the benches, but the general consensus among the writers where I was sitting was that the two teams did not charge the field to fight each other but to restrain Clemens and Piazza from coming to blows. Anyhow, it was all much ado about nothing—no harm, no foul.)

Two days later at Shea Stadium the Mets returned the favor, scoring two runs in the last of the eighth to tack a rare postseason loss on El Duque.

Derek Jeter began game four with a home run, and the Yankees took a 3-2 lead into the fifth inning, when Denny Nagle seemed to falter and David Cone, making his last World Series appearance, got Mike Piazza to pop up in a key situation. After that a triple dose of the Yankees bullpen—Jeff Nelson, Mike Stanton, then Mariano Rivera—sealed the victory. The Yanks had outscored the Mets by just three runs, but were up three games to one.

The final game at Shea seemed to define everything the Yankees had been in the postseason since 1996. The Yankees scored a run in the second, the Mets came back to take a 2-1 lead, Derek Jeter tied it up with a solo homer in the sixth, and that's where it stood into the ninth.

Al Leiter, the Mets ace during the season at 16-8, had told Mets manager Bobby Valentine that "You don't have to worry about pitch counts. I could throw 150 pitches if I had to. I'll give everything I have to, and I'm going to give us the victory tomorrow."

Valentine knew that Leiter wasn't bluffing; he had, after all, won three World Series rings—with Toronto in 1992 and '93 and with Florida in '97. He would take Leiter at his word: If he felt he could throw 150 pitches, Valentine would give him the chance. So would the Yankees.

By the eighth inning Leiter had thrown 121 pitches, and he started the ninth by striking out Tino Martinez with three pitches and Paul O'Neill with five. That made 129 for the game. But then Jorge Posada did to him what Paul O'Neill had done to Armando Benitez in the ninth inning of the first game, forcing Leiter to throw nine pitches, five of them after the count reached 2-2, and drew a walk.

Then Brosius, on a 1-1 count, laced a hard single to left. The wood Brosius put on the ball might have been taken as an indication that Leiter was about spent. But Valentine chose to stay with him against the thirty-five-year-old journeyman Luis Sojo. Leiter threw him a high fast ball; Sojo lunged at it awkwardly and chopped the ball up the middle. Center fielder Jay Payton fielded it cleanly and fired home. Posada, who might have been the slowest runner among the Yankee regulars, rounded third and kept on going. On a normal day, with a throw as good as Payton's, Posada would have been out. On this night, with the World Series on the line, Mike Piazza chose to take the throw in back of the plate. Payton's perfect throw hit Posada in the left hip and bounded towards the Mets dugout, allowing Brosius to score.

Leiter, his left arm hanging limp from 141 pitches, was finally relieved by Valentine. An overworked Mariano Rivera pitched the ninth, with the final out coming from Mike Piazza, who had hit two home runs in the series. He sent a towering fly ball to deep center field that caused Joe Torre, in a rare display of emotion, to jump and yell. But Yankees fans, who by one estimate numbered about 60 percent of the fans in Shea that night, rose to their feet; Mets fans knew better. The ball doesn't carry at night in Shea, and Bernie Williams gathered it a few feet short of the fence.

After the game, Valentine didn't talk about Piazza's last at-bat, he talked about what happened after Sojo's single. "If that ball is a fraction of a second sooner," he said, shaking his head in the Mets clubhouse, "or an inch away from Posada's leg, Mike would have tagged him out. We'd still be out there [playing]." Joe Torre summed up the only difference between the two teams at the post-game press conference: "We may not have the best players, but we have the best team."

This was the fifth year of the Yankees' run. Over that period, including 1997 when they lost to Cleveland in the first round of the playoffs, the Yankees won 487 regular season games and lost 322 for a percentage of .602. That's pretty good, but it's only ten percentage points from mediocre. In the playoffs, though, they were 30-12 for a won-lost of .714, and in the World Series, against the best teams in the National League, they were 16-3 for .842.

Define clutch play however you like, or deny its existence. The fact is that over a five-year period the Yankees won 60 percent of their games during the regular season and then, against the best teams in baseball, won 75 percent of their games in the postseason.

2001

The 2001 playoffs and World Series were the greatest examples of Yankee spirit, pluck, and gamesmanship displayed during the entire six-year stretch. And it was capped by the World Series the Yankees lost.

During the regular season, New York won the AL East with a 95-65 record, finishing 13½ games ahead of the Red Sox. They were third in the league in team ERA behind Oakland and Seattle, and fifth in runs scored behind Seattle, Cleveland, Texas, and Oakland.

Cracks in the Yankees' armor were showing, though. There

were no reliable starters behind Roger Clemens (who won the Cy Young Award with a 20-3 record, though he allowed nearly one hit per inning), Mike Mussina, 17-11, and Andy Pettitte, 15-10. Orlando Hernandez's effectiveness was severely curtailed by injuries (he was just 4-7 all year), and Ramiro Mendoza, with a 3.75 ERA, was the overrated setup man.

Paul O'Neill, at thirty-eight, found his skills swiftly eroding; he batted just .267 and drove in 70 runs while using up 510 at-bats, and many thought that Joe Torre was carrying loyalty too far in continuing to bat him in the third spot. Chuck Knoblauch, who just three years earlier looked like he was headed for the Hall of Fame, suddenly became the man who the Yankees couldn't hide in their lineup. Switching him from second base to left field didn't help his hitting, .250 with 9 home runs, but it did allow Alfonso Soriano to move in at second base and establish himself as a coming star with 18 home runs and 43 stolen bases.

But there were two small market teams that clearly bettered the Yankees' performance during the regular season, Seattle and Oakland. (Within the year, Seattle, with the help of a new ballpark, would mysteriously metamorphose into a major market.)

Let's look at how the teams stacked up going into the playoffs:

	W-L	Runs	OBA	Slg	BA	ERA
Yankees	95-45	804	.334	.435	.267	4.02
Seattle	116-46	927	.360	.445	.288	3.64
Oakland	102-60	884	.345	.439	.264	3.59

I know a lot of people who assumed before the 2001 playoffs started that the Yankees would win the pennant simply because they were the Yankees, and I understand why they felt that way; battling back time and again from long odds does give a team a kind of mystique. But I don't know how you could have looked at those regular season numbers before the playoffs began and concluded that the Yankees were the superior team. I haven't bothered to juggle the numbers and allow for home-park effects, because no matter how you adjust them Seattle and Oakland come out as better teams, which is why they won more games. (The Mariners, in fact, tied the record for victories set by the 1906 Chicago Cubs.) If the 2001 Yankees had played in the same division with the 2001 Mariners and A's, they'd have finished third.

After the first two games of the division series, the Yankees must have wondered if they could have finished third in the West. Mark Mulder and Tim Hudson, the two biggest Oakland winners (a combined 39-18 during the season), whipped Clemens and Pettitte, allowing New York just three runs in eighteen innings—and both games were at Yankee Stadium. It's not possible to get in a much deeper hole than that in a best-of-five series: Your righty and lefty aces have failed you, you're down two games to zip against a younger team that outpitched and outscored you and won more games than you did during the regular season, *and you're headed to their ballpark for the remaining games of the Series.* The Yankees had the A's right where they wanted them.

In game three Oakland's Barry Zito pitched one of the best games of his life, giving up just two hits in eight innings, and found himself on the losing end of a 1-0 score when Mike Mussina and Mariano Rivera combined to blank the A's on six hits. Actually, he combined with Derek Jeter for the shutout.

In the seventh inning, with two outs and Jeremy Giambi on first, Jeter made the signature fielding play of the new Yankee dynasty—maybe the greatest play in the history of baseball's greatest team. The A's Terrence Long, the same man who misplayed Tino Martinez's fly ball in the final game of the 2000 division series, hit a grounder past Martinez and into the right field corner. If the ball had been hit harder, Giambi would have never tried to score, but it faded into foul territory and right fielder Shane Spencer didn't catch up to it till Giambi had already rounded third base. In a spectacular piece of good fortune for the Yankees, Spencer then proceeded to overthrow Soriano, his cutoff man. It wasn't immediately apparent that this might work to the Yankees' advantage, as Soriano had almost no chance of turning and throwing in time to get Giambi, and more than 60,000 fans roared collectively in anticipation of scoring the tying run, as Spencer's throw drifted to the right of home plate towards the on-deck circle. There was no way that the A's could fail to tie the game—unless someone came charging across the entire infield, speared the bail backhanded with two hands across the foul line, and made a perfect backhand flip to the catcher, Jorge Posada.

Which, of course, is what happened. Giambi, so confident he would score that he didn't bother to slide, was easily tagged out. Later, on ESPN and in the papers, he would be roundly criticized for not sliding, but the truth is that not one base runner in a thousand would have thought that Jeter or anyone else would have been able to make that play.

"What in the heck was he even doing there?" the A's Johnny Damon would ask later in a tone of wonderment. What made Jeter's play so remarkable is that it was so completely unexpected. Virtually all other great plays in postseason history—Willie Mays's catch in the '54 series, Brooks Robinson's stab of Johnny Bench's would-be double in 1970, et al.—involved balls hit to a player's position. This play involved a hit down the right field line and a throw back down the line that was in foul territory—*and it was made by the shortstop.*

Lucky? Later, in the Yankee clubhouse, Jeter would say, "A shortstop in a position like that is kind of like a free safety in football. You have to think like Ronnie Lott [the great San Francisco 49ers safety who, like Jeter, earned four championship rings], it's not my job to stand around and look. It's my job to be around the ball." Now there's a man who knows his job description.

Lucky, yes, in Branch Rickey's definition of the word.

Their morale shattered, the A's lost 9-2 the next day in game four, with El Duque coming up big. Then, back in New York for the series final, a combination of Clemens, Stanton, Mendoza, and Rivera hung a loss on Mark Mulder.

For the second year in a row the Yankees had lost the opening game of the divisional series and salvaged it by winning two games on their opponent's home field. All the Yankees had to do now was beat the team that had won more games during the season than any team in American League history.

The Yankees won the first two games at Seattle, both nail-biters, 4-2 and then 3-2, behind Pettitte and Mussina; Rivera nailed down both saves. Seattle expended all their energy in winning the next game at New York, 14-3. The Mariners never made it back to Seattle to claim their home-field advantage in the series. Clemens, Mendoza, and then Rivera again stopped them on 2 hits for a 3-1 win in game six, and the next day, with the brass ring in sight, with Pettitte on the mound, the Yankees pounded Aaron Sele, who had gone 15-5 over the regular season, knocking him out in the fifth inning for a 12-3 win.

Let's recap. For the two series, the Yankees were 3-3 at home and 4-0 on the road against superior teams in their own home stadiums. From 1996 through 2001 the Yankees were 582-387 in the regular season for a winning percentage of .601. From 1996 to just before the 2001 World Series, they were 53-18 in the postseason for a won-lost percentage of .746. At home over that span they were pretty good, going 23-11. But here's the truly amazing part: Of that 53-18 postseason record, *thirty of the thirty-seven victories came on the road.*

The Arizona Diamondbacks presented the Yankees with a different kind of foe. The D'backs were a fundamentally solid team that was unremarkable beyond its first two starting pitchers—but Curt Schilling at 22-6 and Randy Johnson at 21-6 might have been the best one-two tandem ever. Actually, Miguel Batista, 11-8 with an ERA of 3.36, was pretty good, too, but no one knew how good until the Series.

Arizona won the Western Division with an ordinary-looking 92-70 record, but that was deceptive, since in a short series the quality of their first two starters was more important than the depth of the overall staff. They beat the Cardinals in five games in the division series, allowing them an average of just 2 runs per game, and the Braves in five, with Randy Johnson beating Greg Maddux in the first game and Tom Glavine in the last game. Schilling won game number three in a complete-game beauty, allowing just 4 hits and 1 run.

That was the key for Arizona: complete games or at least seven- or eight-inning efforts from Schilling and Johnson. The reason they could pitch so many innings was that they had to throw so few pitches, and Yankee hitters would prove no more successful at wearing them down than National League hitters had been. For the first time in more than six years, the Yankees would go into a postseason series clearly overmatched in first and second game starters. The last time had been the 1995 AL division series against Seattle, and Randy Johnson had been one of the starters in that series, winning the third game and saving the fifth. He would pitch some relief in this series, too.

After the first two games the Yankees seemed overmatched in more than just starting pitching. Mike Mussina, 17-11 in the regular season and 2-0 in the postseason, didn't look to be a bad match against Curt Schilling, but he didn't make it past the fourth inning. The D'backs outhit the Yankees 10-3, the Yanks made 2 errors, and Arizona won easily 9-1. Pettitte didn't pitch poorly in the second game, but he didn't pitch all that well either, losing 4-0.

The Yankees had been outhit 15-6 and outscored 13-1 in the two games, and their vaunted road magic failed them for the first time since '96. But the Yankees' lack of punch really began to show in game three at Yankee Stadium, where they couldn't get good wood on a twenty-nine-year-old journeyman named Brian Anderson. This was supposed to be the soft part of the Arizona rotation, but if not for three crucial errors and a couple of wild pitches by Anderson, the Diamondbacks would have won it. After giving up a run in the second inning, Anderson managed to stay out of trouble until the sixth, when the Yankees scored what would prove to be the winning run. Roger Clemens was terrific, and Mariano Rivera, asked to pitch in both the eighth and ninth, came through again. The Yankees got the win, but had now managed just 13 hits and 3 runs in three games, and the hitting didn't look to get better in game four against Curt Schilling.

One of the more amazing things about the Yankees of this period is how many times they absolutely had to win a game that they shouldn't have won and won it. This was one of those games. I remember it vividly—El Duque, making what would be the last World Series start of his Yankee career, had scarcely pitched an effective game all season, winning just four times in sixteen starts, with an ERA of 4.7 runs per nine innings. The only bright note from the Yankees' point of view was that Schilling would be pitching on just three days' rest—but then, he hadn't had to throw that many pitches in his first start at Arizona.

Arizona scored 2 runs in the eighth, and the brutal probability of being down three games to one muted the Yankee crowd. Down 3-1 in the ninth, sidearming reliever Byung-Hyun Kim got the first out, then gave up a soft opposite field single to Paul O'Neill. Kim then struck out Bernie Williams.

It was one of those situations where nothing less than everything would do, and that's what the Yankees did. Tino Martinez, capping Halloween night by impersonating an actor in a bad baseball movie, hit Kim's first pitch high over the center field wall, and more than 55,000 people erupted. In the tenth Derek Jeter ended one of the most excruciating games in World Series history by taking an outside pitch from Kim and popping it high into right field, where, with no help needed from Jeffrey Maier, it cleared the wall. It was the first, and more than likely the last home run that will ever be hit in the month of November.

Several of my friends tell me that game five was actually better than game four. I don't know, because I never saw the game in its entirety. I was traveling to Phoenix, Arizona, and the screaming at the airport lounges in the fifth inning when the D'backs got two solo home runs off Mike Mussina would have convinced anyone that World Series fever is a virus that can strike anywhere in the country. On the whole, though, Mike Mussina redeemed himself for his lackluster effort in game one, giving up no other runs.

For the second day in a row Arizona was on the verge of winning their third game, thanks largely to their hard-throwing righthander, Miguel Batista, who blanked the Yankees into the eighth inning before being relieved by Greg Swindell. Then in the ninth Arizona manager Bob Brenly again chose Byung-Hyun Kim to hold the lead. Posada opened the ninth inning with a double, but Kim settled down to strike out the next two batters. Once again, the Yankees were down to that moment when only everything would do. And just as Tino Martinez had done in the ninth inning of the previous game on the previous night, Scott Brosius hit a two-run homer to tie things up.

I was at most of the great Yankees postseason home games and a couple of the road games from 1996 through the first four games of the 2001 World Series, but for me this one was my most memorable. I was riding in a van with some friends traveling from Phoenix to Tucson, and at every truck stop or gas station we passed on the way down, the game was blaring on a TV or radio. I'll never forget the scene on a November night at an open-air Mexican restaurant about forty-five minutes from Tombstone. The only noise that followed Brosius's home run was the sound of 56,000 Yankee fans howling through a TV set. The customers stared at the set in stony silence into the Arizona desert night.

In the twelfth inning, with one out, Soriano singled home Knoblauch with the winning run. One of my friends in the van shrugged and said, "Well, that was inevitable." So it seemed.

What were the odds of the Yankees tying games five and six with 2-out, 2-run homers in the ninth inning? Since 1903 to game five of the 2001 World Series, there had been 567 World Series games. Only one other player had ever hit a 2-out, 2-run homer in the ninth to tie a game. It was a Yankee, of course: Tom Tresh in 1964 against the St. Louis Cardinals. Now, again, what were the odds of that happening on consecutive nights? I have no idea. You'll have to make your own. Next time this situation arises, ask yourself what kind of odds you'd give.

The Yankees were now up three games to two, and with one more dose of their road magic would become the first team since the advent of free agency to win four consecutive World Series. Actually, they were already the first team since free agency to win *three* consecutive World Series. They would have matched the record of the greatest baseball dynasty of all, the '36–'41 Yankees, which won five World Series in six years.

But as Casey Stengel (who from 1947 to '53 won six World Series in seven years) must have said, you can't win them all. Andy Pettitte, for some strange reason, was not even competitive on this night, and didn't survive the third inning, after which Arizona was already up 12-0. You can't get a surer lock than Randy Johnson on the mound, pitching at home with a 12-0 lead.

The only surprise was that Brenly let Johnson pitch seven full innings. With such a lead, even the TV announcers were suggesting after the fourth inning (in which the D'backs scored three more runs) that Arizona now had the option of using Johnson in relief in game seven. Brenly later would later justify his decision by saying he didn't want to act until "We had the game well in hand." *Sports Illustrated*'s excellent baseball writer, Tom Verducci, would write that, "Brenly presumably was worried that New York would go to the shotgun and hurry-up offense." But on this night the Yankee offense produced just 7 hits. Game seven came down to Roger Clemens, at thirty-nine the oldest game seven starter in World Series history, vs. Curt Schilling, who was pitching on three days' rest—but with Randy Johnson ready in the bullpen. Nothing is as exciting as the seventh game of the World Series, and this one was a pip.

Clemens and Schilling matched goose eggs into the sixth inning, when Clemens gave up a run. They were deadlocked after seven when the Yankees came up. After game four, Schilling admitted that he had been "running on fumes." Now, he was running on sheer will. In the eighth, the will began to flag, and Soriano, picking a splitter almost out of the dirt on an 0-2 count, whacked the ball into the left field seats.

I'm sure that everyone who thought the Yankees would lose

at this point envisioned a spectacular walk-off home run, or at the very least some sharp liner that eluded the grasp of a Yankees fielder by microinches. What no one was prepared for was the broken bat wiffle-ball hit by the Diamondbacks' only legitimate slugger, Luis Gonzalez, to where Derek Jeter would probably have been playing had the infield not been drawn in to try and cut off the potential winning run at third base.

The Yankees had won forty-five consecutive playoff and World Series games in which they led after eight innings; Mariano Rivera had pitched in fifty-one consecutive playoff and World Series games without a loss. Both amazing streaks came to an end not with a bang but with a blooper.

Don't misunderstand me. I'm not calling this luck, unless it be luck of the Branch Rickey type. Nothing is surer in my mind than that Arizona was the better team and that they deserved to win the Series. In fact, they deserved to win it long before the ninth inning of the seventh game, after which they needed Randy Johnson to pitch 1⅓ innings in relief in order to nail it down.

The wonder is that the Yankees lasted this long. The wonder, in further point of fact, is that it all came down to a bad throw on a bunt attempt. Well, no, that's not entirely fair. Yankee fans have now made it a part of team lore that if Mariano Rivera had made a good throw to second on Damian Miller's poor bunt in the ninth inning, the Yankees would have won their fourth straight World Series. Rivera, whose throw went into center field, helped the myth along by saying later that it was "the key to the game."

It was not. To begin with, the bunt followed a single by Mark Grace, who hit one of Rivera's famous cut-fastballs into center field out of self-defense. "I had to swing at it," Grace was quoted the next day in the *Arizona Republic*, "if I hadn't hit it, it would have hit me in the chest." Anyway, Rivera's throw left runners at first and second with no outs. Brenly then called for another sacrifice bunt from pinch hitter Jay Bell, which was fielded by Rivera and whipped to third base for the force. One out, still runners at first and second.

The real key moment was a pitch to the next batter, Tony Womack, who tied the score with a sharp double down the right field line. Womack is left-handed, and Rivera, who was probably not as sharp as he would have been had he not pitched the entire eighth inning, is supposed to get left-handed batters out. He then hit second baseman Craig Counsell to load the bases.

You can argue the strategy forever, but I think most baseball analysts would agree that positioning your infielders to cut off the potential winning run in the ninth inning was the sound move.

Anyway, perhaps the greatest clutch run in the history of baseball—maybe in the entire history of American professional sports—was over. How superior were the Diamondbacks? They outhit the Yankees 65-42, outscored them 37-14, and their pitchers posted a 1.94 ERA to the Yankees' 4.26.

Really, the World Series it most reminded me of was the first one I ever watched—actually, I don't remember watching it, just reading about it later—in 1960 between the Yankees and the Pittsburgh Pirates. That year the Yankees outhit Pittsburgh 91-60 and outscored them 55-27; Yankee pitchers had a 3.54 ERA to 7.11 for Pittsburgh.

The 1960 World Series might have been a fluke, but the 2001 Series was not. Arizona had better hitters, more speed, and, of course, Schilling and Johnson. But you know it and I know it: If Rivera had thrown that ball properly to second base, or if he had struck out Counsell, or if Gonzalez's soft liner had been pulled in by Jeter, it would have gone down in history as another example of Yankee domination.

I defy anyone to come up with any streak by any team in American sports that featured as many gutsy calls, clutch plays, and thrilling endings as the Yankees' postseasons in '96, '99, 2000, and even 2001. I defy anyone to show me exactly how the Yankees of those years "dominated" anybody. They seldom had the best players, but they almost always had the best team.

Literally the day after game seven of the 2001 Series, the Yankees were placed by the commissioner's office in the crossfire of the negotiations between Major League Baseball and the Players Association; inside of a few months it was gospel in the sportswriting establishment that the Yankees won those World Series rings because Steinbrenner had simply outspent everyone else.

But those of us who followed those seasons carefully and now remember them vividly will always know different. The Yankees of that era were paid obscene amounts of money, and they earned it. They gave baseball a legacy of heart, grit, and professionalism that baseball could have pointed to with pride, much as the NBA did with the Michael Jordan-era Chicago Bulls.

Instead, the 1996–2001 Yankees have, in the minds of many baseball fans, an asterisk next to those achievements in the record book. It's not fair, but then, I guess, neither is life. If Red Sox fans can live with "The Curse," I can live with an asterisk.

8

The Strange Case of Barry Bonds

If Barry Bonds had been killed in a plane crash after the 1999 season, would he have been regarded as the greatest ballplayer of his era? Would baseball fans have reacted to his death with the same anguish that followed the loss of, say, Roberto Clemente?

Let's answer the second question first.

Of course not. Barry Bonds is a churlish, self-centered jerk whose spectacular achievements in the last few seasons should have signaled a turnaround in both his image and that of Major League Baseball. Instead, Bonds's sour personality and petty peevishness towards the demands on his time by the fans and press—surely a small price to pay for the wealth and adoration they have heaped on him—have smothered the public's interest in Bonds and his place in baseball history. He is the great wet blanket of Major League Baseball.

For instance, here's a recent quote from Barry Bonds on the

subject of race in baseball: "Racism is worse than it used to be. Back in the old days, at least it was out in the open. It's just hidden now. Baseball is in trouble. It's becoming a Latin and all-white game."

How many things are wrong with that statement? Where to begin? Well, let's start with the obvious. Of course racism in baseball exists, and of course it is not worse than it "used to be." I agree with Bonds wholeheartedly that it would be far better to bring issues of racism in sports out in the open where they can be dealt with, rather than pretending, as baseball and all other sports want to, that these issues no longer exist, when in fact they have merely evolved into something subtler and more difficult to pin down. Why are there fewer American black players now than twenty years ago? Are the reasons entirely racial, or at least in part socioeconomic, such as the failure of Major League Baseball to promote itself to young black kids in the inner cities? I'm not saying that's not true. In fact, that seems to me to be an entirely logical explanation for the decline in the number of black baseball players, and I won't even deny that that might be partly the result of racism, though we're then faced with the troubling question of why Major League Baseball would prefer black Hispanics to black Americans. I suspect it has much to do with the fact that it is far cheaper and easier to scout black Latin kids than to instruct and develop black American kids. Whatever the answer, I'd like to see this issue come out in the open.

But a statement like Bonds's doesn't bring the issue out in the open: it shuts it off. It closes off the discussion with an oversimplified, ready-made excuse that too many people, white and black, are prepared to accept. And isn't it in some way racially insensitive (as distinguished from racist) to imply that an institution is racist because it includes more Latins than blacks? But I'm digressing into areas I don't have the space to deal with here.

The point I'm getting at is that Barry Bonds was smart enough to pinpoint a problem that baseball is sooner or later going to have to come to terms with, and a problem in which he himself is in an ideal position to help do something about. Who would be a better poster boy for luring young black kids away from a short, body-breaking, and relatively underpaid career in pro football than baseball's greatest player—the godson of baseball's greatest living player? Who better to advertise the long-term rewards of professional baseball than the man who has won more Most Valuable Player awards than any player in the history of the game?

In other words, instead of choosing to become part of the solution, Barry Bonds has self-consciously chosen to make himself part of the problem. It's a shame, really. Bonds has taken an entire generation of fans who wanted to embrace him and made us feel like we're—I hate to phrase it this way because it sounds so, so "California"—invading his space.

All right, enough of this. You didn't buy this book for sociopolitical argument, you want numbers. Let's deal with the first question. If Barry Bonds had been killed in a plane crash after the 1999 season, would he have been regarded as the greatest ballplayer of his era?

The two leading candidates for Player of The Nineties are Barry Bonds and Ken Griffey Jr. Bonds broke in two years earlier than Griffey and has sustained far fewer injuries. Anyway, here's how their career batting records looked after the 1999 season. (The sharp reader will no doubt be puzzled that I don't include the 2000 season, thus capping off both the decade and the century, but since it's what happened to Barry Bonds after 1999 that is so notable, please bear with me.)

	G	AB	HR	Hm-Rd	R	RBI	BA	BB
Bonds	2,000	6,976	445	219–226	1,455	1,299	.288	1,430
Griffey	1,535	5,832	398	212-186	1,063	1,152	.299	747

	OBA	SA	SB-CS	GDP	SLOB
Bonds	.409	.559	460-132	116	22.86
Griffey	.380	.569	167-60	109	21.62

SB-CS = Stolen Bases/Caught Stealing
GDP = Ground into Double Play

I don't know what the argument for Griffey would be even if Griffey had not been injured for more than half of the '95 season. If Griffey had played as many games as Bonds in this period, he probably would have had at least 200 more RBIs and scored about the same number of runs. But this is deceptive, as Griffey played in lineups with much better hitters. Bonds's home parks cut back on his home run total a bit, while Griffey's boosted his slightly. Their SLOBs, which multiplies on base and slugging averages, indicates that the difference between them was slight: Bonds produced about 1.2 more runs per hundred at-bats.

But Bonds holds substantial edges in two statistics not measured in SLOB: GDP (grounded into double plays) and stolen bases. Bonds was much tougher to catch in a double play, hitting into just 7 more in 465 more games. Bonds stole nearly 300 more bases and had a better rate of success, 77.7 percent to Griffey's 73.6 percent. Even giving Griffey credit for perhaps 50 more stolen bases that he might have had if he had played the additional 450-odd games, he doesn't begin to approach Bonds's base stealing ability.

Griffey was a better defensive player and at a more important defensive position. He was a great center fielder over this period, with a 2.66 range factor, almost exactly .30 higher than the league. Like Griffey, Bonds won several Gold Gloves in this period, but from what I can see, he wasn't more than an average left fielder. I don't know how he got the Gold Gloves; in only one season, his first in 1989, did he get to more fly balls than the league average for his position. Griffey was a very good fielder at the key outfield position; Bonds was merely a good one at the least-important defensive position in the outfield. But I don't think the difference in defensive value offsets Bonds's substantially greater ability to produce more runs while using up fewer outs.

So you see the argument for Bonds being the best player of the '90s, and even if you don't agree, you must certainly call him the best player in the National League over that period and the second best in all of baseball. Then something happened that took the debate to a whole new level. No, let me restate that: It eliminated the debate altogether.

From 2000 to 2003 Barry Bonds became the greatest baseball player of all time. He obliterated not merely the batting records of most of his contemporaries but of the all-time greats as well. Even stranger than that, *Barry Bonds from 2000 to 2003, from age thirty-six through age thirty-nine, completely obliterated all of the numbers posted by the young Barry Bonds.*

Let me justify the claim about Barry Bonds vs. The Greats. In 1920, Babe Ruth led all of baseball with a .532 on-base average, the second highest of his career, and a .847 slugging average, the highest mark of all time, before Bonds in 2001. This gave Babe a 45.1 SLOB for the season, which means he created slightly in excess of an amazing 45 runs per 100 at-bats. Ruth's second-highest SLOB came the next season when he led the league in OBA at .512 and slugging at .846 for a SLOB of 43.3. His third best came in 1923, with .545 and .764 for a SLOB of 41.6.

Ted Williams was the only hitter in the twentieth century to even approach these levels, in 1941, the year he hit .406. Williams led the league in on-base at .551 and slugging at .735 for a SLOB of 40.5. He posted some other great SLOBs, perhaps the most amazing coming in 1957 when he was thirty-nine years old, and he led the league in on-base average at .526 and slugging at .731, for a SLOB of 38.5.

Those were the greatest seasons of the two greatest hitters of the twentieth century.

In 2001, Barry Bonds posted an on-base average of .515 and a slugging average of .863 (the highest mark in baseball history) for a SLOB of 44.4, the second-highest SLOB of the century behind Ruth's 1920 season. In 2002, Bonds posted an on-base average of .582 (the highest in baseball history) and a slugging average of .799, for a SLOB of 46.5, surpassing Ruth's best ever. In 2003, he was .529 and .749 for a SLOB of 39.6, higher than any of Ted Williams's great seasons, except 1941.

Many of you are familiar with these stats or are not surprised to see them. What amazes me is how many knowledgeable fans don't realize how entirely unprecedented Bonds's last four seasons really have been. Not only have Bonds's best seasons surpassed those of baseball's two greatest hitters, he did it at an age when both Ruth and Williams were well past their peak years. Let's look at Bonds's 3-year average from age thirty-six to thirty-eight in comparison with those two, and just to get more perspective let's toss in an ordinary superman, Hank Aaron.

Player	Age	HR	BB	BA	OBA	SA	SLOB
Babe Ruth (1931–33)	36,37,38	40.3	124	.338	.475	.648	30.8
Ted Williams (1956–58)	37,38,39	29.3	106.3	.353	.490	.640	31.4
Hank Aaron (1970–72)	36,37,38	39.7	79	.297	.398	.585	23.3
Barry Bonds (2000–02)	36,37,38	56.0	164	.334	.512	.783	40.1

(I didn't make it a four-year comparison because Ruth, by age thirty-nine, was pretty much spent, and I moved Williams up a year so his fantastic 1957 season could be included.)

Those differences are nothing short of incredible, and so is this: Barry Bonds's SLOB from 1986 to 1999, from age twenty-four to thirty-five, was 22.86, the best in the major leagues over that period. From 2000 to 2003, from age thirty-six to thirty-nine, Barry Bonds had an OBA of .513 and slugging average of .795, for a SLOB of 40.8.

I could spend a lot of time comparing Bonds to other great players at the same age, but it wouldn't add anything to the discussion. You won't find anything like it in baseball history.

I'm going to try to sum up how incredible this is in a single sentence. Stick with me because it's going to be a long one:

From 1989 through 1999 Barry Bonds was the best player in the NL and probably all of baseball, and even made a good argument for himself as the greatest all-around player in baseball history; then, beginning at age thirty-six for the next four seasons, he got so much better that a batting order of old Barry Bondses would have outscored a batting order of young Barry Bondses by very nearly two runs to one.

Nineteen ninety-nine was in several ways Bonds's worst season in more than ten years. For the first time in his career, injuries limited him to under 400 at-bats, and he batted just .262, his second lowest batting average since 1989. Then, as if by magic, his performance took a sharp upswing the following year. His batting average in 2000 went up 44 points to .306, beginning a string of four straight years over .300, something he had never accomplished in the years that would normally be considered his physical prime. His slugging average rose 71 points, and he hit a career high 49 home runs. He had previously hit 46 in 1993 at age twenty-nine, and in '96 had 42. You can occasionally find a great player who hits more home runs as he gets older and stronger, but it's hard to find a guy who, at age thirty-six, tops his previous all-time high, achieved at age twenty-nine. But to paraphrase Al Pacino, Bonds was just getting warmed up.

The next year he topped that all-time high by 24. This was nutty. Here's a thirty-seven-year-old guy who more than doubled his home run production from age thirty-five. In fact, in 2001 he more than doubled his home run production from age twenty-eight in 1992. From 1986–99, Bonds averaged a home run for every 15.7 times at bat; from 2000–03 Bonds averaged a home run once every 8.2 times at bat.

I don't know of any player in baseball history who so substantially increased his performance after the age thirty-five. In fact, I can't think of any athlete in *any sport* who so substantially increased his performance after the age of thirty-five. After some study on the subject, I'm prepared to concede that I have found one: Y. A. Tittle. In 1961, Tittle, age thirty-five, came to the New York Giants and had one of his best seasons, leading the New York Giants to the Eastern Conference championship and a championship game with the Green Bay Packers (that they lost, 37-0). For the next two seasons, Tittle, at thirty-six and thirty-seven, had easily the greatest seasons of his career—in fact, two of the greatest seasons ever enjoyed by an NFL quarterback, throwing 69 touchdown passes over 27 games and passing for nearly 6400 yards.

But there are substantial differences between Tittle's situation and Bonds's. Tittle was always regarded as a fine quarterback who had made the best of playing for bad teams; when he came to the Giants he was surrounded by better players than he had been on previous teams—better blockers and better receivers. There were no comparable changes in the personnel surrounding Barry Bonds after the 1999 season.

When someone does something in baseball that's never been done before, there is almost always an obvious reason, and if it isn't obvious it usually reveals itself after some study. But Barry Bonds's is a strange case.

One can only go so far into a discussion of Barry Bonds without dealing with the question of steroids. Last summer, commenting on *Salon.com* about the groundbreaking investigation on steroid use written by *Sports Illustrated*'s Tom Verducci, I wrote that "I really don't know what would account for the Barry Bonds phenomenon . . . There is no precedent in baseball history for anything like a thirty-five-year-old ballplayer who had a career high of 46 home runs when he was twenty-nine to suddenly blossom into a player who could hit 122 home runs at ages thirty-six and thirty-seven. It makes no sense to me, and I can't find any rational explanation for it."

I admit now that it was reckless of me to have written that in a piece on steroid use, even if I qualified it in the next lines with, "This doesn't mean that Bonds has been on steroids. The truth is that I'm not even implying it. . . ." The very fact that I mentioned Bonds within the context of the argument was implying it, and I was wrong to do so.

I got a lot of feedback from readers and friends on the topic, including, finally, an Internet debate among several baseball researchers in which I was quoted. This, in turn, led to an Internet discussion on the subject in September 2002 with Bill James— the baseball analyst, not the psychologist or the British mystery writer—and, among others, Michael Humphries of SABR, The Society for American Baseball Research. Unfortunately, it didn't occur to me at the time to save my own comments, though I'm pretty sure on looking back on it that everything of importance that I had to say has been recapped earlier in this chapter. Anyway, it's Bill's and Michael's input that is important here.

There's no need to bog you down with all the preliminary chat—you can pick up on the gist of the discussion right here. (And my sincere thanks to both Bill and Michael for allowing me to reprint this.)

Michael: Some sort of discount must be applied to Bonds's career accomplishments after age thirty-two (when he started putting on forty, yes, *forty* pounds of lean muscle mass) when comparing him to Ruth, Williams, Mays, Mantle, and Aaron.

Bill: John Holway made this point about the body mass increase of Barry Bonds at Holwayian length and with Holwayian passion in a recent SABR discussion. The interesting thing was that Holway made this point as a part of his lifelong defense of Ted Williams as the greatest hitter ever . . . he talked about how Bonds, McGwire, Sosa, etc. are so much thicker now than they were as young men. But what struck me as odd is I have never seen *anybody*, including Bonds and Sosa, who packed on weight after age thirty the way Ted Williams did. You ever see films of Ted Williams? You see him at age twenty-two, he's like 6'3", 160 pounds. You see him in his late thirties, he's the size of a tree. Not fat, either—he's just frigging *huge*. Babe Ruth was slender as a young player, huge (above the waist) as a mature player.

My point is, it seems to me that some people *may* be overstating the steroid factor by ignoring the portion of this that is natural. *Everybody* gets bigger when they get older. I'm bigger than I was when I was thirty; Allen is. Everybody is.

Michael: Bill, that is all clearly true. However, I'm fairly confident that all of those players added bulk gradually over many years. I don't have the season-by-season playing weight for Ted Williams, but I would be extremely surprised if there was any four-year period during his thirties in which he put on forty pounds of lean muscle mass. What I pointed out earlier is that Bonds has put on lean muscle mass at twice the "maximum" annual non-steroid rate for people under age thirty when he was already half a decade past thirty. (I admit that the "maximum" rate is only the rate reported by self-described experts on the Web, although they are medical doctors, at least. I'm more than open to finding alternative medical authorities. Look, I'd be thrilled if we could all get very comfortable that Bonds has not used steroids.) In addition, Bonds is not just merely "lean"; he's almost freakishly free of body fat. He boasted in a recent *New York Times* article that he has only six percent body fat. Williams was lean in his thirties, but not that lean. Ruth we all know about.

It seems to me that, facing a career crisis, Bonds began using legal medical enhancements that resulted in his achieving higher performance after age thirty-two than before thirty-two. I'm not aware of any top non-pitcher, other than McGwire and Bonds, whose park-adjusted performance after age thirty-two was significantly greater than his performance before thirty-two. By the way, Roger Clemens, power pitcher extraordinaire, has also enjoyed a miraculous recovery during his mid-to-late thirties. I'm not aware of any other power pitcher in the history of baseball whose performance declined significantly over a three-year period in his early thirties who subsequently exceeded his mid-twenties performance levels.

Bill: The point about Clemens, in my opinion, is utterly without foundation. If you define the groups narrowly enough, *every* player is a historical one-of-a-kind. For Clemens, you are requiring that he have a three-year decline phase (which it is questionable that Clemens had . . . what he really had was a kind of off season and two years of real lousy run support), a pitcher who "subsequently exceeded his mid-twenties performance levels" (which is extremely questionable that Clemens had). Clemens had his best year after his "recovery," but four of his five best seasons were *before* the recovery.

Fundamentally, it is *extremely* common for power pitchers to have their best years in their mid-thirties or their late thirties, and I don't believe that there is anything unusual about Clemens's career path. Steve Carlton was a *great* power pitcher—better than Clemens—when he was thirty-six to thirty-nine. I did a data search for pitchers who were substantially better at ages thirty-three to thirty-five than they had been at ages thirty to thirty-two, and found many or all types. Sal Maglie, Preacher Roe, Hal Carlson, Spud Chandler, Ellis Kinder, Bert Blyleven, Doyle Alexander, Ed Whitson, Dazzy Vance, Whitlow Wyatt, Rip Sewell, Jim Bunning, Eddie Cicotte, Dennis Martinez, Burleigh Grimes, Luis Tiant, Gaylord Perry, Randy Johnson, Charlie Hough, Tommy John, Jamie Moyer, Joe Niekro, Whitey Ford, Waite Hoyt, Tim Belcher, Dennis Eckersley, Hoyt Wilhelm, and Kenny Rogers, to name a few.

Michael: Bill, you're probably basically right on this point. What led me toward suspecting Clemens's performance is a recent analysis I've done of pitching stats (using the model I've developed and mentioned to you) of Walter Johnson, Tom Seaver, and Roger Clemens. The model shows Walter and Tom peaking in their mid-to-late twenties, holding steady around thirty and tailing off after that—Walter slowly and Tom more rapidly. Clemens has a sharp decline that seems to trace Seaver's career path, and then suddenly recovers and achieves his highest single season rating in his late thirties, at a time when steroid use came into question. I'd have to do a similar analysis of other power pitchers. Some, no doubt, improved dramatically by improving their control. I do believe, however, that the strikeout rates of the pitchers you cite, when measured relative to their respective league's rate (excluding late-nineties pitchers such as Randy Johnson), followed a normal decline pattern. Clemens's does not. Johnson's does not. Why do 1990s "power" stats have these persistent anomalies?

Bill: With respect to Bonds, your point is not entirely mistaken, but it is subject to the same reservations. If you define the group narrowly enough, *everybody* is a one-of-a-kind. Following your directions, I looked for all players in history who:

a) Were not pitchers,
b) Earned at least 30 Win Shares* total at ages twenty-nine to thirty-two, and
c) Played better after age thirty-two than before.

I ranked these players by the ratio of Win Shares at age thirty-three to thirty-six compared with the Win Shares at twenty-nine to thirty-two. Barry Bonds is ninety-ninth on this list, although this is somewhat misleading, since the ninety-eight players ahead of him include ten to fifteen players like Joe DiMaggio and Johnny Mize, who missed some of the twenty-nine to thirty-two period due to service in the military. (Bonds, on the other hand, wouldn't be on the list *at all* if it wasn't for the strike in 1994, which kept his value at ages twenty-nine to thirty-two lower than his value at ages thirty-three to thirty-six).

---

*Win Shares is Bill James's complex measurement of a player's total value. He wrote a book in 2003 by that title.

Bonds earned 136 Win Shares at ages twenty-nine to thirty-two and 139 from ages thirty-three to thirty-six, a ratio of 1 to 1.022. Among those historically with higher ratios: Gavy Cravath, Eddie Joost, Dave Parker, Lonnie Smith, Mark McGwire, Lay Cross, Brian Downing, Mickey Vernon (no wartime service involved), Lou Piniella, Otis Nixon, Mark McLemore, Ernie Whitt, Bill Terry, Cap Anson, Bing Miller, Edgar Martinez, Andre Thornton, Tony Phillips, Stan Javier, Smoky Burgess, Ellis Burks, Luke Appling, Frank White, Darrell Evans, Elston Howard, Zack Wheat, Rafael Palmeiro, Gene Woodling, Jimmy Ryan, Andre Dawson, Brett Butler, Wally Joyner, Jim Gilliam, Sam Rice, Cy Williams, Mark Grace, Gabby Hartnett, Paul Molitor, Sherm Lollar, Jake Beckley, Lou Whitaker, Dave Winfield, and—Honus Wagner and Babe Ruth.

Now, you may object that I have not grouped the seasons exactly right to capture Bonds's mid-thirties rocket, and you may probably be right, but three points:

1) I was just following *your* grouping; you're the one that said pre age thirty-two and post age thirty-two,
2) If you group it just right to focus on Barry Bonds, of course Barry Bonds will be high on the list. If you define the group narrowly enough, *everybody* is a one-of-a-kind, and,
3) I'd do it again but I've got to run. I'm late to lunch.

Don't respond for an hour or two. I'll get back to this after lunch.

Michael: Sorry, Bill, I just couldn't wait. My grouping is obviously flawed. How about the simpler point that, eyeballing your Career Summaries for Top 40 Players in [your book] *Win*

Shares, pages 643 to 652, I'm not aware of any thirty-seven-year-old with a Win Share total of forty, still less any approaching fifty-four. (Williams did have thirty-eight at age thirty-eight, I think.) Bonds is probably on his way to another fifty-plus Win Share season. By the way, Bonds's defensive ratings as measured by STATS, Inc. have also zoomed in the past few years; he was third in the majors in the field in 2001. Has any thirty-seven-year-old reclaimed fielding prowess in the same way? Also, has any player in his late thirties ever outperformed his "prime" (however defined) peak as much as Bonds has? Has anything like that ever happened to a player who is [age] thirty-five to thirty-seven?

I read the *New York Times Magazine* article on Bonds. He is obviously an extremely dedicated and competitive individual, almost frighteningly so. If he is taking advantage of steroids or legal medical treatments, his success is undoubtedly primarily a function of his extraordinary discipline, as reflected in his exercise regime, diet, and even pitch selection. No one can take that away from him.

I suppose the issue that fans have to grapple with is that it is—and will continue to be—virtually impossible to prove directly whether a player is or isn't taking steroids. I've read a recent Web article by a doctor who specializes in sports medicine and who regularly receives phone calls from players inquiring as to how they can disguise their steroid usage. Said doctor concludes that only an idiot will ever be caught.

With regard to Bonds's past record-breaking performance, it is and will always be absolutely impossible to determine directly whether steroids were a factor. If there never will be "definitive" evidence one way or the other, are we left with no alternative but to forget about the issue?

Being a lawyer by training and having served recently on a

jury in a criminal drug trial, I know that no legal system can work if the law can only be applied when direct and completely incontrovertible evidence is available. Guilt beyond a reasonable doubt is the standard in a criminal proceeding, and in a civil proceeding, questions of fact are determined based upon the mere preponderance of the evidence. In determining guilt or liability under either standard, jurors must weigh the evidence and draw reasonable inferences based upon the credibility of witnesses and the cumulative probability of the evident circumstances occurring if the defendant is or is not guilty or liable, as the case may be.

In the case of Bonds we have the following key circumstances: He gained forty pounds of lean muscle mass during the four-year period ending in 2001, at which point he was thirty-seven years of age, and vastly improved his home-run-hitting ability (previous high was 47 at age twenty-eight).

1997—age 33; height: 6'1"; weight: 190; home runs 40
1998—age 34; height: 6'2"; weight: 206; home runs 37
1999—age 35; height: 6'2"; weight: 210; home runs 34
2000—age 36; height: 6'2"; weight: 220; home runs 49
2001—age 37; height: 6'2"; weight: 228; home runs 73

Not only did his total number of home runs increase, the average distance of his homers also increased—dramatically. It seems beyond any reasonable doubt that his increase in strength contributed mightily to his increased home run total. Of course it was not the only factor behind his success. Bonds already had phenomenal eye-hand coordination, a compact swing, discipline at the plate, and years of experience reading pitchers. That is why no other player who has bulked up during the late '90s has done what Bonds has done. Bonds already had an advantage vis-à-vis other, younger, players, due to his knowledge of hitting, which, when you think about it, can continue to improve over time. His increased muscle strength simply kept him from suffering physical decline, and probably reversed it. When many ballplayers are hitting 30, 40, 50 home runs a year, which happened for the first time in the mid-to-late '90s, it isn't all that surprising that the most skilled among them hits 73.

What is surprising, and in fact completely unprecedented, is that the most disciplined hitter in baseball also has, at age thirty-seven, the strength and bat speed of a much younger man. (By the way, Bonds at thirty-eight is currently leading the majors in slugging percentage and, I think, home run percentage.)

Now we must deal with the question of how he acquired such strength. Skip Bayless has written:

> An expert on steroids-and-sports research, Dr. Joey Antonio, who wrote a column for *Muscle and Fitness,* once told me: "Unless you're a genetic freak, it's impossible to put on more than about five pounds of muscle a year without using steroids. That's eating five or six high-protein, low-fat meals a day, following a very strict training program and using creatine to speed recovery. After age thirty or so, it gets even harder. I've recently heard from several doctors and bodybuilding experts who believe [Bonds's] muscle mass explosion had to be steroid-fueled. Several say [his] face exhibits the puffiness of a man who cycles steroids.

Dr. Charles Yesalis, a Penn State professor of health and human development, believes "The talk about creatine and other supplements is a smoke screen, that as many as one half of major league ball players are using anabolic steroids." Author of the book *The Steroid Game,* Yesalis says, "Over the last decade, I've seen lean-mass increases in players that I frankly cannot attribute to changes in strength training alone. Forget about creatine. To me, it's very obvious that steroids have taken a major foothold in baseball."

Players are using andro, creatine, and other performance-enhancing supplements to mask strength gains from actual anabolic steroids. They are not bulking up with steroids during the actual season. Rather, it is happening during their workouts over the winter. "Players who use steroids are taking shortcuts, putting up numbers fraudulently, setting the wrong example for impressionable kids, and risking their own long-term health," wrote Jerry Crasnick in *Baseball America.*

Bonds put on 40 pounds of lean muscle mass (actually, "38," as his reported weight rose from 190 to "228") in a four-year period. (And it was all muscle; Bonds boasts in the *New York Times* article that he has only 6 percent body fat—an absolutely incredibly low figure.) In other words, he put on lean muscle mass at a rate twice the "impossible" rate for athletes in their twenties, and furthermore added such muscle when he was already far past thirty. The enhancement that Bonds (eventually) admitted using, creatine, could not have this effect, at least according to the only expert opinions I've been able to find.

Unless we can find a precedent somewhere in the history of sports for someone adding that amount of muscle mass that quickly at such an age without steroids, I don't know what else we can reasonably infer from the facts at our disposal other than that Bonds has used steroids and such steroid use has enabled him to put up unprecedented numbers that distort the history and very integrity of the game. Of course, proving a negative is, strictly speaking, impossible. Do we therefore just throw up our hands and say, "Who knows for sure?"

Now let's consider the issue of credibility. Bonds's initial responses were defensive and evasive. He later said, "They can test me any time they want." That sounds an awful like what Gary Hart sounded like during the '88 presidential campaign, in which he challenged reporters to follow him around to see if he was cavorting with what's-her-name. Bonds eventually crafted an explanation involving creatine, which simply isn't sufficient. Do you really believe him?

Finally, let me address what I think is your most important point:

The fact is, as you note, there is no one who has ever done what Bonds had done, and it is for that reason that I feel that there's no definitive explanation. We both realize, of course, that plenty of players have likely used steroids. But we also know that none of these players have done anything like Bonds, either.

As explained above, Bonds is besting the competition today because he has the skills and savvy of an old man and the strength and bat speed of a youth. So far the only plausible scientific explanation for such strength and bat speed is steroids. Furthermore, I believe that Bonds is on his way to achieving the highest sabermetrical (in the narrow sense of the word) ranking in the history of the game because he is the first and possibly only likely first-ballot hall-of-famer to enter the decline phase of his career during the beginning of a "youth serum" boom. A great player beginning his physical decline but continuing to build upon his relative advantage in experience and saw will clearly benefit more than anyone from a youth elixir, particularly during a period when such elixir is beginning to be used,

22222222

but is not yet universally used. Once everybody is using the magic technology from the beginning of their careers, players will probably not obtain nearly so great a relative benefit compared to their respective leagues as they get older.

So, in a sense, the "problem," at least as it relates to evaluating ballplayers over the course of their careers against their respective leagues for purposes of all-time career rankings, could go away—by becoming universal! (I suppose that's some comfort.) Context-adjusted career performance patterns would revert to normal, and no one would enjoy high ratings relative to their league during their late thirties. Thus Bonds, who does have the highest ratings in the history of baseball relative to his league for a player in his late thirties—ratings much higher than those when he was in his "prime"—may end up enjoying career rankings that no player ever has or ever will. Timing, as they say, is everything.

Does all this really matter? I think it does. I'd like to hear the arguments why it doesn't. In any event, I will always consider Mays the greatest player in the history of the game, and a much better player than Bonds, no matter what numbers Barry puts up in the next few years. When Bonds is elected in his first year of eligibility for the Hall of Fame, I hope at least a few members of the baseball writers association will see things the same way and vote accordingly.

Bill: Attempting to be fully responsive to Michael's thesis, that Bonds's late-in-life surge is remarkable, I took a data file of all players in history who were not primarily pitchers and who earned at least fifty Win Shares in their careers—1,962 players, as it turned out. In that data file I "penciled in" a 44 for Bonds in 2002, which is about what he will have. (Michael's suggestion that he will top 50 again is very improbable. A Win Share 44 is a historic season.)

I then figured, for each of those 1,962 players,

1) their peak production in a three-year period ending no later than age thirty-two, and
2) their peak production in a three-year period beginning no sooner than age thirty-three.

Of the 1,962 players:

- 1,839 had a higher peak before age thirty-two than after age thirty-three;
- 118 had a higher peak after age thirty-three than before thirty-two; and
- 5 had the same.

Bonds is one of the 118—one of the 6 percent of players who peaked after the age of thirty-two. He is near the bottom of the list. With a three-year peak of 125 before the age of thirty-two and 130 after the age of thirty-two, Bonds has a ratio of 1 to 1.040, which ranks 108th on the list.

At the top of the list (the highest ratio of post-thirty-three peaks to pre-thirty-two peaks) we have a series of fluke players—nineteenth-century players who were thirty-two before baseball started, Negro League players, guys who didn't reach the majors until late, etc. Actually, the top five are Joe Start, Eddie Mayo, Candy Nelson, Al Todd and George Crowe, none of whose examples are at all instructive about Barry Bonds.

Later on the list, however, we have a good many Hall of Fame players and Hall of Fame candidates, about whom one would have difficulty saying anything except simply that they were better players after age thirty-three than before age thirty-two. Among these are Elston Howard (53-80), Paul O'Neill (56-76),

Tommy Henrich (59-80), Frank White (40-54), Cap Anson (60-78), Mickey Vernon (57-74), Lay Cross (50-63), Bill Terry (75-93), Edgar Martinez (61-75), Mark McGwire (79-96), George Davis (73-85), Nap Lajoie (95-106), Willie Stargell (79-87), Luke Appling (81-89), Max Carey (73-80), Gabby Hartnett (64-69), Fred Clarke (82-88), Indian Bob Johnson (71-76), Davey Lopes (65-69), Dolph Camilli (78-82), Paul Molitor (83-87), Mark Grace (65-68), Jose Cruz (78-80), and, most interestingly, Honus Wagner (135-145) and Willie Mays (125-130).

In other words,

a) While *most* players have their best seasons before the age of thirty-two, it is certainly not unprecedented for a superstar player to have his best seasons after age thirty-two, and

b) Bonds's godfather, Willie Mays, had exactly the same ratio of pre-thirty-two to post-thirty-three peaks that Bonds has.

Even more interesting: If you take these 123 players, who have peaks post-thirty-three as high as their peaks pre-thirty-two and rate them as to their peak seasons before age thirty-two, the top four are:

1) Honus Wagner
2) Barry Bonds
3) Willie Mays
4) Nap Lajoie

If you rank them on the peak seasons *after* age thirty-three, the top four are the same four players, in the same order—Wagner, Bonds, Mays, Lajoie. In other words, Bonds's position relative to this peer group is the same *after* age thirty-three as *before*.

In short, it is unusual for a player to play his best ball in his mid-thirties—but it is not nearly as unusual as you may believe it to be. Bonds's mid-thirties explosion in value does, in fact, have precedent.

One of the differences here is that you focused on Barry's *power* increase, whereas I focused on his overall value to his team. But I did it the way I did it because I believe it is a better way to do it. The business of focusing on power, it seems to me, has two problems:

1) It targets Barry. One player can be proven a historical fluke (and therefore presumed to be a steroid abuser) based on hitting for average, another based on steals, another based on defense or whatever. You can wind up with multiple players proven to be historical flukes.

2) Isolated power is not a historical constant. It is variable over time, and is higher now than it has ever been—hence, we would naturally expect players in recent years to increase more than they have in other eras.

Michael: At the very least, we must conclude that players who reached their mid-thirties during the late '90s benefited from new medical and or conditioning regimes unavailable to players in prior eras.

Bill: By the same logic you could prove that it must be witchcraft. *Nonsense.* If Barry Bonds does something that no one has done before, all we can conclude is that Barry Bonds has done something that no one has done before. We can make no conclusion whatsoever on *why* this is.

My sincere belief is that the role of steroids in increasing power in recent years has been dramatically overstated by many people, for the simple reason that people are attracted to nefarious, underhanded, "secret," paranoid explanations, and prefer them to straightforward, above-board, "honest" explanations. Some, much, most, or *all* of the increase in power can in fact be explained by other factors, including:

1) Laser eye surgery. Ted Williams was famous for his eyesight. Now *everybody*—every hitter—has perfect vision because of eye surgery. Think about what a difference that makes. *Many, many* hitters now have the precise advantage that for many years was routinely cited as the key to Ted Williams's excellence.
2) Maple bats. What do they really mean? Nobody actually knows.
3) Double-dipped bats. In the late 1990s bat manufacturers realized that there was a hole in the description of what was a legal bat, which allows multiple coats of shellac to be put onto the bat, which makes the bat much harder. It makes a very real difference—but no one knows exactly how much.
4) Legal strength training.
5) Smaller ballparks.

Michael: Assuming these medical and conditioning techniques become widely applied by all ballplayers of all ages, relative performance over the course of a career should return to norm sometime soon. In other words, older players who have recently been able to combine youthful vigor with experience have derived an "unfair" benefit in terms of league-relative career performance measurements typically used for making all-time career assessments.

Bill: This is *precisely* what Ford Frick was thinking. That damned Maris has an unfair advantage on Babe Ruth; we've got to do something about that. By the same logic, Babe Ruth had an unfair advantage on everyone before Babe Ruth, in that fresh baseballs were kept in play post-1920, whereas dirty, old baseballs were used pre-1920, so we would have to make some sort of adjustment not only for Babe Ruth, but for everybody post-Babe Ruth. Not only that, but what about the expansion of the schedule in 1903 or whenever it was—why shouldn't we "adjust" the record for the fact that Pete Rose was playing 162 games a season, whereas Ty Cobb played only 154, and why shouldn't we "adjust" Cobb's record for the fact that Cobb played 154 games, whereas Cap Anson, the first person to hold the record for any length of time, started out playing 60 games a season. Michael, *every* generation of players has "unfair" advantages over the previous generation. So what? That's just life.

What makes Bonds special is, *Bonds is the guy who figures out how to take advantage of everything.* That's what Bonds is, that's what Ruth was, that's what Cobb was, that's what Clemens is—that's baseball. I have absolutely zero sympathy for this idea that we need to "adjust" these things out of existence.

I will let Allen have the last word on the subject.

Well, thanks, Bill. The problem is, I really have no idea what to do with this last word. I'm not even sure there can even be a last word on the subject, at least not until we know a great deal more than we know now.

For the time being I have not a single answer and nothing to offer but questions. Principal among them is, will we eventually see the question of Barry Bonds's late career performance not as a matter of someone peaking after age thirty-two, for which I admit I see many precedents, but someone peaking after age thrity-five, for which, as far as I know, there are none. This will depend on whether other players in the next several years upgrade their performances after age thirty-five, won't it?

One thing I can say definitely is that I don't see any single factor that would explain what Bonds has done since the year 2000. His fanatical conditioning routine? No doubt Bonds *is* a fanatic when it comes to conditioning; his routine, as outlined in the May 2003 issue of *Men's Journal,* is as rigorous as any I have seen in sports. But it's not *more* rigorous than several others I've seen in sports, and, for that matter, Bonds has always been a conditioning nut. The question is why should his conditioning have so much more to do with his performance now than it did six or eight or ten years ago?

And don't other major league ballplayers, in fact all other professional athletes, have access to the same trainers and same methods as Barry Bonds?

What about Bonds's savvy and experience, his improved knowledge of the strike zone? Okay, I'll accept these. But wouldn't we expect them to be offset just a bit by the decline in his physical skills? I mean, whose body gets better from age thirty-six on, no matter how they take care of it? And again, could Barry Bonds be the only great player who got *that much* smarter and savvier *after* turning thirty-six?

Besides, is that the entire issue? It isn't just that Bonds hit more home runs, but that he hit *longer* home runs. In fact, I don't recall anyone ever saying that Barry Bonds hit tape-measure shots before the year 2000.

"I've watched baseball for sixty years," wrote Branch Rickey in *The American Diamond.* "I've never heard of any ballplayer adding power . . . you cannot add power. You cannot add it to a batter or a runner or pitcher or put it in the arm of an outfielder. A man is born with power, and that is it." Of course, Rickey was talking about baseball before steroids, and not only before steroids but before all the other factors we've been discussing. But Barry Bonds has not only added power, he's added more of it faster than any player ever to play the game.

Could laser eye surgery be responsible? Could be. I hear on TV all the time how much better Barry Bonds "sees" the ball in recent years, but without some kind of medical help, why would he be seeing the ball better now than when he was twenty-seven? After several inquiries, I can't determine that Bonds has or hasn't had eye surgery. I can't find anyone who even thinks there's a rumor that he has, but maybe if I had had similar surgery I'd keep quiet about it to discourage pitchers from getting it, too.

The wood the bats are made of? I'll buy this—and if I were a ballplayer, I'd certainly buy some of those bats, too. But that's just the point—couldn't anybody buy maple bats if they increase home run production? In another chapter I quote Branch Rickey on the subject of the new whip-handled bats, such as the one Babe Ruth used, and how they changed the game. But in Ruth's time there was a definite prejudice against that kind of bat and the kind of baseball they engendered. It took years for the majority of players to accept them. Can anyone say the same about Barry Bonds's bats? If Bonds has indeed discovered a new kind of bat that enhances the hitter's power, wouldn't everyone be using them inside of a year? No one can argue that today's players can't afford such bats.

The ballparks, perhaps? How about Barry Bonds's own home ballpark? Bonds steadfastly maintains that Pacific Bell Park is the most difficult in the National League to hit home runs in, but in 2001, when he set the all-time record of 73, he hit 37 homers at home. In 2003, he hit 23 of his 45 home runs at home. How hard can it be to hit home runs there? At least for him?

And if the rest of the NL ballparks are that home-run–friendly, why hasn't some stud even younger and stronger than Barry Bonds come along and hit 80?

Has pitching really declined so much in the last four seasons that Barry Bonds could not only dramatically increase his home run output but *hit for the two highest averages of his career—* .370 in 2002, 34 points higher than his previous best in 1993—at ages thirty-eight and thirty-nine? And if so, why hasn't this bad pitching manifested itself in the batting averages and home run totals of all other hitters?

How about something we haven't focused on yet, like all that body armor that Bonds wears? If it really does reduce the fear of being hit with an inside pitch, perhaps it gives him a decided edge when battling pitchers who need the inside of the plate. For several months I received E-mails from a strength coach in California who swore that the gear Bonds was wearing was well known to "power lifters," and that it gave their muscles some kind of power surge that instantly energized their muscles and reflexes. Well, it sounds a little weird to me, but what do I know? If Bonds was the first ballplayer to discover these, then more power—literally, in this case—to him.

Steroids, of course, tie all of these questions up in one neat little bundle and toss them all out the window. Or, at any rate, they seem to, until you look at it more closely, because the problem with the steroids argument is the same with all the others: If steroids are the reason that Barry Bonds's power (as expressed by his home run total and slugging percentage) and consistency (as expressed in his batting and on-base averages) and, yes, his speed (for his first fourteen years, his stolen base percentage was 78 percent, while over the last four seasons, it has been 83.3 percent), then why hasn't some other older player shown similar increases? For that matter, why hasn't some *younger* player, say age thirty-two or thirty-three, shown some similarly dramatic improvement?

It isn't really increased performance beyond the age of thirty-two or thirty-three that we're discussing here: It's increased performance at age thirty-six, thirty-seven, thirty-eight, and thirty-nine that we're talking about. And there's only one man in all of baseball history who is in this category: Barry Bonds.

And so, I can't have the last word on this subject because I simply don't know enough about it. I really don't have a clue as to why Barry Bonds has been a better player over the last four seasons than he was in the previous fourteen, or, more to the point, why over the last four seasons he suddenly developed into the greatest player in baseball history.

Until we do, I have to agree with Bill that it's wrong for us to taint his achievement with talk of drugs. But there would be no taint on Bonds's record at all if this ridiculous steroid situation didn't exist in the first place.

Tom Verducci's story on steroids in *Sports Illustrated* was important, not because of what it revealed but because of what it forced us to acknowledge that we already knew. You can't even call steroid use a dirty "secret"; the secret has been out in the open so long that no one regards it as a secret anymore. What we didn't know was how prevalent steroid use is. And now that we do, it's going to dominate our view of sports until it's eradicated.

Make no mistake: The use of steroids in baseball is, in the long run, a more important issue than the phony revenue sharing war currently being waged between the owners and the players' union. Not that the problem is confined by any means to baseball. Far from it. Basketball and football players have bulked up far more over the last two decades than baseball players, and might there not be a well-known wrestler here and there whose physique and temperament suggests unrestricted steroid use?

But the average fan expects more from baseball than from other sports; he doesn't so much care if hundreds of anonymous offensive linemen whom he wouldn't recognize if they took off their helmets in front of him are inflating their bodies and shrinking their testicles with drugs. (And, yes, I know there is supposed to be a strict antisteroid policy in the NFL, but we all know that it's violated with impunity. In Mike Freeman's eye-opening book on pro football, *Bloody Sundays,* he cites a videotape in which "The union informed its membership that a significant number of players had failed drug tests . . . but were not punished or suspended, because of a secret agreement between the league and the union.") The average fan cares very much if it's a baseball player whose performance he follows every day.

It may seem trivial to pursue the argument from this perspective, but let me ask the question anyway: What happens when the average fan's faith in the integrity of baseball records is shattered? I mean, what happens to the game over the long run? The lifeblood of baseball is statistics, numbers, and records that fans must take on faith, as they can never see but an infinitesimal fraction of the actual games. What happens when fans no longer accept the numbers as a true reflection of the players' on-field performances? At the very least—and this is perhaps the most truly terrifying thought of all—what happens if they stop buying books like this one?

What if the breaking of a new record is simply written off to the belief that "Oh, he's just on steroids"? Do you think that baseball is on the verge of that kind of reaction right now? I do.

Of course steroid use is bad, and *of course* performance-enhancing steroids need to be eliminated from sports. Let's not pretend we don't understand why they haven't been eliminated from baseball. Unlike cocaine, which devalues their property, the baseball owners have actually benefited from steroids in the form of extra ticket sales and more media attention when records are pursued and broken. The owners have no reason to stamp out steroid use. The harmful effects of steroids take years to show up, by which time the owners have lost interest in aging hunks of meat and found new beef to replace the old.

Let's stop putting all the blame for this problem on the Players Association, which on numerous occasions has submitted what it believes to be highly effective drug control plans, only to see management cynically exploit the drug issue by asking players to step forward voluntarily for drug tests in defiance of union agreements. (The union has never denied the necessity for drug testing, but it has resisted and will resist random drug testing programs under the control of management as a means of overriding agreements with the union.)

Is it really possible that MLB can prepare no program for drug testing that doesn't violate someone's constitutional rights?

Somehow I just can't believe that. Steroids is a cancer eating at the core of the game's integrity. This is an issue that Major League Baseball, the Players Association, the press, and the fans should have no trouble agreeing on.

Postscript: Two weeks after this chapter was completed, Barry Bonds and Jason Giambi, along with other well-known professional athletes, were subpoenaed to testify before a federal grand jury probing BALCO, a "Bay Area Laboratory Co-Operative" (as described by the Associated Press), founded by a man named Victor Conte. BALCO was raided by the Internal Revenue service and drug agents in September.

The home of Bonds's personal trainer, Greg Anderson, had previously been raided in conjunction with the raid on Victor Conte's lab. According to the *San Francisco Chronicle*, "BALCO is under investigation for selling a previously undetectable steroid—and steroid-related substance—tetrahydrogestinone ('THG'). The U.S. Anti-Doping Agency found the substance in several athletes at a major track and field event."

As of November 10, 2003, the scope of the investigation is unclear and federal officials have refused to comment.